Illustrated

MOTORSCOOTER
BUYER'S ★ GUIDE™

Michael Dregni & Eric Dregni

Motorbooks International
Publishers & Wholesalers

First published in 1993 by Motorbooks International Publishers & Wholesalers, PO Box 2, 729 Prospect Avenue, Osceola, WI 54020 USA

Motorbooks International books are also available at discounts in bulk quantity for industrial or sales-promotional use. For details write to Special Sales Manager at the Publisher's address

Library of Congress Cataloging-in-Publication Data
    Illustrated motorscooter buyer's guide /Michael Dregni, Eric Dregni.
        p. cm. – – (Motorbooks International illustrated buyer's guide series)
    Includes bibliographical references and index.
    ISBN 0-87938-791-2
    1. Motor scooters– –Purchasing. 2. Motor scooters– –Collectors and collecting. I. Dregni Eric. II. Title. III. Series: International illustrated buyer's guide series.
    TL450.D74 1993
    629.227'5'0297– –dc20   93-13170

On the front cover: To scooterists around the world, Vespa is synonymous with motorscooter. The classic Vespa shape is epitomized by the GS models of 1955–1964, a high-performance version of Piaggio's scooter that became popular as a Mod hot rod. This 1962 GS 160 Mark II is owned by Sam Pitmon of The Pacesetters Scooter Society of Minneapolis-St. Paul. *Michael Dregni*

On the back cover: Two classics and one modern scooter: Cushman Model 52 Step-Through owned by Roger McLaren of Excelsior, Minnesota; Lambretta TV 175 Series 2 owned by Tim Gartman of St. Paul, Minnesota; 1992 Honda Elite 80.

Printed and bound in the United States of America

Contents

Acknowledgments

Many people have given time, energy, and the loan of valuable information and material to help us write this history.

We must begin with a toast to Vittorio Tessera, Rodano, Italy, scooter collector straordinario and keeper of the Lambretta flame. In addition, we salute Herb Singe, Hillside, New Jersey, with his phenomenal collection of prewar American scooters; and Keith and Kris Weeks, Mound, Minnesota, for sharing their beautifully restored collection of Allstate, Cushman, and Doodle Bugs.

Secondly, we raise a cup of coffee to the Minneapolis-St. Paul scooter mods: Tim Gartman, Jeaneen Gauthier, Kris Adams, Will Niskanen, Mark Preston, Steve Jacobs, Jim Kelly, John Pierson, Sam Pitmon, as well as Zachary Zniewski for inspiration in many matters. Many a cup of Dunn Bros. coffee was consumed in both dreaming of and writing this book.

We also thank, in alphabetical order: Joe Baker, St. Paul, Minnesota; George Edwards and Welles Emerson, Minneapolis, Minnesota, for the loan of their collection of the 1959 American magazine, *Scooter*; Randolph Garner, Cleburne, Texas; Eric Halladay at First Kick Scooters, Berkeley, California; Jim Kilau, St. Paul, Minnesota; Philip McCaleb at Scooterworks, USA, Chicago, Illinois; Roger McLaren, Excelsior, Minnesota; Vince Mross of West Coast Lambretta Works, San Diego, California; Halwart Schrader, Germany, for clearing up the ages-old Ilo/ILO/Jlo/JLO mystery; Mick Walker, Wisbech, England, for the loan of archival photos when he was thinking of doing a similar book himself; photographer Paul Verlangieri; Steven Zasueta and the *Classic Scooters of America* newsletter.

For making sense of bizarre French and German, we owe thanks to Aimee Roberson and Barbara Vogel, St. Paul, Minnesota.

And for assistance with specific marques, we thank:

For Cushman, Robert H. Ammon for his interviews and loan of materials; Linda Churda at OMC, Lincoln, Nebraska; Ray Gabbard, Portland, Indiana.

For Iso, Winston Goodfellow, Menlo Park, California.

For Mustang, Walt Fulton for his recollections; Michael Gerald for sharing photos and his definitive history, *Mustang: A Different Breed of Steed*.

For Parilla, Larry Wise at Cosmopolitan Motors, Hatsboro, Pennsylvania; Joe Rottigni; and Bruno Baccari, Modigliana, Italy.

For Powell, Wallace Skyrman, North Central Point, Oregon, for allowing us to quote from his Powell Cycle Registry history.

For Rumi, Riccardo Crippa, Bergamo, Italy; and Gösta Karlsson, Sweden, who also provided material on Swedish scooters.

For Salsbury, E. Foster Salsbury for his interviews and loan of materials.

For Triumph-BSA, Lindsay Brooke, Birmingham, Michigan.

For Zündapp and other German marques, W. Conway Link, Shreveport, Louisiana, and the Deutsches Motorräd Registry; and Roland Salbon, Exeter, New Hampshire.

We also thank everyone at Motorbooks International, including Tim Parker, Greg Field, Zachary Miller, and Michael Dapper, who were always polite when the subject of scooters was mentioned.

Mille grazie a Stefano Pasini, Giorgio Nada, é tutta la famiglia Erba. Thanks as well to Evie Yiannoussi and the Yiannoussi family for information on Greek scooters: as far as we know, there has not been a Greek scooter, but if there was it would certainly be the best. And for archaeological research into Bolivian scooters on the altiplano, thanks to Sigrid Arnott.

Prolegomena to Any Future Motorscooter Metaphysics

Motorscooters have had many nicknames. Scoots. Putt-putts. Italian Hairdryers. Dustbins on Wheels. People give nicknames to things they love—or hate. With scooters, there's no middle ground; like licorice, you either love scooters or you hate them. You laugh at them or you ride them.

The Pioneer Motorscooters

The history of motorscooters begins at the turn of the century. The motorscooters evolved in the 1900s from the child's push scooter, an image it was never able to outrun.

There was a scooter craze in the 1910s and 1920s with a host of upstart scooter makers offer-

The scooter that saved the world. Piaggio's Vespa was created by helicopter engineer Corradino d'Ascanio, who brought advanced aviation principles to scooter design and developed the most long-lived and loved of all motorscooters. The Vespa was not the first, but it was the best—and proved that with motorscooters, beauty is more than just skin deep. This restored 125cc Vespa added extra power, a spare wheel, and a second seat to the original Vespa 98 of 1946. Owner: Vittorio Tessera.

The idea was simple: take a child's push scooter and get rid of the push by adding power in the form of a gas engine. And folks took to scooters like fish to water. The American-made Motoped, shown here, and Autoped scooters arrived in 1915-1916, followed by the British ABC Scootamota in 1919. These early scooters were faddish gimmicks at most, ostensibly designed for ladies to travel downtown for afternoon tea without having to hike up their dresses. It was a fun idea but didn't last long because many of the scooters didn't last long, mechanical reliability being but a dream.

ing cheap and cheerful scooters that often made it from point A to point B, but not back again. The first motorscooters featured a small, raspy, oil-spewing engine mounted above the front or rear wheel, usually with chain drive to a wheel sprocket or direct roller drive running onto the tire. Some had gearboxes. Some had clutches. Many were single-speed and boasted of such weak power they did not even need a clutch. A tall steering rod ran from the front forks ending in handlebars, often equipped with a throttle and brake lever. These early scooters had a central floorboard to stand on, usually just inches from earth, so the driver could put a foot down to the safety of solid ground should anything untowards happen.

The first motorscooters were quaint, faddish vehicles at best, and they were not taken seriously at the time. Created for pithy ladies to putt-putt to town for shopping or afternoon tea, the scooter was ideal with its upright driving position because the driver's neatly ironed dress did not get wrinkled. That was the motorscooter's first sales pitch.

The American-made Motoped is believed to be the first motorscooter to enter production, in 1915. It featured an engine mounted atop the front fender driving the front wheel. A twist-grip throttle controlled the engine speed. For convenience, the handlebar column could be folded away for portability.

The Motoped was followed by the Autoped of 1917, created by the Autoped Company of New York, and powered by a miniature 1.5hp engine mounted on the front fender above the wheel. The reputation of the Autoped spread far and wide: US Army doughboys tested it for a military draft in the late 1910s, and it was soon being license-built by Krupp in Germany with a 155cc four-stroke and by CAS in Czechoslovakia. Production of the Autoped was halted in 1921.

Meanwhile, in 1919, British engineer Granville Bradshaw created the ABC Scootamota with 147cc intake-over-exhaust engine, later supplanted by a 110cc overhead-valve engine. Other pioneering English scooters included the Autosco and Autoglider from the 1920s.

A second type of scooter evolved from the standup push scooter; these bore a chair for the lady rider to sit down upon. The American-made Militaire of 1911-1920 was half scooter and half automobile, with a steering wheel, cozy armchair seat, and a set of side wheels that were lowered to keep the scooter stable at rest. Couthness had come to the motorscooter, and other machines followed in the Militaire's image, including the American and English versions of the Neracar, the French Monet-Goyon Vélauto, German Megola and DKW Golem, and English Wilkinson.

The scooter was just a passing fancy in the Roaring Twenties, going the way of the Charleston and steam-powered automobiles. The first wave of scooters died by the side of the road as quickly as it was born. In 1935, the English magazine, *The Motor Cycle*, bemoaned the death of scooter and what might have been: "Had the scooter lived, and not died stillborn as a result of makers rushing into production with untried and crude machines, we should probably have seen it develop into a most useful type of vehicle." Little did anyone know what loomed on the horizon.

Born From Economic Necessity

A second wave of scooters began in 1936 in Southern California and spread across the United States. These scooter makers took up where the first scooters had left off, but they now built reliable machines with hardy engines, solid gearboxes, brakes that actually braked, and most importantly for the scooter's future acceptance, they added bodywork that covered the engine and other dirty mechanical bits so drivers never had to soil their hands. The scooter had been civilized.

Following World War II, scooter makers blossomed throughout Europe and Japan. In both Italy and Japan, the first scooters hit the road in

1946; France, Germany, England, and others had their own makers within several years, often licensed builders of the Italian makes.

This second wave of scooters shaped a clause in the definition of a scooter: Motorscooters were born from economic necessity. The first scooters of the 1910s and 1920s had been gadabout toys, and failed. The second wave of scooters, sparked in the United States, was a byproduct of the Great Depression; bad times were the fertile breeding ground for scooters. All scooter ads of the late 1930s hailed the go-forever-on-a-teaspoon-of-gas fuel consumption, inexpensive operating costs—"Cheaper than shoe leather," shouted one Cushman ad—and promoted a scooter instead of a car, or as a second car, for struggling working families.

During World War II, scooters were shanghaied into service and fought for peace, dignity, and the American way with all the nationalistic fervor the elfin engines could muster. But more importantly, some US makers received dispensations to build scooters as civilian wartime transportation, whereas car makers were converted solely to military contracting. Riding a scooter became a wartime duty, as patriotic as flying the flag. As American motorcycle maven Floyd Clymer prompted while lauding the aptly named Victory Clipper scooter, "If you want to conserve Gasoline and Tires . . . and save money to invest in War Bonds, you should consider our Motor Scooters . . . . Remember a 'D' Ration book is good

for 1 1/2 Gallons a week . . . at 100 miles per gallon that's better than a 'B' Book."

Sidecar models were also for sale to tote the whole family about like sardines in a motorized tin.

Postwar, the European and Japanese economic recovery rode atop the midget wheels of motorscooters, as well as other mopeds, commuter motorcycles, and micro cars. Cushman even helped establish the Belgian Cushman firm under the auspices of the US Recovery Act. And during the Suez Crisis of 1956 when gasoline supplies were threatened, scooter sales boomed again in Europe. By the 1960s, many scooterists had forsaken their trusty steeds and moved up to motorcycles or cars.

But scooters did not go away. Instead, they became a youth vehicle, providing economical transportation to youths, offering freedom and mobility, and playing a supporting role in the development of an international youth culture—and counterculture.

Today, the scooter makers that survive sell to these two markets: the market of necessity for economical transportation, primarily in Third World countries today, and the teen market.

The Great American Motorscooter

The second wave of scooters was sparked by a tiny vehicle built in the back of a plumbing and heating shop in Oakland, California, by E. Foster

FIVE YEARS AHEAD
OF THE MOTOR CYCLE WORLD

THE UNDERSLUNG MILITAIRE
The Machine They're All Talking About 1912 THE MILITAIRE AUTO CO., Inc.
CATALOGUE SENT ON REQUEST 301-304 Columbia Bldg., Cleveland, Ohio, U.S.A.

The American-made Militaire was half scooter and half automobile. In sum, it was an audacious attempt to create a new form of motorized vehicle. As this 1912 ad boasted, it was "five years ahead of the motor cycle world." The best feature of the Militaire was the set of side wheels that were lowered to keep the scooter stable at rest. Numerous other scooter-car-motorcycles were created in this image in the 1900s through 1920s era, but they all eventually went the way of the dodo bird—until Honda revived the concept with its Helix, adding plastic bodywork to create an 80mph Barcalounger.

The United States was the birthplace of the modern motorscooter, with the Salsbury Motor Glide from California and the Chicago-based Moto-Scoot leading the way in 1935-1936. American collector extraordinaire Herb Singe stands with just some of his early American scooters. In the front from left: 1939 Crocker Scootabout, 1936 Motor Glide, and 1937 Motor Glide. At rear from left: 1937 Moto-Scoot and 1936 Keen Power Cycle.

Salsbury and inventor Austin Elmore. In 1935, Salsbury had seen the great feminist and aviator Amelia Earhart frolic around the Lockheed airport at Burbank on a leftover Motoped scooter. "It got me started thinking about building a real scooter," Salsbury said in 1992. "I wish now I had gotten to meet her."

The design of Salsbury and Elmore's 1936 Motor Glide spread like a contagious disease: Powell, Moto-Scoot, Cushman, Rock–Ola, and others were offering their own scooters in the Motor Glide mode by the end of 1936. And by late 1937, Salsbury introduced its most revolutionary feature: the Self-Shifting Motor, a radical new automatic clutch and transmission torque converter. Again, the others rushed to follow the leader; Salsbury even sent a licensing agent to Europe in 1938 to offer his scooter to possible manufacturers, including Piaggio.

The Salsbury Motor Glide defined the Five Commandments of a motorscooter that set the style for all scooters that were to follow: A small motor placed next to or just in front of the rear wheel; a step-through chassis; bodywork to protect the rider from roadspray and engine grime; small wheels; and an automatic transmission/clutch package. All other scooters that came after the Salsbury had at least three of the five tenets.

In the late 1930s, motorcycle tuner, racer, and builder Albert G. Crocker created his Scootabout scooter, also in California. The Scootabout's engine and solid front suspension were typical of the time, but not so its flowing bodywork. Crocker followed the tenets of Salsbury's mechanical design but added the Sixth Commandment of a scooter: Styling. With its Art Deco teardrop shape and two-tone paint, the Scootabout foreshadowed the spirit of the Jet Age scooter styling that was to come.

The Second Italian Renaissance

Following World War II, the Piaggio Vespa was born. Today, many people call the Vespa the first scooter, an erroneous statement considering the dozens of prewar American makes. The Vespa

Toro! The scooter was quickly accepted and adopted to find a place in culture—even going so far as to replace the horse in bullfighting! These toreadors straddle a Parilla Levriere scooter as they prepare to lance a bull during a fight in Lisbon, Portugal, in 1956. Just hope the two-stroke engine didn't die at an inopportune moment. The crowd was taking it seriously!

was not even the first Italian scooter; the Gianca Nibbio wears that crown. Instead, the Vespa was more important than being simply the first; the Vespa was the best.

The Vespa was reliable. It was economical. It protected its rider from roadspray and motor oil. Its superior engineering demanded the respect of even motorcyclists. As a Calabrian scooterist told *American Mercury* magazine in 1957, "Wherever donkeys go the Vespa goes too." The Vespa was a scooter a grown person could ride with dignity to work or on vacation, and so the Vespa spread the good word about scooters throughout the world.

Just months on the heels of the Vespa came Innocenti's Lambretta, a more social scooter as it added a second seat and the horsepower to carry a second rider, an important feature for the times. Innocenti called its scooter a "social appliance" in what was perhaps an off-target Italian-to-English translation. Nevertheless, the term *social appliance* carried a much larger truth.

The scooter became essential to the Italian economy. Vittorio De Sica's 1948 film, *Ladri di biciclette* or *The Bicycle Thief,* depicted the plight of a Roman man who had his bicycle stolen, his one essential possession. In much of Italy, the scooter had already supplanted the bicycle by the time of De Sica's film, but *The Vespa Thief* would have lacked poetry.

By 1956, 600,000 scooters were buzzing around the roads of Italy. Tourists to Italy despised the unpicturesque sight of the buzzing "insects" swarming around the Trevi Fountain, ruining their snapshots for the folks back home, and filling the air with the choking scent of two-stroke exhaust. But the social consequences of the scooter boom were just starting to be felt.

In the 1930s, Benito Mussolini and his Fascists were able to dominate Italy because the country was largely agrarian with little communication between villages and even cities. Italian towns were worlds unto themselves; people were born, grew up, married, lived, and died in their own village, often without ever venturing past the surrounding fields. Culture was regionalized; local economies were largely self-sufficient but subsistent. While Il Duce later built roads and railways, in his fledgling years his Fascists were forced to march on Rome, and he used this lack of communication in Italy to divide and conquer. Postwar, scooters changed all this.

The scooter brought the city to the country, and vice versa. It brought people together, spread ideas and culture, and almost overnight carried Italy into the modern world; it was the dawn of a second Italian renaissance. The prodigal son could borrow the family Vespa and travel to the next town to court girls. Soon, women were on scooters as well.

Motorscooters played a starring role in the emancipation of the modern Italian woman. The British magazine, *Picture Post,* documented "A New Race of Girls" in 1954, stating that "the motor scooter gave her new horizons," as quoted from Dick Hebdige's semiotical analysis of the scooter in *Hiding in the Light.* A 1954 Innocenti promotional film for England, entitled *Travel Far, Travel Wide,* showed an airplane stewardess (in itself an image of the modern woman) on her Lambretta. The narrator announced that "The air hostess can become the pilot herself—and there's plenty of room on that pillion for a friend!" And who should climb on to the pillion but the airplane's male pilot.

Along with freedom of mobility, scooters were a catalyst in changing female fashion, sym-

La felicità va in **lambretta**

Innocenti's Lambretta offered 125cc power and a second seat from the beginning, marking it as the social scooter over the Vespa's single-seat, bare-bones functionality. It was ideal for courting and cruising the piazza, as scooters opened Italian horizons postwar, giving mobility to youths and spreading culture far and wide. In the 1940s, the woman rode on the pillion seat, sitting side-saddle as a lady should. That was all about to change forever, in a large part due to the motorscooter.

bolic of changes in status. *Picture Post* showed Gina Lollabrigida on her Vespa and chronicled the fashion changes: "The pocket handkerchief fashion which swept the women's world in 1949 was devised to keep a pillion girl's hair tidy at speed. The following winter, the headkerchief was developed by the Florentine designer, Emilio Pucci, into a woollen headscarf. Next year, the blown hair problem was solved by the urchin cut. The narrowing of the new-look skirt was dictated in order to prevent it getting tangled up with the wheels. The slipper shoe was created for footplate comfort. The turtleneck sweater and the neckerchief were designed against draughts down the neck." Meanwhile, Innocenti's prudish *Lambretta Notiziario* owners' magazine lamented that "one is all-too-frequently tormented by the sight of badly trousered women on motor scooters."

The Romantic Putt-Putt

After Audrey Hepburn and Gregory Peck fell in love on a Vespa in the 1953 film, Roman Holiday, love and scooters were never the same. Plunged into the spotlight, scooters facilitated the many splendored thing. Since, as the New York Times Magazine noted in 1958, "It's an unwritten code for scooterists to greet each other," the youth movement instantly had friends, and love.

Piaggio soon realized the importance of a dual-seated scooter and added the second seat to their Vespa, something that Innocenti's Lambretta had from the beginning.

Through advertising of scooters in exotic countries with beautiful people, the media was hooked. *American Mercury* followed Piaggio's lead in February 1957 with an article about the relationship between Vespas and teen love: "young couples, she riding side-saddle prettily and revealingly and he, heading deliberately for every bump to jounce her into holding him tighter." And *Popular Science*, in 1957, stated that, "Sports riders in this country are mostly either single or newly marrieds (scooters are so conducive to romance that there is a fast turnover between these categories)."

From her window, Juliet pines, "Romeo, Romeo, wherefore art thou, Romeo?" And then, over the hill, approaches the amorous putt-putt of a Triumph Tigress TW2 ridden by fair Romeo beaming with scooter-inspired virility. Juliet can't help but swoon. Love rode on two wheels for many a youth from Italy to England to the United States. And prudish dates didn't need to worry about any backseat gymnastics as there was no backseat. The real concern, however, was having the scooter break down in some out-of-the-way spot—whether planned or not. Mick Walker archives

Picture Post even went so far as to say that the scooter—along with beauty competitions and films—"consummated" the Italian woman's emancipation. As proof it pictured film stars Anna Magnani and Sophia Loren and talked about a new breed of "untamed, unmanicured, proud, passionate, bitter Italian beauties"—all riding scooters. Italian women had come a long way from sitting side-saddle on the pillion.

The Worldwide Scooter Boom

Scooters were, to paraphrase Immanuel Kant's categorical imperative, the greatest good for the greatest number. Alongside bicycles, scooters were inexpensive to build and inexpensive to operate—everyone could afford one. As the American *Popular Science* magazine discovered in 1957, "Cheaper than walking and lots more fun"; the second statement was true, the first doubtful, but the idea was sound. Scooters were the true democratic machine. Enrico Piaggio even saw them as a way to fight the encroaching tide of communism. And so Europe and Japan's postwar recovery rode on two wheels.

Vespas and Lambrettas were soon built under license in England, Germany, France, and Spain. By the late 1950s, factories in Belgium, Czechoslovakia, Mexico, Poland, Yugoslavia, Chile, Argentina, and India were turning out their versions of the smallest wonder, to paraphrase the Volkswagen's nickname. A *New Yorker* reporter wrote in 1957 (with a touch of panic in his tone) that "This is more than a fad, it's a revolution and I don't see how anything can stop it."

Japan also quickly recognized the scooter's value, with its first scooter offered in 1946, the

---

Lambretta Twist and Other Scooter Hymns

Cars have always inspired singers to break into song. Mississippi Delta bluesman Robert Johnson sang of the Hudson Terraplane with thinly veiled sexual allusion. And the Beach Boys longed for their little Deuce coupe to the sounds of twanging surf guitars. Even motorcycles had their fair share of bel canti, from the Ducati Cucciolo theme song ("The little engine beats like my heart") to Brigitte Bardot's hit promising that she needed nothing but her Harley-Davidson.

Scooters, however, have probably inspired more innovative swear words than heavenly hymns. But there have been several songs sung to the scooter.

In 1947, Innocenti announced the arrival of its first Lambretta A 125 scooter with a catchy tune played day and night over RAI radio. The ditty was one of those you could not get out of your mind no matter how hard you tried—and is still whistled to this day by Milanese caught off guard.

Then in the 1960s came the Italian hit, "Lambretta Twist," and on dance floors everywhere the crowd was twisting—everyone, that is, except Vespisti.

The most eloquent testimonial to the scooter was surely The Who's *Quadrophenia*, a rock'n'roll opera telling the tale of the Mod-Rocker clashes in 1960s England. A Vespa graced the album cover as well as the movie poster and the sinking of a scooter ended the film with symbolic eloquence.

And in between there was the music. Mods rode to the downbeat of ska and the upbeat of soul. The Who were turned to 11 with Pete Townsend smashing Rickenbackers and Roger Daltry yodelling in "The Punk Meets the Godfather": "I ride a GS with my hair so neat/wear a war-torn parka in the wind and sleet." Amen.

LO SCOOTER 4 MARCE 150 CC. "59"

By the 1950s, the Italian woman's emancipation rode on two wheels. The scooter brought easy-to-use mobility to women, and fashions soon evolved to suit scooters, from shorter skirts to keep the hem out of the engine to—gasp!—slacks. In the 1950s, you only sat side-saddle if you wanted to show some leg. This 1950s Iso ad reflected a new era; to mix national metaphors with *The Wizard of Oz*, Dorothy and Toto were no longer in Kansas. *Vittorio Tessera archives*

11

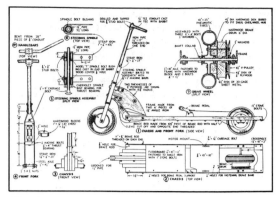

"First find an old washing machine motor," began this 1938 *Science and Mechanics* instruction on how to build your own scooter. Scooters were so popular in prewar America that dozens of manufacturers sprouted like weeds, offering everything from mail-order scooters to build-your-own plans for 25¢. In almost every issue, science magazines told everyone with a wrench and hammer how to use what would usually be considered junk to build a scooter that was definitely junk. As these directions went on to say, "The body frame is of scrap lumber and it is assembled with corrugated fasteners." Inspiring, to say the least.

same year as the Vespa. The premier scooter was built by Fuji of Tokyo and called the Rabbit. Mitsubishi, builder of the great Zero-San fighter for the Japanese Air Force, followed in 1947 with its Pigeon scooter. While these first scooters were clear copies of postwar US designs and were rustic at best, Japan soon developed an efficient luxury scooter as good as any ever built by the Germans. The Japanese scooter industry followed the same rise as the Europeans and had many of the same effects on the economy and culture.

The Soviet Union and Eastern Europe also caught on and built scooters for the masses. Many of the Soviet scooters simply copied Western designs, hiding their patent infringements behind the Iron Curtain. The Russian Vjatka was a brazen Soviet Vespa; the Tula was a Goggol–Isaria in disguise. While a scooter was the ultimate democratic machine, it was also the ultimate communist machine.

Mods, Scooter Boys, and Rumbles in Brighton

In the late 1950s and early 1960s, the teenage market was born. The standard of living was rising throughout Europe, and the youth had money in their pockets from allowances or part-time jobs. In the United States, plenty of old Ford deuce coupes with Flathead engines could be had for cheap and hot-rodded in the backyard; but in

Europe, scooters were the hot rods of a generation.

As an inexpensive form of transportation, scooters were ideal for the younger set while their mums and pops popped for an automobile. And of course, teenagers wanted quick machines with styling galore. The two main scooter makers, Piaggio and Innocenti, responded with high-performance models for youths who wanted to get from point *A* to *B* with a stop at the local coffeeshop or record store for their friends to ogle their ride.

British teens led the way. Groups of teenagers jumped on the latest fad, searching for their own image while outdoing their peers with style. The Teddy Boys bloomed in England as a distinct set of teens that eschewed the schmalz English culture of their parents to dress slick and bop to American rock'n'roll.

Then came the Mods. Clothes, hair, music, and scooters ruled in the Modernist mindset. Richard Barnes defined his peers in *Mods*, his remembrance of things past: "The Mod way of life consisted of total devotion to looking and being 'cool'. Spending practically all your money on clothes and all your after hours in clubs and dance halls." Originally the music consisted of new jazz from the likes of Thelonius Monk and Charlie Mingus, then later turned to ska, American soul, and The Who. Mods were crazed for anything continental; they strolled Carnaby Street and the London West End in sleek Italian suits, tailored shirts, and French crepe-soled shoes, topped by the haircut of the week.

Scooters came to the Mod scene as an afterthought, or as a rebuttal against the other great youth force of the time, the Rockers. Scooter boys wearing hooded army parkas were another youth group of the time that eventually melded into the Mods, and the chic modernistic styling of the Lambretta caught the Mod fancy. Suddenly, a scooter was quintessential cool.

Meanwhile, Rockers were hopping to Eddie Cochran and doing the jukebox drag race: you popped your coin into the Ace Bar jukebox, punched the buttons for your fave song, ran outside, kicked over your Triumph, squealed out of the lot, did the town down to the designated turnabout, and blasted back before the song was over. Mods were silly fops to the working class Rockers, and their scooters were prissy and sissy.

Mods and Rockers formed their image by what their enemy wasn't. Rockers donned leather jackets, hair grease, and lived to ride while riding to live on their BSA Gold Stars and Triumph Bonnies. When the *Daily Mirror* interviewed young Mod, Teresa Gordon, in 1964, she said it like it was, "You've got to be either a Mod or a Rocker to mean anything. Mods are neat and clean. Rockers look like Elvis Presley, only worse." It was difficult to imagine anything truly worse.

The rivalry between Rockers and Mods became violent in 1964 when both groups converged for a Bank Holiday on the beaches of Brighton to stroll the boardwalks and check out the latest fashions. What started as an Innocenti-sponsored scooter meet, soon turned into a melee: scooters were tipped over wheels up, beach chairs were thrown, and haircuts ruffled. The British nation was (enjoyably) shocked.

The Mods' scooters went through various stages of modification. In the beginning, the scooter was left alone as the classic look. Then fancy two-tone paint jobs were the rage fronted by an endless assortment of mirrors, trophies, and chrome frou-frou as well as enough headlamps to light up half of London. One day, the scooter went minimalist; it was stripped of its side panels and horn cover to reveal what looked more like a petite Rocker's motorcycle than a scooter. And then, of course, the styles turned back and started all over again.

The Modern Motorscooter

In the late 1960s and early 1970s, scooters fell out of favor. In the United States, Cushman and Harley–Davidson had thrown in the towel due to declining sales; both firms began building golf carts instead, so the grown-up kids in kelly green who had once buzzed Main Street on a scooter

Even in the United States, the land of land yachts, the scooter held a fascination. The 1955 Ice Capades show toured the country featuring such spectacles as a re-enactment of Peter Pan on skates as well as the grand finale of Ravel's Bolero. The true spectacle was watching the traffic police in the Autorama section ride their Lambretta LD 125 Series 1 scooters on ice without augering in. The Ice "Cop" Ades, Ice Ca"Pets," and the El-Dorables pirouetted around the buzzing scooters wearing gas pump caps and skating outfits with car grilles on the front, all while trying not to choke on two-stroke fumes. This really did happen. *Courtesy Hymies' Vintage Record City*

could now tour the links. In Europe, most adults had graduated from scooters and were now happily ensconced behind the wheel of a car. Most Europeans looked back on scooters with the same fondness they felt for carpet bombings.

The Modern Age of the Motorscooter arrived in 1978 when Piaggio launched its Nuova Linea of P Series Vespas. To many people, modern meant plastic and ultra-modern meant all-plastic, but the new Vespas offered more. The P Series boasted of electronic ignition, rotary-valve induction, automatic transmission, electric start, and other luxury features, and other scooters soon followed Piaggio's lead.

Never mind the nicknames, scooters had a history as mechanical marvels. The legacy began with the torque converter on the Salsbury Motor Glide in late 1937. It continued with the unitized stressed-skin chassis of the Vespa in 1946. It went on with the mechanical disc brake offered in 1961 on the American-made Midget Motors Autocycle and in 1962 on the Lambretta TV3 (not the first disc brake on a motorcycle; the Maserati motorcycle of 1955 holds that honor). In between there was hydraulic suspension and electric starters, often long before they became common features on motorcycles. Scooters always offered a lot for a little.

And then there was the styling. From Art Deco to Jet Age to Futuristic, scooters had it all: tailfins, jetpods, turbine ducts, two-tone flairs, fender skirts, chrome jewelry, and even integrated sidecars.

The long-lived appeal of the scooter can be seen in the Piaggio's attempt to retire the Vespa. In the mid-1980s, Piaggio announced plans to replace the Vespa with the new Cosa scooter, which featured much of the Vespa's technology under a new body. Outcry came from all sides inspiring many a former scooter riders to dig the old machine out of the shed, restore it to better-than-new condition, and parade about town while all passersby waxed poetic about the good old days. Membership in vintage and Mod scooter clubs skyrocketed worldwide, and suddenly everyone was wiping a nostalgic tear from the corner of their eyes and daydreaming about scooters, from Cushmans to Lambrettas, Bastert Einspurautos to Fuji Rabbit Superflows.

So Piaggio gave in to the demand and brought back the Vespa. The company even began selling a line of vintage-styled scooters with modern mechanicals on into the 1990s. And Honda, Yamaha, Suzuki, Benelli, Aprilia, PGO, Peugeot, and others offered their own modern scooters to a renewed market interest.

And this story continues.

Brutish British rockers on their grimy, uncouth working class Triumphs gang up on poor Mod Chalky and his Italian Hairdryer in this still from the film, *Quadrophenia*. The Mods and the Rockers were on the road to the 1964 Brighton Beach Bank Holiday fracas that shocked a Great Britian that wanted to be shocked—JDs, or juvenile deliquents, were the stylish outrage of the era. The movie summed up the Mod lifestyle to the sounds of The Who with Pete Townsend's Rickenbacker and Marshall turned to 11 harmonizing with packs of Vespas and Lambrettas at full, unmuffled two-stroke bore. Italian suits, army parkas, and scooters were the signs of the times.

Treachery and Treason Amidst the Subcommittee of Vespa Paint: A Report by Eric Dregni

In Italy, motorscooters are not just inexpensive transportation or kitsch artifacts. As with many things Italian, scooters are another reason for a good argument.

I recently infiltrated a weekly Vespa Club d'Italia Milano meeting, which took place in a Vespa-crazed insurance agent's office (the location seemed all too convenient for him to also acquire new clients). Ten Vespisti were in attendance, although they bemoaned having to meet in the front office while in the prestigious backroom, the Moto Gilera club was holding its gathering. More horsepower, more pull.

I was introduced to the club members, all of whom had illustrious titles and ranks in the heirarchy; only a handful were simply "members." These ranks were essential to note: the VIPs were those respected enough to be allowed to talk uninterrupted (sometimes).

Although the club was desperate for new members, they suspiciously asked me what I wanted. I flattered them, saying I had ventured all the way from the US just to attend one of their famous meetings. They bought this statement wholeheartedly, proudly replying that people often come from all over the world to consult with them. When asked for specifics, however, they were a little vague but they pointed to one of their members who had recently returned from a Piaggio business conference in Rio; he produced photos of himself arm in arm with two towering Brazilian dancers. These snapshots were passed around to a chorus of "Ooh-la-las," which was interrupted by Gino, who rhetorically asked, "Have we come here to talk about women or scooters."

There was no dissent to this logic, and Gino announced the first order of business: the absolute, dire necessity of charting the correct green paint finish of the early Vespas. It had come to his attention that some early Vespas were slightly more metallic looking than others.

The insurance agent interrupted him to talk about an upcoming scooter rally, which caused Gino to raise his voice, demanding that if Vespisti the world over want the "correct" finish, the club must form the Subcommittee of Vespa Paint staffed by experts who would determine exactly the right shade for all restorations.

This was countered by one of the younger members, who stated that he personally may not know about paint but he did know all the brake specifications of every Vespa model—not just the early ones.

Naturally, this statement outraged Gino, who demanded that no one change the subject from paint. Next week, they could discuss brakes all they wanted and even form a Subcommittee of Vespa Brakes. Now was the time to talk paint.

Sig. Rossi then interrupted, opining that instead of forming exclusive committees, wouldn't it be better to teach younger Vespisti the joys of restoring early Vespas? Gino was on his feet, insulted to the core, insisting that if the club designated certain members as experts in specific fields they would have to learn every last bit of information on that topic and then others could never question their word.

A younger member boldly replied that Gino just didn't want anyone to question him when he talked about paint. This obvious statement infuriated Gino and he banged his fist on the desk. Alas, he could not be heard over the din of argument. Sig. Rossi then said they needed to ask their president, who was already an hour late (as usual). In the meantime, they all turned to me, asking what the proper procedure should be: disseminate the valuable information or consolidate it within subcommittees.

After all the shouting, the silence was painful, especially under the hard stare of all eyes. I fidgeted in my seat and could feel the sweat running down my neck. Had they aimed the lights at me as well?

And then the moment arrived: I confessed that I didn't even have a Vespa. I was a Lambrettista.

The silence turned to shock. I was afraid for my kneecaps and certain that I had definately lost my chance of ever achieving a prestigious title in the Vespa Club d'Italia. But then Sig. Rossi, ever the kind ambassador, reassured me, saying, "Well, actually Lambrettas are better scooters: more powerful, steadier, and two seats."

The room reverberated with outrage. How could one of their own Vespisti prefer Lambretta to Vespa? A traitor in their midst! Treason! Besides, the insurance agent insisted, even if Lambrettas are more powerful, there are six times more Vespas than Lambrettas!

Before lines were drawn and knives pulled, the president miraculously appeared. The grave dilemma of the Subcommittee of Vespa Paint was posed and a fuming silence reigned awaiting his decree. He calmly ignored the question and began telling about the phenomenal soccer game he had just seen: his team had won! The insurance agent and several others were outraged. His team was terrible! They did not deserve to win! Pandemonium broke loose and the insurance office boomed with screams. In the midst of it all, I grabbed my coat and ran for the door as Gino pounded his fist and screamed that they were not to change the subject from paint.

Star Ratings

The star ratings system developed for the Illustrated Buyer's Guide series is general and subjective at best, but, taken with a grain of salt or a full saltshaker in some cases, it does give a broad hint of a scooter's collectability or desirability.

The star ratings run from your basic, barebones, no-frill scooter at one star all the way up to five stars for the best, the tops, the coolest, the rarest, and the weirdest. The rankings in between are gradations on the theme.

With scooters, there are several ways to decode all of this. Some scooteristi rank the odder, more eccentric scooters as the tops. For these people, the Cushman Model 53 with packed parachute or the Italian FM with its eccentric rear suspension are the best. Others are loyal to one brand only.

You must also think in terms of frames of reference. In balancing our star ratings, we attempted to look at scooters of the world and give relative ratings. But if you're an American scooter collector, you may care little for a Rumi and sell your soul for a Rock-Ola. If you're a Mod, you wouldn't be seen dead on a Cushman Super Silver Eagle at the local coffeehouse; only a Vespa GS with enough headlamps to light a night baseball game will do.

You need also consider what you want in a scooter when deciphering the stars. If you collect prewar American scoots, then a 1936 Motor Glide ranks five stars and a Honda Helix none. But if you are looking for a daily rider with class, style, and history, then a Vespa P200 ranks five and a Nibbio is passed over.

As we said, general and subjective.

On the other hand, if you meet the scooter of your dreams and fall for it hard, forget the star ratings and go with your heart.

Alphabetical Listing of Scooter Makes of the World

Achilles Germany ★

Achilles built motorcycles for the Austro–Hungarian empire in the days when Princess Georgiana, the White Rose of Hungary, was to wed his majesty King Zog of Albania.

Achilles offered its Cushman Eagle-like Sport scooter with the choice of a Fichtel & Sachs 147cc or 175cc engine from 1953–1957. The Sport was half scooter—small 10in wheels and floorboard—and half motorcycle with the gas tank between the legs and engine ahead of the rear wheels. The Achilles had power to scale its native mountains, with the smaller Sport at 6.75hp at 4500rpm for a 85km/h (52.7mph) top speed, and the larger had 9.5hp at 5250rpm for 90km/h (55.8mph). After Achilles closed shop in 1957, the British Norman motorcycle works bought its machinery.

Adler Germany

At the turn of the century when bicycles moved the masses, Adler led the way with 100,000 bicycles built by 1898. With the development of the internal-combustion engine, Adler shifted from bicycles and typewriters to automobiles, motorcycles, and motorscooters.

Junior 1955–1957 and Junior Luxus 1957 ★★

"Live joyfully with wings—drive an Adler" urged ads for the Junior. Unfortunately, competition raged so fiercely, the Junior practically died in its nest. Upon realizing that the 98cc 3.75hp engine was no match for the larger scooters, Adler designed the 125cc Junior Sport prototype that also never went into production. Instead, it updated the standard Junior to the Luxus with 4hp and other minor changes.

In describing the power of the Junior engine, ads touted "its quick starting, easy hill climbing and steady perseverance on the motor highway can be taken for granted and need hardly be mentioned at all." Was this purple prose a plot to cover up its weak engine?

Fortunately for manufacturers, however, when riding a scooter speed is magnified far beyond reality. In 1957, a *New Yorker* reporter was taken for a test ride on an Adler and "a moment or so later, hanging on for dear life, we found ourself breezing down Broadway at what he told us was twenty-five miles an hour, though it felt like

Here's what Mr. Smith likes best about the Adler Junior: 98cc engine, electric starting, and opportunity to get forty extra winks in the morning. As this brochure pointed out, Adler was German for egle and the Junior would certainly "lend you wing." The Junior was one of the few German scooters imported into the United States, but it only had limited success next to the scooter giants Cushman, Innocenti, and Piaggio. *Mick Walker archives*

17

ninety." In fact, the top speed of the Junior was 70km/h (43.4mph) on its 14in wheels.

Aermacchi Italy

Like Piaggio, Aermacchi came to motorcycle construction from an aviation background. Aeronautica Macchi, located on Lago Varese, was famous for its racing seaplanes that contested the Schneider Trophy, setting in 1934 the world speed record for piston-engined seaplanes of 440.69mph, a record that still stands today.

Macchi 125, Ghibli, and Zeffiro ★★

In 1950, the firm introduced its Macchi 125, which, like Moto Guzzi's Galletto, was a motorscooter on large, 3.00x17in tires; Aermacchi's flyer called it "Lo scooter trasformabile"—the transformable scooter. The engine was a horizontal two-stroke single of 52x58mm delivering 5hp at 4300rpm. Several versions were available: the S; the more luxurious N with fuller fenders; and the Grand Luxe and the C, both with added, protective bodywork.

Scooter Police: "Fuzz With A Buzz"

In Westerns, the Law was always on horseback. When motorcycles arrived, it was only natural that police should take to them like doughnuts. And when scooters first became available in 1936 California, scooter police units hit the mean streets.

Salsbury flyers showed scooter police mounted on Motor Glides—often with dubious looks on their faces. Other American police forces bought Cushmans and had crime on the run.

With the European postwar scooter boom, it was only natural for cities to equip their cops with economical transport. If the Baddies were escaping at a top speed of 40mph, why not chase them down with another scooter? In 1956, Dublin, Ireland, armed a police squad with Vespas.

In 1964, New York City took the cue to save the dark metropolis from crime by fighting evil with scooters. The SCRAMBLE Patrol (Scooters in Communication with Range and Mobility for Better Law Enforcement) was broken down into TSU (Tactical Scooter Units) of seven policemen each. The eighty police Vespas and Lambrettas on the streets by 1967 had brought the level of muggings down by 30 percent in Central Park and 40 percent in Brooklyn's Prospect Park in 1964, as reported in *Time* in 1967.

In an article titled "Fuzz with a Buzz," the magazine hailed the good scooters brought to Gotham: "The zippy little vehicles provide all sorts of extra benefits. The putt-putting noise daunts would-be lawbreakers; the potential speed (60mph) and mobility enable wheezy cops to outrun juvenile delinquents, mount sidewalks or even bounce up shallow steps to bypass traffic."

Who needed Batman?

Buzzing fuzz: the tactical scooter law enforcement team of Inglewood, California's finest mounted atop 1938 Motor Glides. The five scooters at left were De Luxe models with lighting; the model at right a Standard. All of the officers have tenative looks on their faces. E. Foster Salsbury archives

Aermacchi also released the Macchi 125 U, named Ghibli after the Saharan wind. The U was a basic, utilitarian version of the standard S model.

The Ghibli was soon replaced by the Zeffiro, or Zephyr, with 125cc and 150cc version available. Two 150cc models were offered: the base 150 Luxe and the 150/N, a sportster.

Chimera 175 and 250 ★★★

In 1956, the futuristic Chimera was offered based on Ing. Bianchi's great four-stroke 175cc horizontal pushrod single. Riding on motorcycle wheels, the Chimera was clothed in pressed-steel bodywork that was pure Jet Age. But even when offered in 250cc form, the Chimera failed to find a market; it was years ahead of its time in styling and technology.

Brezza ★★

In the early 1960s, Aermacchi was split in two. The motorcycle division was partnered with Harley–Davidson; the aeronautical side went to Lockheed. In 1962, the motorcycle group released the Brezza, or Breeze, scooter in the style of the Zeffiro with a 150cc two-stroke engine.

By 1973, Aermacchi disappeared totally from the motorcycle scene, swallowed up by Harley–Davidson.

Agrati–Garelli Italy ★★

Agrati introduced its Capri scooter in 1958 based on a brilliant yet simple idea: build a single scooter and equip it with a series of engines and gearboxes to create a complete line to satisfy all markets. Thus, Capris were available with the following powerplants: 3.3hp 50cc with three speeds; 4.3hp 50cc with four speeds; 3.3 hp 70cc with three speeds; 4hp 80cc with three speeds; 5.5hp 125cc with four speeds; and 5.6hp 148cc with four speeds.

The styling was also simple. Bodywork covered the machine with lift-off side covers in a contrasting color. Two-tone schemes were red and beige, gray and light blue, and light blue and dark blue.

But the Capri had one problem: competition. Piaggio and Innocenti controlled the scooter market and the Capri could not edge its way in; thus, the scooter was doomed to be an exile. The vast majority of Capris were exported throughout Europe from Greece to Great Britian and on into the United States. It was an odd success story for an Italian scooter.

The Agrati–Garelli merger was formed in 1961, made up by Agrati and the Garelli firm that built the ubiquitious post-World War II Mosquito clip-on bicycle engine. In 1961, Agrati continued with a 98cc Capri while Garelli offered a 125cc Capri De Luxe.

Aldimi Belgium ★★

Launched in 1953, Aldimi of Brussels built a scooter named, in all seriousness, the Prince de Liège. It used a 125cc Saroléa engine of 6hp at 4800rpm riding atop 3.50x10in tires. In 1954, the Prince de Liège's ego got even larger with a 200cc Sarolèa. But even with such regal endorsement, the scooter did not go far. In 1956, Aldimi switched to building Piatti scooters for Belgium, with little success.

Allstate USA

Allstate was a fitting brand name for Sears, Roebuck and Co. to sell motorscooters under; after all, Sears saturated the United States with its mail-order catalog and outlet stores.

Sears management must have seen the success the Gambles mail-order company had with its Doodle Bug since 1946, and began shopping for a scooter line in the late 1940s. By 1950, there was only one reasonable choice: Cushman. Salsbury had gone the way of the nickel Coca-Cola and

The idea behind the Capri was brilliant: one scooter offered with a variety of engines to create a whole model line. Thus, Capris were offered by Agrati–Garelli in two- and four-stroke form from 50cc to 150cc. But the Capri had one problem: competition in Italy. In the end, it was destined to exile, being sold throughout the world but only in small numbers in its native country.

Piaggio's Vespa, which Sears would begin importing in 1951–1952, was unheard of in the United States at the time.

Cushman was happy to sign on. The Sears deal offered it a new outlet for sales—never mind what Cushman's own dealers said under their collective breath—but it also prevented Sears from offering a competitive line. By 1951, the first Cushman badge-engineered Allstate motorscooters were listed in the famous Sears tome, sent to millions of households across the United States.

Standard Model 3hp 1951–1958 ★★

The basic model was the Standard 3hp, although Sears was inconsistent in calling it either the Standard or the 3hp on and off from 1951–1958; throughout its production run it was given consecutive Sears catalog numbers and the Sears 811.30 model number, all of which were important for locating parts. The 3hp was a thinly disguised Cushman Model 61 Highlander. The 811.30 model name denoted the Cushman Husky 12.3ci engine stamped with 811 for Allstate use; the 30 suffix stood for 3.0hp.

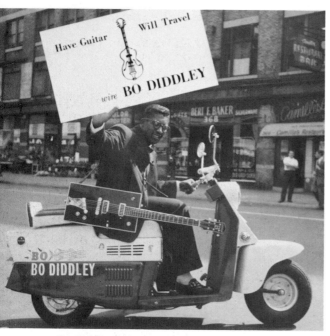

Bo Diddley had guitar (a custom solid-body rectangular Gretsch) and traveled (on an Allstate Jetsweep). Truth be told, however, Bo traveled further with his single signature guitar lick and his Grestch than he did with his scooter; Gretsch even named a model after Bo, which is more than Allstate ever did. Nevertheless, this was high rock'n'roll style in the 1960s. *Chess Records/Quality Records*

Differences from the 61 were subtle yet all-important. While the 61 was what Cushman called a Sport, meaning it had no rear bodywork, the Allstate was well dressed with bolt-on side covers. Large Allstate decals depicting the outline of the USA with the word Allstate superimposed were placed on the side covers under the seat. The 3hp was only ever available in bright red enamel.

The 3hp could be yours in 1951 for $179.50 cash or $36 down with monthly payments. The Sears installment plan advantage sold many Allstates through the years when you needed cash in hand at the Cushman dealer.

By 1953, the Cushman tow hitch was offered. In 1957, the rear bodywork of the 3hp was subtly redesigned and catalogued without fanfare; the Allstate decal was now smaller and placed at the rear near the taillamp. The new 3hp Allstate lasted only one more year; in 1959 it was replaced by the Standard 4.8hp.

De Luxe Model 4hp 1951–1957 ★★★★

Sears called its advanced scooter the De Luxe 4hp but as with the Standard, Sears was inconsistent in terming it the De Luxe, Deluxe, or 4hp through the scooter's career. The Allstate was based on the Cushman Model 62 Pacemaker with one-speed transmission and automatic centrifugal clutch.

The engine was the famed 14.9ci Husky; Sears ads ballyhooed its "automotive-type camshaft," which was certainly superior to other camshaft types. The rear drum brake was also of the "automotive-type," giving "Dependable 'stop on a dime' braking power," in technical terms. "Runs easily in slow traffic, zooms up to 40 or more for speedy get-away," the catalog stated. The "or more" top speed was 45mph with a tailwind.

The De Luxe 4hp was one of the most stylish scooters of all time, blending a funky "streamlined windsplitter" front fender with avant garde rear bodywork. The look was set off by chrome trim, swank Allstate decals, and arrow-shaped nameplate. As the Sears catalog pointed out, the styling was "exclusive and advanced!"

The Allstate's look was indeed exclusive compared with the 62. The Cushman had progressed little from the first Auto-Glide—traditional styling was a polite way to say it. The Allstate redesign created a scooter that was a vision of the future on two 4.00x8in wheels at a time when American automobiles were largely still 1940s designs. The windsplitter front fender "quoted" the Salsbury Model 85 design while the tail foreshadowed the chrome and tailfins of the 1955 Chevrolet.

The De Luxe first appeared in the 1951 Sears catalogs available at $219.95 cash. Or you could pay only $44 down and have it shipped in a crate to your front door and offer up monthly payments while you wheeled your way about town.

During its production run, the two chief items that changed on the 4hp were its price, which usually went up, and the color scheme. In 1951-1952, it was offered in bright red or "gay" yellow baked-on enamel; for 1953, only red was available; by 1954, red was supplemented by glass green; in 1955, you could have your 4hp in two-tone only with red highlighted by ivory trim; for 1956-1957, two-tone was out and it was back to red with black trim, although the latex seat cover was now striped.

In 1957, the fabulous Allstate 4hp was retired to be replaced by the equally fantastic Jetsweep.

Jetsweep Model 4.8hp 1957–1960 ★★

The 4.8hp replaced the 4hp in late 1957 as the Cushman 722 Pacemaker replaced the 62 Pace-maker earlier in the same year. Sears initially called its new scooter the 4.hp in 1957 ads, retitling it the Jet-sweep in 1958 and subtly reworking the name to be the Jetsweep for 1959.

"Look forward to miles of pleasure on this sleek, strong scooter of the future," read the catalog. The Jetsweep "carries you miles in minutes," a claim that certainly could not be challenged.

The Allstate changed during the years along with Cushman's version. Cooling woes had plagued the 722 and cooling louvers were stamped into the rear bodywork to help along the 14.9ci Husky. In 1957, the Allstate was free of louvers; by 1958, cooling louvers appeared on the top deck; by 1959, louvers were on both sections.

From 1957–1959, the Allstate was painted Coronet Red and Dover White two-tone. In 1960, the Allstate reversed Cushman's color scheme with the body painted Mist White and the trim and top deck in Hunter Red.

Standard 4.8hp 1959–1961 ★

"All-new fresh-as-a-breeze styling!" the Sears catalog shouted; it should have been a cry of warning. The replacement for the old Standard 3hp was based on the new Cushman 721 Highlander, an ungainly scooter design if there ever was one.

Based on the the 12.3ci Husky, the Allstate was painted Hunter Red with reflective silver trim

Sears Roebuck and Co. flyer for its Allstate "mile-making" scooter line of 1955, including the 3hp Standard Model and the 4hp Deluxe Model. Sears introduced its top-of-the-line 4 1/2hp Vespa in 1953 as the Allstate Cruisaire, but did not include it here. In 1955, chief competitor Montgomery Ward was just launching its Riverside line of scooters, which were Japanese-made Mitsubishi Silver pigeons. *Sears Roebuck and Co.*

The De Luxe was based on the Cushman Model 62 Pacemaker with the 14.9ci Husky, one-speed transmission, and automatic centrifugal clutch. The body was built by Cushman based on styling reworked by Sears, marking it as one of the most distinctive scooters ever built. Allstate was never consistent in naming its models. The Sears catalog termed it the De Luxe Model in 1951 and called it simply the 4hp Model 1952–1957; Sears copywriters made a slip of the tongue, terming it the Deluxe in 1955. Owners: Keith and Kris Weeks.

and a black engine and seat. It came to your home "partly assembled," which may have been another warning.

3hp 1960 ★

For one year only, Sears offered a revived 3hp model with an 8.4ci engine based on a 2 15/16x2in bore and stroke. The styling was distinctively slab-sided, set off by a two-tone Temple Gray and Cascade Blue paint job topped by a bare-bones cushion seat.

Compact 1961–1962 ★

Sears began selling Austrian-built Puch motorcycles under the Allstate nameplate in 1954; by 1961, it also offered a Puch scooter as its Compact model.

This compact was a beginner's supplement to the Piaggio and Cushman line, as the catalog promised: "Even if you've never driven one you'll soon handle this like a pro." Never mind that the Compact was faster at 42.5mph than the Cushman, had three speeds versus the Cushman's one, as well as front and rear drum brakes.

The engine was an aluminum two-stroke with flywheel magneto ignition. "Listen to its Puch-built engine purr," the catalog copy said by way of seduction. The Puch arrived at your doorstep painted in "lustrous" cream and red two-tone.

Sears and Cushman Part Ways

In 1961, Sears and Cushman went their separate ways. Sears chose to concentrate on its Piaggio and Puch lines, and Cushman made the odd decision to retire its step-through scooters and challenge Sears by also importing Vespas. Sears' decision to sever its relations with Cushman prob-

ably helped spell the end of Cushman scooters as much as Cushman's own decision to switch to Piaggio. And in 1963, Sears dropped all scooters from its catalog. It was a sad finale to years of mail-order scootering.

Alpino Italy ★

Alpino built a small motorcycle of 75cc in the early 1950s that by virtue of its extensive bodywork and smaller, 18in wheels, deserves the esteemed mantle of motorscooter. Legshields and a full engine cover protected the rider from unpleasantries.

Alpino later offered its 150cc and 175cc two-stroke scooters. The larger version had electric start.

Ambassador UK ★★

Ambassador of Ascot built a healthy number of small-capacity motorcycles for the English market in the 1960s, including a foray into the scooter world. Ambassador's scooter was known simply as the Ambassador.

Based on a fan-cooled two-stroke 173cc Villiers 3L engine of 59x63.5mm, the Ambassador had a four-speed integral gearbox with primary and secondary drive by chain. A heel-and-toe pedal shifted the gears. As *Motor Cycle* reported in 1960, "acceleration nippy up to maximum speed of about 55 m.p.h."

The Ambassador was of classical scooter construction with a 2 1/4in diameter main tube frame enclosed by unstressed bodywork. A swing arm at the rear was damped by springs on both sides but a Girling shock absorber on just the right. Tires were 3.50x6in and 12in brakes were fitted front and rear.

The Ambassador was fitted with luxury features over and above its call of duty, including a Siba Dynastart electric starter—which was "silent," according to a flyer—a speedometer and idiot warning lights for ignition, neutral, and low gas level.

In the tantalizing terms of an Ambassador flyer, the bodywork was "styled from stem to stern on graceful modern lines, with an appealing decor." Two-tone paint colors were Raven Black, Sun Valley Cream, or Royal Gold each paired with Grey-stone White, or Carnation Pink and Oyster Grey.

In 1962, Ambassador was sold to the English DMW firm, which ended the scooter's career in the same year.

Ambrosini Italy ★★★★

In 1952, the Società Aeronautica Italiana Ing. A. Ambrosini & Co. of Milan offered its Freccia

Allstate's 1957–1960 Jetsweep was a rebadged Cushman 722 Pacemaker, and just as Cushman had numerous problems perfecting its 722, the same changes in engine cooling were made year to year on the Jetsweep. Owners: Keith and Kris Weeks.

Azzurra, or Blue Arrow, scooter. The Ambrosini was a classic scooter mixing style, inventive creativity, and folly—the esssence of a motorscooter.

As befitting an aeronautical firm, the scooter's bodywork was perfectly aerodynamic, an essential feature when the Italian government limited scooters to 80km/h. If nothing else, the avant garde bodywork was pure Jet Age: the headlamp was streamlined into the fender; the horn blended into the legshields; and long, shapely ducts along the side fed air to the engine.

That engine was a Sachs two-stroke 147cc of 57x58mm giving 7.5hp at 5000rpm. A four-speed gearbox was shifted by a foot lever. Tires were 3.00x12in and had, of course, whitewalls.

Essential luxury features of the Ambrosini included a radio with antenna and an automatic engine cut-out gravity switch if the top-heavy scooter turned wheels up.

Aprilia Italy ★

The modern firm of Aprilia offered its Amico 50 scooter in the 1980s and 1990s based on a compact 49cc two-stroke of 40x39.2mm. While the frame consisted of steel tube, the formed-plastic bodywork enveloped the metal in dynamic colors.

At the 1992 Bologna show, Aprilia unveiled its *animale da città*, the Lama scooter. The spaceship styling was created by Frenchman Philippe Starck and topped by a handlebar cover that integrated turn signals to the front and rearview mirrors at the back, the whole affair angled skyward like llama ears.

Ardent France ★

Cannes may be known for its film festival and beautiful beaches, but its scooters have plunged into the abyss of anonymity. In 1951, the petit Baby was displayed, pedals and all, with a VAP-4 engine. The following year the Azur was sold with the added incentive of "super ballon" tires and either a 49cc 1.25hp Le Poulain engine for a 45km/h top speed or a 85cc 3hp Le Poulain motor for 70km/h. Finally in 1952, Ardent showed off "le plus beau scooter de Salon [de Paris]" known as the Estérel. Its 65cc Lavalette engine pumped out 2.8hp moving the scooter to a 65km/h top speed.

Ariel UK ★

Ariel was a once-proud motorcycle manufacturer, renowned for its Square Four models. But by the 1960s, the firm was singing its swan song through the muffler of such creations as the Ariel Pixie scooter-moped.

With a 50cc engine, the Pixie's frame was a pressed-steel spine similar to BSA's Beagle and

The Bangor Scootmaster bore a suspicious resemblance to the Cushman Auto-Glide of its day, but then again, imitation is the sincerest form of flattery. Styling, placement of the 3hp Clinton engine, controls, and even the inadequate front suspension were all telltale signs of where the idea originated. Owner: Jim Kilau.

Ariel's interesting if odd Leader and Arrow motorcycles.

Bangor Manufacturing Company USA ★★

Bangor of Bangor, Michigan, sold its Scootmaster in the late 1930s. Powered by a 3hp Clinton and riding atop 4in wheels, the Scootmaster was a no-frills vehicle that bore a suspiciously close resemblance to the Cushman Auto-Glide of the day.

Bastert West Germany ★★★★

Bastert of Bielefeld built its Einspurauto, or Single-Track Car, a monstrous spaceship of a scooter bedazzled by jetpod accents and chrome trim. Although the name rings less than beautifully in English, Bastert's exotic hovercraft with 13in wheels was a rare specimen since only 1,200 Einspurauto's were produced 1952–1956.

The Einspurauto had only one easychair seat with a backrest but could easily carry two people due to the powerful engine. The extended fenders added weight making for an 85km/h top speed for the 174cc 7.6hp model and 90km/h for the 197cc 9.5hp model.

The Einspurauto's main competition was the Maico Mobil, but Bastert's design was "outstanding perfection," according to advertising braggadocio, and included such extravagant luxuries as a fully optioned dashboard. Such high style made for a scooter that was "elegant + schnell"; but it was expensive even in the 1950s when, for the same price, a three-wheeled midget car could be had.

Bastert also produced prototype 120cc, 150cc, and 174cc scooters that unfortunately never saw production.

Beam USA ★★★

In the years after World War II, the Gambles Stores competed with chief rivals Sears Roebuck and Montgomery Ward. Gambles decided it wanted a motorscooter to market; management had seen the sales success of Cushman and Salsbury and believed that with its nationwide outlets, mail-order catalogs, and household name, it could make large profits from selling the little scooter to eager young putt-puttniks.

In 1946, Gambles signed the Beam Manufacturing Company of Webster City, Iowa, to build the Doodle Bug, a scooter more elfin than most. The chassis was a simple tube frame covered by scant rear bodywork and a cylindrical gas tank cantilevered off the tail, waiting for a rear end collision to blow up the machine in the best Ford Pin-

to manner. A simple cushion seat sat atop the engine; buckhorn handlebars were welded to the steering rod. In place of front forks, the sheet-steel fender cradled the wheel.

Beam chose the tried-and-true 1 1/2hp Briggs & Stratton engine to power the Doodle Bug via a belt drive. For a short period, the B & S engine was out of stock and Beam filled in with the Clinton 1 1/2hp. Beam always favored the B & S engine, and the Clinton-powered Doodle Bugs were rarer insects.

The Webster City factory hatched Doodle Bugs in four build lots of 10,000 scooters each for a total of 40,000. Sold through Gambles and Western Hardware stores, these specimens were the dream of many a young American boy.

Benelli Italy ★

Benelli of Pesaro was one of the pioneer motorcycle makers of Italy that turned to scooters

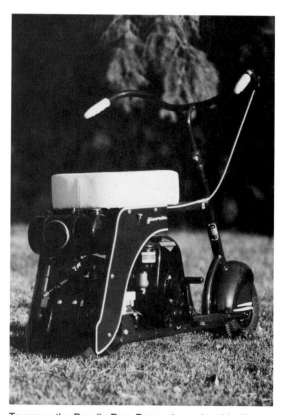

Mobilizing the masses with all the comfort of an easy chair on wheels, miles of smiles were found on every citizen exiting from the Bauhaus-styled Bastert factory. Keep your workers happy and productive with the 197cc 9.5hp Einspurauto.

To power the Doodle Bug, Beam chose the ubiquitious 1 1/2hp Briggs & Stratton engine with a belt drive. The Doodle Bug was hatched from the factory in four batches of 10,000 units each, mostly with the B&S engine but some with Clinton 1 1/2hp power. Owners: Keith and Kris Weeks.

during the boom years. It offered its Monaco scooter in the 1960s, which was an awkward blend of moped and scooter powered by a 125cc engine.

The Monaco's lack of success was symbolic of Benelli's troubles, and by 1971 the august firm was bought by Argentine Alejandro de Tomaso, who also would own Innocenti and Guzzi. To meet the ongoing demand for scooters, Benelli offered its S50, S50S, Laser 50, and S125 plastic scooters in the 1990s. At the 1992 Bologna show, Benelli displayed its KB-X50 Race scooter with high-performance components.

Bernardet France

After the liberation of France, the three Bernardet brothers began building automobiles and motorcycle sidecars at their factory in Bourg-la-Reine. Realizing that scooters are little more than motorized sidecars, the frères went to town in 1947.

Bernardet A.48 and A.49 1947–1948 ★★★

The Bernardets designed a scooter that went into production in late 1947 as the A.48 model, making them one of the French scooter pioneers. The two-stroke 128cc Ydral engine was backed by a four speeds and situated by the rear wheel without suspension. The totally enclosed scooter had a large front legshield with a Bernardet-Frères coat of arms on the front fender looking like an elf's cap with the headlamp as the tassel. The A.49 updated the A.48 with better cooling among other things, but retained the 4x12in wheels.

B.250 1949–1951 ★★

Presented at the 1949 Salon de Paris, the frères Bernardet's 250cc scooter had a split-single Violet engine designed by the famous engineer Marcel-Violet. The bodywork remained much the same as the earlier models but with rear suspension and a left-side kickstart for the 10hp engine. A shielded spare tire was mounted on the legshield's inside and leather saddlebags hung at rear.

BM and C.50 1950 ★★

The first series of Bernardets were updated as the BM with a 9hp 250cc engine and the C.50 with a 125cc Ydral engine.

E.51 1951; D.51 and Y.52 1952-1954 ★★

The second series appeared as the E.51 prototype at the 1951 Salon de Paris with smaller, 8in wheels, lighter in weight, and a 125cc Bernardet motor producing 6hp via four speeds and a right-side kickstart.

The D.51's 250cc Bernardet hit a 90km/h top speed with the kickstart and rear suspension on the left side. The front section was refined with an immovable fender and headlight mounted on the

This 1950 250cc Bernardet came in a vicious two-tone of lime green and white to fit in with prevailing 1950s kitchen styling. The front headlamp in the shape of a miner's helmet set the Bernardet's bizarre lines apart from its contemporary French conterparts. Owner: Vittorio Tessera.

apron. The design differed little from the Y.52 with the half-moon airscoop on the rear sidepanel that gave the impression of the eyelids of an animated scooter. The Y.52 kept the left-kick 125cc Ydral engine with the same 70km/h top speed as the 125cc Bernardet motor.

The French stereotype of the American cowboy came to life in the coveted "Texas" version of the Y.52. The cowhand's scooter came complete with rhinestone saddlebags, fringed handlebars, and studded seats with a saddlehorn on the rear pillion. Displayed at the Salon de Paris on a rug of simulated white cowhide, the only thing missing was cowhorns on the front fender.

Cabri L6 and M60 1954–1959; Guépar 1955–1959 ★★

"Easy to park" was about all that could be said for the Cabri since the classy designs of the early Bernardets were lost. The tall, horizontal 50cc—later 85cc—engine raised the rear section to look like a metal fez, but instead of a tassel, a bicycle seat rose out of the top. In 1955, Bernardet came under the control of Le Poulain, installing its 50x50cc Comet with the Servomatic system. This new model was also sold in Belgium with two-tone paint as the Hirondelle Passe-Partout, or the All-Purpose Swallow.

The Guépar, or Cheetah, first appeared in 1955 as the Jaguar but its name was soon changed due to litigation threats from the British car maker. The Guépar was powered by a two-cylinder engine.

Bianchi Italy ★★

Edoardo Bianchi was one of the early motorcycle makers of Italy. After decades of crafting beautiful racing and road cycles, in 1960 Bianchi built its first scooter, the 71.5cc BiBi. The engine was a two-stroke horizontal engine pumping out 3hp via a three-speed gearbox.

In 1960, the BiBi was replaced by the 80cc Orsetto, or Bear Cub. The 4hp 48x43mm engine was hung in the center of the scooter below the tube frame with rear drive by a long, enclosed chain.

Binz West Germany ★

Binz of Lorchin Württemberg—not to be confused with Benz of Mercedes-Benz fame—exported its Binz-Roller to such faraway places as Belgium. One of the major selling points was the exotic "Klaxon électrique," the electric horn. The Binz-Roller would be categorized as a mere moped due to its 20x2.25in wheels and bicycle handlebars, but was saved by its scooter-like floorboard and body covering.

The choosy scooterist of 1954–1955 could decide between a Fichtel & Sachs 47cc for the S50 model or an Ilo 49cc for the J50. Ilo was short for Ilo-Werke Norddeutsche Maschinenfabrik, a German proprietary engine maker also referred to variously as ILO, Jlo, or JLO.

The two scooters had identical bodies as well as speed (40km/h), weight (50kg), gas tank capacity (1.5liters); in fact everything was the same except for the zesty 0.5hp advantage of the J50.

Bitri The Netherlands ★

Made by the Nederlandse Scooterfabrik NV in Dokkum, the Bitri was presented in 1954 with a German Ilo 118cc engine delivering 4.5hp at 4500rpm via a two-speed gearbox. Soon, a 150cc Ilo was offered, and in 1957, the Bitri added a 200cc Sachs with four speeds and 10.2hp; electric start was optional.

In 1960, you had four Bitri models to choose from: 150-4 KS Standard and Luxe and the 150-4 ES and 200-4 ES, both with electric start.

BMW Germany ★★★★

BMW never built a production scooter but in 1953 at its early Munich factory, engineers created a prototype for a shaft-driven motorcycle-scooter with bodywork covering its obviously motorcycle-based frame and riding atop 16in wire-laced wheels.

In 1954, BMW created the R10, a prototype for a true scooter, this time based on a 200cc sin-

Bianchi's Orsetto, or Bear Cub, scooter was based on a horizontal two-stroke 80cc engine that was housed in the middle of the scooter below the central tunnel. The scoop on the front fender fed cooling air directly into the tunnel. The layout gave optimum weight distribution although the engine was also prone to being soaked down by road spray. Raleigh in England bought Orsettos to be sold as Roma scooters.

BMW created this styling mockup in 1954 while considering production of its R10 prototype scooter. Based on a 200cc single-cylinder four-stroke engine delivering 8–10hp, final drive was via a shaft, like the BMW motorcycle and Lambretta scooters of the era. If BMW had built a high-quality scooter in line with its motorcycles of the time, the world could have been a better place. *BMW archives*

gle-cylinder four-stroke engine delivering 8–10hp. Final drive was via a shaft, like the BMW motorcycle and Lambretta scooters of the era. Earless-style triangulated front forks held the front wheel. The bodywork was unadorned, fully enclosing the engine in the Vespa fashion.

Whether the BMW scooter would have been a success is a question for the academics. But amid the market of inexpensive, jangly two-strokes, the scooter would have brought all of BMW's refined engineering to the field, perhaps transforming people's demands.

In 1992, BMW showed its C1 scooter prototype to the Köln Motorcycle Show with a choice of 125cc or 250cc engines. The C1 was a modern plastic scooter with turn signals molded into handlebar covers and topped by a streamlined windshield. The seat was a full sports car-style bucket seat with four-point seatbelt.

Bond ★★

Bond was the Piaggio of England, one of the firms that provided the wheels beneath Great Britain's postwar recovery. Yet whereas the Vespa was ridden with dignity and is remembered with respect by the Italians, Bond's various two-and three-wheeled creations are recalled by the British with much the same fondness the country feels for the V-1 rocket.

Minibike 1950–1951 ★★

Lawrence Bond started his empire by building the Bond three-wheeled car, moving to the two-wheel Minibike in 1950, an oddity that defies categorization even as a scooter. The engine was simple enough: a ubiquitous Villiers 1F 99cc two-stroke with two-speed gearbox. The frame, however, was pure creativity—or eccentricity, depending upon your point of view.

Made of sheet aluminum, it was rolled and lap-riveted into an oval-section spine with a tube subframe holding the engine. This construction was the main weightsavings in the Minibike's mere 45kg.

Cavernous legshields protected the rider from all but a flood while sheet-aluminum fenders showed but a little of the 4.00x8in tires.

Suspension was lacking, unless you counted the two springs on the saddle seat; by 1950, the front forks were telescopic. In 1951, a De Luxe model was added with 125cc JAP engine and three speeds.

BAC Gazelle 1952–1953 ★★

Bond Aircraft and Engineering Company (BAC) created its Gazelle scooter in 1952 based on a Villiers 122cc 10D two-stroke with 4.00x8in tires. The frame was a standard tube affair with front and rear fenders and legshields but only a gawky

Bond's P4 scooter was one of the first scooters to use a fiberglass body—and the bizarre styling flourishes possible with a mold. Note that the jetpod tailfins were purely ornamental. *Mick Walker archives*

cage enclosing the engine, much like the German Ferbedo.

By the end of 1952, a second Gazelle based on the 99cc 1F Villiers engine was offered as well as a sidecar with aluminum bodywork. By 1953, rights to the Gazelle were purchased by the Projects and Developments firm. In 1953, Bond two-wheeler production was halted as the firm concentrated on its car.

P1 and P2 1958–1959 ★★★

In 1958, Bond created a true scooter in its P1. Powered by a fan-cooled two-stroke 31C Villiers 148cc with a Siba Dynastart electric leg and three-speed gearbox. The chassis possessed an interesting design—for a scooter and for Bond—with the engine as a stressed member of the frame. Stub axles held the wheels and 4.00x10in tires.

The P1 body was made of fiberglass and the modernistic styling was garnished by two-tone paint scheme, tailfins, and chrome portholes on the sides. In mid-1958, the P2 was added with electric-start 197cc 9E Villiers and four speeds.

P3 and P4 1960–1962 ★★★

In 1960, the 147cc 6.3hp P3 and 197cc 8.5hp P4 were released. The new scooters had a different frame that mounted the engines 2.25in lower. The bodywork was also restyled for a curvaceous yet still refreshingly odd look—the styling was "contemporary," according to *Scooter Weekly*. Options included a windscreen, spare wheel and carrier, and chrome wheel discs.

Bond continued building scooters until 1962 when it returned to producing solely its three-wheeled cars. It was a sad day for the scooter faithful but a joyous occassion for the mini-car fraternity.

Brockhouse Engineering UK ★★★

The Corgi was based on the Welbike, a lightweight foldable paratrooper scooter built by Excelsior during World War II. Postwar, Brockhouse Engineering of Southport civilized the Welbike as the Corgi, believing that people would need an economical commuter machine and that the Welbike's heroism would serve the Corgi well

As a precursor to the Mod-Rocker wars on the beach at Brighton, this old BSA poster showed its Sunbeam catching some rays complete with saddlebags. Scintillating was the word. *Classic Scooters Newsletter/Steven Zasueta*

in the marketplace. In retrospect, Corgi also seemed a better name; the scooter's low-bellied chassis duplicated that of the Queen's favorite dog.

Corgi power was a two-stroke 98cc Excelsior Spryt engine of 50x50mm built by Brockhouse, similar in design to the Villiers Junior de Luxe. The cylinder was on the horizontal, fitting snugly beneath the steel-tube frame in the center of the wheelbase. A Wico-Pacy flywheel magneto provided spark. Bodywork was minimal and the Corgi rode atop 2.25x6.25in tires.

Although announced in 1946, two years passed before the first Corgis were available, thereafter selling well to transport-hungry commuters. A bare-bones sidecar was soon marketed as a sort of motorized shopping cart.

In mid-1948, a Corgi Mark II was offered with a dog-clutch that disengaged the drive to provide a neutral gear; the basic Corgi was then named the Mark I. In 1949, a two-speed Albion gearbox and telescopic front forks were options for both models.

Aftermarket bodywork was made by the Jack Olding firm in 1950. A Mark IV was offered in 1952 with the two-speed and telescopic forks standard. The Mark IV continued its career until 1954 when (slightly) more sophisticated cars took over the market.

BSA UK

Birmingham Small Arms was one of the stalwart British motorcycle pioneers, but in 1960 it created a motorscooter. As part of World War II reparations, BSA had won the German DKW firm's prewar two-stroke engine design, which it shared with the lucky Harley–Davidson, Yamaha, WSK in Poland, MZ (formerly the DKW factory in East Germany), and Voskhod in Russia. The two-stroke design was used in BSA's Bantam and inspired the firm's first scooter, the Sunbeam, as well as the Triumph Tigress, since Triumph was owned by BSA at the time.

BSA Beeza prototype 1955

The Beeza was based on a 198cc single-cylinder side-valve engine with a four-speed gearbox cast in unit and a finned muffler. Where the Beeza, or Beezer, failed, the Sunbeam succeeded with its sleek lines and power engine.

Dandy Scooterette 1955–1962

The Dandy finally started rolling off the production line in 1957, two years after the moped-like vehicle was promised in the form of a prototype. The gearshift for the 70cc engine was placed on the handlebars with an awkward levered chooser controlling a series of springs.

Sunbeam B2 and B2S 1959–1964

The scooters were designed by Edward Turner, who up to that time had a great reputation based on his Triumph Speed Twin vertical engine. By 1959, nearly identical Triumph Tigress and BSA Sunbeam models were offered, each in two versions, a 175cc two-stroke single and a 250cc four-stroke twin.

The B2 250cc shared engine parts with the 175cc from the clutch back but the block and heads were cast in aluminum and were special to the four-stroke twin. The B2S added electric start and a second battery.

The 250cc engines zoomed the scooters faster than the 10in wheels and 5in drum brakes were made to handle. The front fork followed the Vespa design with a single-sided, stub axle with the damper and spring units enclosed.

Sunbeam B1 1960–1965

The B1 mirrored the Tigress 172cc TS1 with an engine based on the Bantam motorcycle although most engine parts were not interchangeable. The scooter had a foot shift and flywheel magneto fan to cool the ever-overheating two-stroke.

In 1960, the Sunbeam was garnished in the classic Vespa metallic green, but by 1961 it was offered in a choice of blue or red with an option of a cream weathershield.

BSA-Triumph built its scooters in an attempt to thwart the Italian-dominated scooter market, but it was too late. By 1960, much of the craze had faded away, and the Tigress and Sunbeam also died a quick death.

B. S. Villa Italy ★

Based in Crespellano, near Bologna, B. S. Villa offered its 50cc AX and GZ scooters in the 1990s. At the 1992 Bologna show, Villa displayed a scooterone—larger scooter—with Buck Rogers styling and disc front brake.

C & E Manufacturing USA ★★

The Argyle Scooter Cub was built at C & E's Memphis, Missouri, factory in the 1960s as a foldable scooter based on the 2 1/2hp two-stroke Clinton.

Carnielli Italy ★★

Carnielli's Vittoria scooters, named after the firm's home of Vittorio in Veneto, were based on tube frames. The bodywork had an odd feature: the engine covers ended below the pillion seat and a separate rear fender continued the lines.

The first Vittoria, Tipo 75, of 1951 was a lightweight scooter showing the firm's heritage of bicycle building. The engine was a 65cc two-stroke of 43x44mm giving 3.2hp at 5450rpm. Tires were 3.50x7in, later switching to 8in.

In 1952, Carnielli showed its Vittoria Luxe based on a 125cc NSU two-stroke. While many French, Germany, and English scooter makers used engines from other sources, the Italians almost always used their own engines, so Carnielli's NSU powerplant was an oddity—especially since *it* was based on a Lambretta C/LC engine.

The Luxe was soon replaced by the Grand Luxe with redone bodywork, chrome luggage rack, and 3.50x10in tires.

Casal Portugal ★

The Casal Carina S170 scooter followed the classic step-through design with a tube frame covered by sheet steel bodywork. The two-stroke 50cc engine was 40x39.7mm delivering 5.2hp at 7500rpm. A four-speed gearbox was shifted by a foot lever giving power to the 3.00x10in tires.

Casalini Italy ★

Casalini began production in 1958 with its David scooter, believed to be the only scooter with a biblical name. But Piaggio was the Goliath of the market, and Casalini lasted but a short time.

Cazenave France ★

Known for its mopeds, Cazenave decided to brave the scooter market with three models: the Belina, Super-Belina, and Alpina. The first two, in

The Argyle Scooter Cub folded up to 14 1/2x18 1/2x22 1/2in—and it took exactly 15 seconds to do it, according to *Popular Mechanics*. The layout of the Argyle was ingenious in its compactness: the horizontal two-stroke nestled under the seat with the carburetor feeding the crankcase at back. The frame and fenders were made from cast aluminum alloy. Owner: Jim Kilau.

1954 and 1955, resembled the Rumi Scoiattolo with an odd rear section overshadowed by a large boomerang-shaped chrome piece that was perhaps designed to reassure the quizzical buyers that the scooter would return them home as well as get them there. The two different models came with a choice of three different engines, a VAP, Mistral, or Ydral for a total of six possible combinations.

The Alpina appeared in 1960 with your choice of an Italian Demm or German Sachs motor.

Claeys-Flandria Belgium ★

Based at Zedelgem, the firm showed its Flandria scooter in 1954 based on a German Ilo 175cc engine with four speeds. In 1956, Flandria started building the Italian SIM-Moretti Ariete scooter for Belgium.

In 1960, Flandria offered its Parisienne scooter with a 49cc two-stroke with four speeds.

Clark Engineering USA ★★★

When the Powell scooter firm turned to war contracts during World War II, Clark Engineering of South Pasadena, California, bought the remaining stock of Powell's innovative A-V-8 scooter. Clark renamed its scooter the Victory Clipper in a burst of patriotic pride—and salesmanship as it offered the scooter during the wartime dearth of car production.

All Victory Clippers were leftover 1942 model A-V-8s: as Clark's brochure stated, "We cannot supply new Clippers," hinting, however, that "a very few near new ones [were] available!" And while you needed to be issued a buyer priority certificate by the US War Department as a war contractor to buy a new car or motorcycle, Clark noted that no priority was necessary to buy a used scooter. The Victory Clipper was doing its part to win the war.

In 1947, Clark was back, building the A-V-8 as the Clark Cyclone scooter.

Columbus Cycle Company USA ★

Named after its home base of Columbus, Nebraska, Columbus built the Discoverer scooter in the 1960s with a four-stroke 2.5hp engine. Suspension was by "frame and seat," according to *Popular Science* magazine. It was a sobering thought.

Comet Manufacturing Company USA ★★★

The Comet scooter was built prewar in Minneapolis, Minnesota, with at least three models available. The standard model had a rubber-mounted front fork, 1/2hp engine, automatic clutch, and two-tone blue and white paint scheme. A Pick-Up version had an extended tail section. An open-frame sport model was also available with a bicycle seat and a crossbar to stabilize the frame.

Condor Switzerland ★

The famous Condor firm built the Austrian Puch scooter under license.

Cooper USA ★★★

Frank Cooper affixed his own decals to the Powell Aviate scooter to create his "decal-engineered" Cooper Aviate in 1941–1942.

When the US Army requested bids for a lightweight scooter to drop by parachute behind enemy lines, Cooper added a new engine to meet

The Cooper War Combat Motor Scooter could have scared the Nazis into submission just by its name. This photo, from a US Army test, showed the maze of cross-bracing added to your basic Powell A-V-8 to make the Cooper withstand the parachute drop behind enemy lines. But alas, America's secret weapon was never unleashed.

Comet Manufacturing located on scenic Nicollet Avenue in beautiful Minneapolis built these early putt-putts. The two scooters on the right were the standard 0.5hp model, while the coveted Pick-Up version added a rear luggage compartment. *Herb Singe archives*

mil-spec, and offered the Army his Cooper War Combat Motor Scooter.

With such a belligerent name, the Cooper scooter should have won a Medal of Honor merely for striking fear into the hearts of the enemy. Alas, America's secret weapon was never built, as the Cushman Model 53 Airborne won out in bidding.

Still, Cooper's airborne was quite a machine. The 5hp Wisconsin engine was mounted in the chassis center with a long chain driving the rear wheel. The motor displaced 17.8ci or 290cc and created 5hp and 7.7lb-ft of torque at 3400rpm with a Wico magneto. The transmission was by Plymouth, although an Army Characteristics Sheet noted that it had been "altered."

But the chassis is what deserved the medal. With the aid of a welding torch, Cooper added a maze of triangulated reinforcing bars to the Aviate frame to stand up to the shock of a parachute drop. A single cantilevered saddle rode atop a sole coil spring with an odd-shaped gas tank nestled on top of the frame rails. Mil-spec required 6.00x6in tires, interchangeable with USAAF training planes. Naturally no lights were needed.

While the Army rated the Cooper better than the Cushman 53, Army inspectors were unimpressed with the Cooper Motors, Inc.'s "factory," and awarded the bid to Cushman. A small number of Coopers were built circa 1944 for Army evaluation and probably destroyed in parachute testing.

Cosmo USA–Italy ★

Cosmopolitan Motors of Hatboro, Pennsylvania, sold Puch scooters under its own name in the late 1950s.

Crescent Sweden ★

Crescent was a small bicycle maker starting production in 1954 in Varberg. It was soon bought by the Swedish Monark firm, which made bicycles and motorscooters as well as some of the world's great motocrossers. After the sale, Crescent sold Monark scooters under its name, usually in different color schemes.

The Monark Skoterett 901264 was renumbered as the 921264 and painted in yellow or blue and white two-tone for Crescent. It was powered by a 48cc Husqvarna two-stroke 1hp single.

Monark's version of the Honda Cub, the Skotermoped Model 901269, was also redesignated as the 921269 and sold by Crescent. Today both firms are part of Volvo.

Crocker USA ★★★★★

Albert G. Crocker was the builder of the great Crocker V-twin motorcycles of the 1930s that sin-

Military Motorscooters: The Mouses That Roared

Nowhere in the classic treatise of modern warfare, Prussian General Carl von Clauswitz's On War, is the military potential of the motorscooter mentioned. And probably with good reason. But never fear; it's been tried.

As early as 1917, the US Army drew up milspecs for a dispatch scooter and the Autoped Company of New York created its Autoped motorscooter, based on Junior's push scooter where the doughboy perched precariously on the chassis center, balancing above the dwarf wheels. But the Autoped had power—1 1/2hp via a miniature engine mounted above the front wheel.

During World War II, armies worldwide sponsored development of lightweight scooters to be dropped with commando paratroop units behind enemy lines. The collapsible British Welbike by Excelsior, Italian Aeromoto by Volugrafo, and American Cooper and Cushman Model 53 all roared their little engines in patriotic anger.

Even in modern times, the military motorscooter lives on. The French have dropped Vespas by parachute, which are then mounted with 75mm cannons. The Italians procured Vespas fitted with bazookas, which must do a back gainer when the bazooka is fired.

In 1993, scooters reached an ignominious low when they were packed with explosives and used as budget car bombs by fundamentalist terrorists in a series of attacks in Calcutta, India.

Scooters remain the ultimate stealth weapon to slip in behind enemy lines, a motorized version of Hannibal's elephants.

Forget about the Trojan Horse or even paratrooper scooters, this Vespa had firepower. The Italian army procured Vespas mounted with bazookas in the 1960s and 1970s as mobile tank killers. Don't laugh—this drawing was made from a photo of the real thing.

glehandedly caused Harley–Davidson and Indian more grief than any event up to the British motorcycle invasion of the 1950s. Crocker was a former colleague of Harley–Davidson's famed engineer William Ottaway when the duo worked for Thor motorcycles; Crocker was later an Indian dealer and racer, so he was well placed to be a thorn in everyone's side.

The high-performance Crocker V-twins put the other motorcycles to shame on the speedways and dirt tracks of southern California where they were bred. But neither Harley–Davidson nor Indian gave a hoot about Crocker's other endeavor of the late 1930s, his Scootabout motorscooter. In the end neither did Crocker himself.

The most interesting feature of the Scootabout was not its Lauson engine or solid front suspension but its flowing bodywork. Following the tenets of Salsbury's step-through design, Crocker added a further clause to the definition of a scooter: Styling.

The Motor Glides and Auto-Glides initially did not venture beyond single-plane folds in their bodywork; afterall, scooters were built on a budget and sold as a utilitarian device. The Crocker, on the other hand, was formed of sinuous bodywork with two-tone paint that added a further dimension to the curvaceous lines. The tail section covered the wheels with fender skirts, the design coming together at the rear in a teardrop shape. The Scootabout foreshadowed the Vespa in spirit.

But the Scootabout never scooted about much. In fact, production probably numbered less than 100—as did Crocker's infamous motorcycle.

Csepel Hungary ★★

Part of a large steel works in Budapest, Csepel was once upon a time the largest motorcycle maker in Hungary. The firm offered its Tünde scooter based on the Puch Alpine of the early 1950s. Csepel was reorganized by the State as Danuvia and Pannonia in 1952.

Cushman USA

Cushman Motor Works' decision to build a motorscooter in the 1930s was a serendipitious afterthought from a company that was successful-

Albert G. Crocker brought an eye for styling to the American prewar scooter field with his Lauson-powered Scootabout. The look was Art Deco with curvaceous fenders and two-tone paint at a time when Motor Glides and Cushmans were boxes on wheels. *Ken Gresiak archives/Lindsay Brooke*

Restored 1939 Crocker Scootabout alongside a 1936 Salsbury Motor Glide shows how radical Albert G. Crocker's vision of a stylized scooter actually was. Full, flowing fenders and a curvaceous tail section made this a dandy among scooters in the 1930s. Owner: Herb Singe. *Herb Singe*

ly producing industrial equipment and engines. Cushman played follow-the-leader into the scooter market, recognizing Salsbury's novel scooter as an economical option to a second car during the recovery years after the Great Depression. With the success of its first scooter, Cushman continued to construct the most long-lived American motorscooter in a dazzling variety of unique models. And as Vespa became synonymous for scooter in the rest of the world, Cushman stands for scooter to most Americans even today.

Cushman's Auto-Glide motorscooter was inspired by the innovative Motor Glide built by E. Foster Salsbury in Los Angeles. Looking for a more powerful engine to propel the Motor Glide, Salsbury sent blueprints of its scooter to Cushman and requested a bid in mid-1936 for 1,000 units of its renowned Husky engine. When Salsbury declined the bid, Cushman decided to use the 1,000 engines to build its own scooter.

Colonel Roscoe Turner, the famed Motor Glide–endorsing aviator, indirectly led to the startup of Salsbury's chief rival. In 1936, his barnstorming antics came to Lincoln, Nebraska, Cushman's hometown. In a 1992 interview, Cushman's former president Robert H. Ammon told the tale: Turner buzzed the airfield on his Evinrude-powered Motor Glide, prompting a local boy to fashion his own scooter out of angle iron, wheelbarrow wheels, and a Cushman Husky lawn mower motor. "We found out about this scooter by chance," Ammon recalled. "One day my dad looked out the window and he saw the kid on his scooter buying parts at our parts depot."

The writing was on the wall: Cushman built a scooter prototype that was to become the Auto-Glide Model 1-1.

"We were in the business of building and selling engines," Robert H. Ammon stated. "The idea of making a motorscooter was to build and sell more engines." It was that simple.

Salsbury's interest in the Husky motor was well founded: the Husky was a venerable, hard-working engine. According to a Cushman promotional history booklet published in the 1950s, Cushman was founded by cousins Everett and Clinton Cushman, who began building two-cycle gas engines in their basement in 1901 to power pleasure and fishing boats. They were issued their first patent in 1902 for a two-stroke gas engine

Cushman's first series production scooter, the Auto-Glide Model 1 of 1937-1938. As this ad stated, the heart of the Auto-Glide was the Cushman Husky; and as

Robert H. Ammon, the scooter's inventor, noted in 1992, "The idea of making a motorscooter was to build and sell more engines."

that was used on farms to drive everything from separators to washing machines. The duo later created several successful racing marine one- and two-cylinder two-stroke engines before venturing into a series of four-stroke, water-cooled engines.

In 1913, a full-fledged factory was built on the site that would become the current OMC works. In 1922, Cushman developed the Husky, its first air-cooled, four-stroke engine. The one-cylinder Husky ran on roller bearings, and was used to power its Bob-A-Lawn mower, aptly named for the Roaring Twenties era of bobbed haircuts.

But by the 1930s, Cushman Motor Company was in trouble due to the Depression and the hard-hit farm economy. In 1934, John F. Ammon and his son Charles, founders of The Easy Manufacturing Company, also of Lincoln, took over Cushman. The Ammons had a long relationship with the Cushmans, using Cushman castings and engines in their pipe layers, cultivators, and other industrial tools.

With this staid background in industrial equipment and no-nonsense engines, the creation of the Auto-Glide motorscooter by Cushman in Lincoln, Nebraska, was as far-fetched as a trip to the moon at the time. But "Uncle Charlie" Ammon had a son.

That scion, 19-year-old Robert H. Ammon, had heard tell of Roscoe Turner's barnstorming Motor Glide and seen the local boy's homemade machine. Robert and Charlie Ammon had a vision of a motorscooter.

Auto-Glide 1-1 and 1-2 1936 ★★★★★

The first Auto-Glide was designated the Model 1-1, denoting the first scooter, first model.

Auto-Glide Model 1 of 1937 with add-on battery-powered headlamp, a common addition of the time. The frame was made of 2in channel iron with minimal sheet-steel bodywork enclosing the steering head and engine; as an ad promised, "It will stand up." Owner: Jim Kilau.

Robert H. Ammon built the first scooter in the Motor Glide mold with the 1hp Husky engine mounted directly below the seat in front of the rear wheel.

Ammon remembered that he copied the local boy's scooter in using 1 1/4in angle iron for the first frame but the angle iron soon broke. "So I used 2in channel iron, which did the job," he said. "I learned early on that a rigid frame was essential, and the channel-iron frame lasted a long time for Cushman."

Pressed steel made up the step-through chassis with spindly fork tubes holding the fenderless front wheel and channel iron enclosing the engine and holding the seat aloft. There were no lights and no suspension. And as with the local boy's scooter, Ammon said he used wheelbarrow wheels on the prototype mounted with 4.00x8in tires.

Ammon's aim was to build "just a good, sturdy, two-wheel scooter," as he told *The Lincoln Star* for a retrospective article on June 21, 1984. "We finally had an engine in it and had it running in, oh, I'd say, 30 days. And it was a very crude-looking thing, of course."

A series of prototypes were built. Development continued, and by late 1936 the 1-2 was tested featuring similar mechanicals to the 1-1 but with a front fender and simple bodywork made of welded steel sheets enclosing part of the tail section. The "styling" eschewed any compound curves, foreshadowing the familiar Auto-Glide shape.

After designing the rigid frame, Ammon worked on getting the steering geometry correct He recalled in 1992, "I had read an article at the Engineering School of the University of Nebraska about the correct geometry for a bicycle or motorcycle. I developed the first scooter's steering head angle so that the tail end of the steering head was at a point behind the point where the wheel first touches the ground. When I got the scooter stable enough so I could drive it without any hands, I knew it was ready."

According to Ammon, less than twenty Models 1-1 and 1-2 were built and sold.

Auto-Glide 1 and 3 1937–1938; 1T, 1V, 3T, and 3V 1939 ★★★★★

By 1937, Cushman was serious about motorscooters. Production began at a pace with two models offered: the Model 1, called a Sport version, and the 3, which included the Kari-Pac, a bolt-on rear section with a 16x18x16in luggage box similar to Salsbury's Parcel Carrier attachment. And instead of Roscoe Turner's Salsbury endorsement, Cushman had more advanced technical support; one ad stated that "Prominent Engineers proclaim Auto-Glide the greatest advance ever made in low cost, motor transportation."

At the heart of the Auto-Glide was the Husky engine, as Cushman promotion always reminded buyers. But like E. Foster Salsbury before them, the Ammons had decided the 1hp Husky motor was not enough power for the prototype. With these first production models they stepped up to the 1 1/2hp Husky based on a bored version of the 1hp motor. The 1hp engine had measured 2 3/8x2 1/2in bore and stroke for 11.08ci; the 1 1/2hp engine was 2 5/8x2 1/2in for 13.53ci.

At the heart of the Husky were Lincolnite aluminum-alloy strut-type pistons with three rings and a steel x-section drop-forged and heat-treated connecting rod riding on die-cast "high-speed" bearings. The cam- and crankshafts were both drop-forged and heat-treated steel with fully enclosed taper roller main bearings. A flywheel fan forced cooling air over the engine and an Eisemann magneto fired the 1937 models; by 1938, a variety of Wico magnetos was used.

Cushman expected to sell its scooters to novices with little mechanical or engineering skills and the Husky was an easy engine to use. Yet it did have its quirks, typical of most engines of the 1930s, that required expert care. The instruction book chided owners to de-carbon the cylinder head every 5,000–8,000 miles, grind the valve seats, and adjust valve-to-pushrod clearance by grinding the valve stem end with a margin for error of 0.02–0.03in. Scooter ownership in the 1930s was not for the faint of heart.

In an odd twist of marketing, early Cushman ads promoted the *slow* speeds of the Auto-Glide: "Low speed ensures safety. Auto-Glide is *not* a 'speed wagon.'" Instead, the ads promised economy: 30mph at more than 120mpg. As other ads featuring businessmen in suits speeding along atop Auto-Glides promised, "Operates for actually one tenth the cost of an auto!" And the ultimate sales point, "Cheaper than shoe leather."

Like the power curve, the chassis of the 1 and 3 was also strengthened over the 1-2. The frame was still of one piece from the engine mounts to the steering head. A side frame of 2x1/8in channel steel and five steel crossmembers braced the unit construction. As an ad promised, "It will stand up."

The 1 and 3 rode on disc wheels with "non-skid" 3.50x12in balloon tires filled by inner tubes, which supplied the scooter's "suspension." Operation was easy: the "smooth-as-velvet" clutch to the single-speed drive was operated by the left foot, the rear-wheel drum brake was controlled by the right foot, and the handlebar-mounted throttle

by the right hand. For optional accessories, a bicycle light could be mounted on the handlebars.

The bodywork had developed slightly from the 1-2 to enclose the engine with louvers for venting—and was now painted. The paint was sturdy tractor paint and the colors were Ford blue or Farmall red.

For 1938, the 1 and 3 continued, supplemented by Deluxe 1T and 3T versions, which featured two-speed transmissions and a 6 volt lighting and horn kit with generator and battery. The generators were rebuilt Ford Model T units, according to the Cushman instruction and parts book: "The bearings, field windings, brushes and brush holders are usually new. The armatures are rewound. The commutators are new or newly sized." Call it built to a pricepoint, but according to an ad, the lighting "Complies with all State Highway requirements."

The heart of the Auto-Glide Model 1, the Cushman Husky 1 1/2hp four-stroke engine with a 2 5/8x2 1/4in bore and stroke for 13.53ci. This was the engine that had enticed E. Foster Salsbury to contact Cushman about using it in his Motor Glide; Salsbury changed his mind and Cushman decided to build its own scooter.

By 1939, Cushman was reaching a nationwide audience through the space ads at the back of magazines such as *Popular Mechanics*; before the advent of television, this was the most inexpensive and most effective route to inform possible buyers. This ad showed the new Auto-Glide Model 2 with the larger-bore 2hp engine as well as the three-wheel Model 9 Package-Kar.

The V suffix models denoted a V-belt clutch added to the two-speed 1T and 3T.

The Kari-Pac was optional for the Model 1. And either model could add on the Trail-It Attachment, which hooked the Auto-Glide backward to a car's rear bumper for towing. Yet, unlike Salsbury's Cycletow with its two-wheel attachment, Trail-It left the scooter to run on solely its front wheel, easy prey to things like potholes and corners.

Auto-Glide R-1 1938 ★★★★

The R-1 was a stripper model of the 1. R stood for rental, and Cushman hoped to sell the model to what it foresaw as a blossoming scooter rental business.

The R-1 retained the 1 1/2hp Husky but with a simplified starting procedure for novice riders. The unskilled simply pushed the scooter to start it, pulled in the compression release on the handlebar to allow the engine to turn over, released the release, and let the engine take off.

Standard color for the R-1 was green with an Auto-Glide logo decal on the frame side near the steering head.

Auto-Glide 5, 5T, 7, and 7T 1938 ★★★★★

Cushman continued to refine its scooters with each model change. As Robert H. Ammon stated in 1992, "I saw other scooters—Moto-Scoot, Salsbury, Powell, and others. We would buy them to look them over to see what good features they had that we could incorporate. We also had lots of suggestions from dealers and employees within the company."

In late 1938, Cushman introduced the 5 and 7 DeLuxe battery-ignition versions of the magneto-ignition 1 and 3; the 5 was the Sport and the 7 had the Kari-Pac. These models featured lighting via a 6 volt generator with a large headlamp mounted atop the steering head and an electric horn on the fork tubes above the fender. The 5 and 7 retained the 1 1/2hp Husky, the T models grafted on a two-speed transmission.

The new models featured a two-tone paint scheme with the front fender, forks, and handlebars as well as the scalloped area down the back in the light color. Auto-Glide decals were glued to the rear above the taillight and the frame side near the steering head; a Husky decal was affixed to the engine fan cover.

Auto-Glide 2-4 1938–1939; 2T-4T 1938–1939; and 2V-4V 1939 ★★★★★

In 1938, Cushman went for more power, releasing the 2 and 4 as 2hp versions of the 1 and 3; the 2 was the Sport and 4 had the Kari-Pac. The 2 and 4 continued with the single-speed transmission and magneto ignition but had larger, 2 5/8in bore 13.53ci engines.

Along with changing the bore of the 2hp engines, a new cylinder head was introduced with a freer flowing exhaust exit angle and eight retaining bolts instead of the smaller engine's six bolts.

For 1938, the 2hp Huskys were fired by Eisemann magnetos; in 1939, both Eisemann and Wico were used.

T-suffix models added the two-speed transmission; V-suffix models added the V-belt clutch.

Auto-Glide R-2 1938–1939 and RV 1939 ★★★

With the arrival of the 2hp Husky, the rental model was also upgraded as the R-2. The RV added the two-speed transmission and V-belt clutch for 1939.

Auto-Glide 6-8 and 6T-8T 1938 ★★★★★

The 6 and 8 were 2hp, battery-ignition versions of the 5 and 7, respectively. Again, the T models added the two-speed transmission.

Auto-Glide 12 and 14 1940 ★★★★

In 1940, Cushman introduced its Models 12 and 14, the latter being the DeLuxe model. While both had 2hp and Wico magneto ignition, the 12 had the one-speed and the 14 the two-speed transmission. The clutch control moved from a foot pedal to a handlebar lever mounted on the same side as the throttle. Lights and 6 volt generator were optional.

The major change in the new models was a wheelbase lengthened to 54in and the move from 12x3.50in to 14x4.00in tires, which increased ride stability, as noted in the instruction book. The new front forks were reinforced by small section tubes at the front.

Cushman also recognized the advantage of suspension for the first time. A trailing-axle lever-action setup damped by a preloaded light-gauge coil spring held the front wheel; coil springs mounted in the center of the scooter cushioned the rear.

The bodywork of the new models was also updated. The squared one-piece rear section now completely covered the entrails of the Husky, lifting away for servicing. This cover incorporated the seat into the bodywork , adding a 1cu-ft package compartment to replace the add-on Kari-Pac. The styling update also included a full front fender featuring—for the first time—compound curves.

Auto-Glide 22 1940–1942 and 24 1940 ★★★★

The 20 Series Models 22 and 24 quickly replaced the 12 and 14 respectively, although changes were minimal. The 24 retained the two-speed transmission, which Cushman noted was ideal for use with the new optional Side-Kar.

The 22 came with Cushman's new Floating Drive, an automatic clutch and transmission. Salsbury had introduced its revolutionary Self-Shifting torque converter in 1937, and Cushman was not to be outdone. Its ads proclaimed the Floating Drive "just like a fluid drive on the latest models of automobiles," which was something of a simplified misnomer. Instead, the Floating Drive was a drum clutch with three shoes that pushed outward against the inside of the drum as speed increased their centrifugal motion.

As well as the optional lighting system, other Cushman accessories included a windshield and speedometer for 1940. The Auto-Glide was moving upscale.

Auto-Glide Economy Model 21 1940 ★★★

The 21 was a step forward and backward at the same time: it replaced the stripper R-2 but used the old 1 1/2hp Husky with the new Floating Drive. It also retained the old-style 12x3.50in tires, it moved into modern times with the coil-spring suspension. And while the new body style incorporated a luggage compartment, the 21 did not; instead the Kari-Pac was once more available.

Auto-Glide 32 and 34 1942–1945 ★★★★

The 32 and 34 replaced the 22 and 24 respectively in 1942 as the 30 Series scooters. These were also the last to be called Auto-Glides; like Salsbury, Cushman chose to promote its own name as a scooter manufacturer following World War II.

The US Army formed much of the specifications for the 30 Series by requesting bids for military scooters. As part of the military requirements, the small Huskys were shelved and a new 4hp version was the sole engine available. While the 2 5/8in bore of the 2hp Husky was retained, the stroke went from 2 1/2in to 2 3/4in for 15ci. Wico flywheel magnetos provided spark. The brawnier power output gave the Auto-Glides new life.

The 32 came with the Floating Drive while the 34 used the two-speed. Lights and horn were now standard equipment. The engine cover of the 30 Series was redesigned with a larger package compartment and louvers on the sides to cool the more powerful engine.

While the US Army had formed the 30 Series and was pleased with the outcome, it purchased only 495 Model 34s with Side Kars for use as administrative mules, according to Fred W. Crismon's *U.S. Military Wheeled Vehicles*.

But the majority of 30 Series sales went to civilians. While production of civilian cars, trucks, and motorcycles was all but halted during the war to concentrate industry on war materiel, Cushman got an exemption from the War Department as its vehicles were deemed ideal for wartime civilian transportation: they were economical both to build and ride. During the war, Cushman was constructing up to 300 scooters daily.

"This was tremendous thing," Robert H. Ammon told *The Lincoln Star*. "We were making scooters when Ford couldn't get tires to make cars."

And when the war was over, Cushman would be in full swing for civilian production while other manufacturers had to retool. "That's when they really took off, right after World War II," Ammon remembered.

Model 53 Airborne Scooter 1944 and 53A Civilian 1946–1948 ★★★★★

In the history of warfare, there have been few such fantastical strategies as the US Army's notion of parachuting motorscooters with the famed 82nd or 101st Airborne behind enemy lines so they could putt-putt their way to attack the nearest Tiger tank. Rank it up there with Hannibal's elephants and the Trojan Horse, both of which succeeded; the Army's plans for an airborne scooter did not.

None of which diminishes the fascination or collectivity of the Model 53. In fact, it was a great scooter.

In requesting bids for an airborne scooter, the US Army followed the lead of the Fascist Italian army and the British Red Berets. The Italians spawned the Volugrafo paratrooper scooter while the British built the collapsible Corgi Welbike.

The Army requested bids on April 29, 1943, for a lightweight airborne scooter, and received

Cushman's Model 53 Airborne scooter was the US Army's Trojan Horse of World War II. Model 53s were dropped behind enemy lines with paratroopers and came ashore at Normandy as well as seeing action in the Mediterannean and Pacific theaters. No lights were desired and suspension was deemed an unnecessary luxury. This 53 featured its own parachute. Owners: Keith and Kris Weeks.

prototypes of the Cushman 53 and the Cooper War Combat Motor Scooter from Cooper Motors, Inc., of Los Angeles. The competing scooters were assessed by Army Ordnance in Detroit on Characteristics Sheets filed February 17, 1944. While the Cooper had a more antagonistic name, the better to drive the Nazis back into the Fatherland, it also outpowered the Cushman Husky 5hp to 4hp. Overall, Army project engineers ranked the Cooper superior to the Cushman, but after inspection of the two factories, the Army recommended a contract be awarded to Cushman to build a first batch of 600 Model 53s. By the end of 1945, the Army had bought 4,734 Model 53s, according to Crismon.

The 53 was a Model 34 that had done the mail-order Mr. Universe course. Stripped down to shed unneeded bodywork, it showed off its muscle: a reinforced, rigid chassis and sturdy bracing surrounding the engine. It also shed the coil-spring suspension of the 30 Series; the tires were to handle the 53's heaven-sent arrival.

Cushman legend has it, according to Somerville's *A History of the Cushman Motor Works*, that to test the operational durability of the 53 dropped from C-47s by parachute behind the Normandy beachhead, prototype scooters were hoisted by rope over the branch of a tall tree out back of the Cushman workshop and dropped to make certain they could stand the impact.

Other military requirements dictated the design of the 53. The tires were 6.00x6in, interchangeable with USAAF spotter aircraft. And the nuts and bolts were the eccentric English Whitworth spec—as were lend-lease P-51 Mustangs—to standardize tools needed.

Along with its planned airborne duties, the 53 was drafted for flightline work in the USAAF. Mil-spec required the 53 to be painted olive drab green, but many were repainted yellow for airfield use.

After the war, the 53 was just too good to be laid to rest with a twenty-one-gun salute, and so Cushman offered the 53A, a civvy version of the Army model with an honorable discharge. And the 53 was too good to be changed; the 53A merely added a lighting system with 6 volt generator, reinstalled the 30 Series coil springs to the forks, and added a Cushman decal to the gas tank. An optional Buddy Seat could be had that perched at the rear, supported by long barrel springs.

52, 52A, and 54 1946–1948; 54B 1948–1949 ★★★★★

Following the war, it was the Cushman rather than Auto-Glide motorscooter, but the 52 and 54 continued the lineage of the Auto-Glide Models 32 and 34 respectively. There was no 40 Series due to the 1940s war years.

Cushman regaled the new line as "The Family Scooter," and instead of the old Auto-Glide decals featured the script Cushman logo on the rear sides of the engine cover, termed the "tail sheet" in the instruction manual.

The chief update was the arrival of the automatic clutch on the two-speed 54 model. Cushman promoted the addition of the knee-action suspenion to the rear wheel, which "gives a smooth velvety ride—that F-L-O-A-T-I-N-G sensation. . . . Road shocks and jars never reach the hands and arms." The main advance was the use of "moder"n barrel springs replacing the coil springs; with their different-size windings, the barrels were crude but (sort of) effective variable-rate springs. The 50 Series glided along on standard 4.00x8in tires or optional 6.00x6in tires left-over from the mil-specs for the 53.

But the most exciting item on the 50 Series was the new lighting system that could be turned on by tightening the generator belt with a control lever; all you had to do was lift the seat to turn on the Cushman Permalite generator. And the new scooters had a dazzling hi-low beam controlled by a "tilt-ray" foot switch.

The new Model 52A was a Sport version of the 52 sold without the engine cover "tail sheet" in the style of the 53A. The 52A was not widely promoted by Cushman, appearing only in rare ads. The instruction manual listed it, however, stating that the 52A and 53A had a special "sport-type frame," leading one to believe that the frame differed from the standard models, when in fact the frames were identical. As the 50 Series instruction manual noted parenthetically, "The frames of all machines are alike, allowing a conversion from one model to any other model." This can leave a black hole on the subject of scooter identity for restorers today.

The 52A and 53A were altered during their production runs as well. Later brochures show them with full rear fenders mounted with tail-lamps and long dual leaf springs holding single or optional tandem cushion seats.

In late 1948, Cushman debuted its new belt-drive torque-converter automatic clutch and transmission, called the Variamatic and denoted as the B-suffix to the Model 54B. Cushman had attempted to do battle in the motorscooter mar-ketplace with Salsbury's cutting-edge belt torque converter when it introduced its Floating Drive centrifigal automatic clutch in 1940, but it just wasn't the same. And neither was the new Variamatic.

Cushman's Variamatic was a troubleprone design that "almost ruined the Cushman reputation for reliability," according to Somerville. Finding a 54B with the original Variamatic today is like searching for a proverbial needle in the proverbial haystack; most were retrofitted with the tried and true but less-sophisticated Floating Drive.

Cushman offered a variety of accessories for its 50 Series scooters as listed in ads of the era. Chromed "spill bars" were available that bolted to the chassis front to protect the paint finish on event of a rollover. A plastic windshield could be had with a snap-on "fabricoid" cover to serve as legshields. The speedometer was driven off of the front wheel by cable and bolted to the steering head; different speedo packages were listed for scooters with 6in, 8in, and three wheels. Two different tandem seats were offered, a saddle type and a cushion. A chrome headlamp was also available to add "glamour."

The most interesting and rare option was a front wheel brake, part number S22-456. The drum mounted to the right side of the wheel and could be used with the speedometer. The Cushman Side-Kar was also available. It was a box on

Post-World War II, the name Auto-Glide was retired and the scooters were called Cushmans, as noted in this 1949 *Popular Mechanics* ad announcing the new 50 Series. The name was changed, but the styling and mechanicals were largely the same.

Cushman Model 52 with optional rear bumper. The major advance was the new automatic clutch on the two-speed 54 model, although this 52 had the old two-speed gearbox. The 50 Series glided along on standard 8.00x4in tires, as here, or optional 6.00x6in tires. Owner: Roger McLaren.

wheels with a lid equipped with slip hinges that could be "removed in ten seconds," according to a brochure. A steel seat could be added to the Side-Kar but no one weighing over 200lb could ride.

62 Pacemaker, 62A Sport, 64 RoadKing, and 64A RoadKing Sport 1949–1956 ★★★★

Cushman advertised the new 60 Series as "Twice the Scooter!" depicting a monstrous Model 62 surrounded by dimunitive people straight out of *Gulliver's Travels*. But for Cushman, the 60 Series ushered in a new era of gigantic scooter sales numbers.

The run of the new 60 Series was fraught with changes, alterations, and updates from year to year. Robert H. Ammon recalled examining the new Italian scooters as soon as they were imported to the United States, and as with the other American competition in the prewar years, Cushman compared them with its own products for updates and new features. "We got some ideas from Vespa and Lambretta," Ammon stated in 1992.

Bowing in late 1948, the first 60 Series scooters featured parts from the old 52 and 54. But by 1949, the style was defined until 1952 when a new, square-block engine was introduced.

The 62 Pacemaker replaced the 52 while the 62A was variously called a Sport or Super version of the Pacemaker but eschewing rear bodywork in the style of the 52A and 53A. The 62A was initially offered with only the Variamatic but soon switched to follow the rest of the 60 Series. Like-

---

Belgian Cushman

In 1950, the Belgian Cushman firm was erected in Anderlues to build Cushman scooters for the Belgians under license. Cushman supplied components including Husky engines, transmissions, wheels, and more to the firm as part of the European Recovery Act. The Belgian firm made its own frame, forks, bodywork, and other parts.

In 1951, Belgian Cushman offered its Single model with a 300cc Husky engine. The bodywork was odd when compared with the Cushman 50 Series of the day and weird compared with any other scooter. The tail section was a standard rounded covering; the front legshield was a large sheet that looked like protective armor on an artillery cannon. A luggage compartment sat in front of the apron with styling that appeared to be based on a mailbox. As an early brochure tentatively offered, the Single could "perhaps by piloted by anyone without apprenticeship."

Belgian Cushman also offered a three-wheeled Delivery scooter with "robust construction."

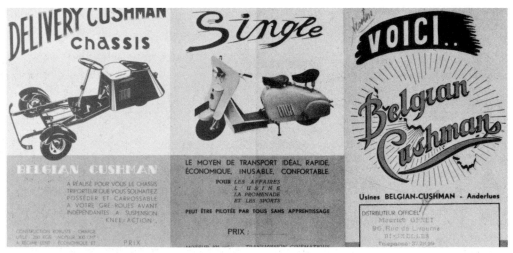

As part of the European Recovery Act, Cushman helped start scooter production in Belgium by licensing its patents to the Belgian Cushman firm. This flyer shows what the Belgians could do with the American design, reworking the Cushman 50 series scooters into the oddly styled Single. Never imported to the United States, a Belgian Cushman would be the ultimate addition to an American Cushman collection. Vittorio Tessera archives

wise, the 64 replaced the 54 but included a new two-speed sliding-gear transmission, and the 64A appeared in its Birthday Suit as a Sport.

The bodywork of the clothed 60 Series scooters was much like that of the 50 Series except it was smoothed over and rounded off. The rear was wider, with a turtle-back look.

The 60 Series were powered by a dazzling variety of engines all available from 1949 on. The 4hp Husky was the staple engine with bore and stroke of 2 5/8x2 3/4in for 14.89ci displacement. A 5hp version was optional according to ads based on a larger 2 7/8in bore for 17.80ci. The 5.4:1 compression ratio of the 4hp Husky also climbed to 5.9:1 for the 5hp.

Beyond that, the 60 Series continued in the Cushman tradition. The frame was still "sag-proof," as one ad proclaimed, and the automatic clutch still "has not four speeds, not ten, but actually hundreds of speeds," as another ad stated in purely technical terms.

In 1949, an updated Husky engine was quietly introduced, which revolutionized the Cushman. That the new engine design bowed without fanfare was probably an attempt by Cushman not to draw attention to any sort of change in the engine that may have cast doubts on its reliability among the nonmechanical buyers. Cushman ads simply denoted the new engine as the "heavy duty" Husky.

The square-barrel Husky engines still produced 4hp, 5hp, or the new optional 7.3hp, but they were better and cooler running as well as quicker in acceleration. The new Husky would power Cushmans until their demise, even after the 1960 introduction of the Super Husky.

And the 60 Series continued to sell. In 1950, Cushman produced some 10,000 scooters, including the new Eagle; by 1954, it was up to 12,000 units, according to *Business Week*.

61 Highlander 1949–1950 ★★★

The new highlander carried on Cushman's old tradition of offering a stripper economy model alongside its regular line of scooters. The 61 was offered alongside the naked 62A Sport but used the old 3hp engine, which mounted directly to the frame without benefit of rubber bushings and caused more than its share of vibration.

Riding on 4x8in tires and fitted with a bare-bones tractor-like seat, the Highlander 61 was built for less than two years before being upgraded.

711 Highlander 1950–1958 ★★★

The 711 was a refined 61 with the engine now mounted on rubber bushings and the fender bolted to the frame whereas it had been bolted directly to the engine of the 61.

The Model 53 Airborne's lineage continued through to the Model 61 Highlander of 1949–1950. This was an economy scooter stripped of its bodywork and powered by the old 3hp Husky, which mounted directly to the frame without benefit of even rubber bushings. Owners: Keith and Kris Weeks.

714 Highlander 1952–1953 ★★★

In 1952, Cushman released the 714, which was a 711 upgraded into a deluxe stripper model, a contradiction in terms to everyone except scooter manufacturers. The upgrades must have brought the 714 into conflict with the 60 Series as it now boasted the 4hp engine and full bodywork.

The bodywork was a curious blend of the 60 Series styling and the unclothed 61. An engine

The Highlander was reworked in 1958 as the 721 Series; this was a 721-28 DeLuxe with the larger-bore 4.8hp engine. The 721 Series was a 722 Pacemaker without the fiberglass bodywork. Owners: Keith and Kris Weeks.

cover was added that was reminiscent of the early Auto-Glides.

715 DeLuxe Highlander 1953–1958 ★★

The 715 was a development of the 714 with added floorboards, a two-person padded cushion seat, and the new Cushman 100 tires.

711-51 DeLuxe Highlander 1958 ★★

The 715 was renamed as the 711-51 to bring it in line with the standard 711 Highlander that had lasted through three new DeLuxe models unchanged.

721 Highlander Special
and 721-28 DeLuxe 1958–1964 ★★

The 721 Series Highlanders were all new for 1958. As the brochure stated, "The Highlander proves you can have all you want in a scooter—sleek beauty, powerful performance and safe roadability."

The 721 Special continued with the 3.2hp engine and rode on 4.00x8in tires while the 721-28 had the 4.8hp engine and Cushman 100 tires.

The new Highlanders rode on a completely new frame (same frame from the 720 Series) with lever-action leading-link front forks, a splash shield, and fiberglass rear bodywork.

The DeLuxe was fitted with the 12 volt flywheel magneto, sealed-beam headlamp, and electric horn whereas the Special continued with 6 volts.

By 1960, the 3.2hp engine was shelved and for a short time just the 4.8hp Highlander could be had; by 1961, both the 4.8hp or 7.95hp Husky were available. At about the same time, the 721 Series moved up to Cushman 200 tires measuring 9.75x3.75in. An optional pillion seat was also available made of vinyl and polyurethane foam.

722 and 722-45 Pacemaker and
725 and 725-46 RoadKing 1957–1961 ★★

For 1957, Cushman turned its attention to a replacement for the 60 Series standard scooters. The new 720 Series Step Thru scooters featured the Pacemaker and RoadKing models, carrying over the names form the 60 Series but little else.

The chassis for the 720 Series was completely redesigned and based on a large-diameter main steel tube that ran from the headstock to a rear subframe, which held the engine. The new front forks featured a knee-action leading-link design.

The 722s were clothed in bodywork that was either as "modern-as-tomorrow" or just boxy, depending on how you looked at it. Cushman said the new design had "eye-catching beauty" and termed the styling "streamlined". Whether

The going is great on

It wasn't essential that you had an astronaut's haircut to ride a Cushman, but OMC always promoted a clean-cut image with its scooters. When the 720 Series made its debut in 1957 it was a modernistic vision of the scooter of the future with fiberglass bodywork and Jet Age styling. The 725 RoadKing may lead the Super Eagle down the street on the cover of this 1959 ad, but its sales were far behind. By 1961 the 720 Series was gone and—surprise of surprises—Cushman sold the Vespa instead.

Cushman created its Eagle line styled as a miniature motorcycle based on the whim of a Cushman salesman, as Robert H. Ammon recalled in 1992. Powell and Mustang's models had also been examined. Whoever came first, the Eagle was the sales success. This 1949 765 Eagle is from the first series built, which used barrel-spring front suspension as on the 50 Series scooters of the same era. Owner: Jim Kilau.

you agreed or not, the value of any streamlining was dubious anyway at a 40mph top speed.

The bodywork was finished in bright two-tone paint schemes of Sapphire White with Castle Grey, Festival Red, Cascade Blue, Tahiti Coral, or Nugget Gold, or Safety Orange with Black; as an option, a clear overcoat of "reflective safety paint" could be had.

The seat was a monstrous padded cushion providing "arm-chair comfort" and finished in two-tone gray and white. It was redesigned in 1960 with contours but retained the color scheme.

The rear deck of the new 720s was hinged to tilt forward for access to the engine, gas tank, and a package compartment. The hinged cover could be removed by pushing a single button—no bolts held it in place. The Side-Kar was again offered for delivery or passenger use.

The Pacemaker was available in two models, both with single-speed transmissions: the 722 DeLuxe with the 7.95hp Husky and the 722-45 Special with the 4.8hp engine.

Likewise, the RoadKing was available in two similar models, but using the new two-speed sliding-gear transmission: the 725 DeLuxe with the 7.95hp and the 725-46 with the 4.8hp. The two-speed gearbox resulted in the RoadKing weighing in at 310lb, 35lb more than the Pacemaker.

The first series of 720 scooters had problems with engine overheating and in their second year, additional louvers were cut into the side panels.

In 1959, the front apron was redesigned in line with the styling of the new Super Eagle. A chrome plate with a C and M logo was placed just above the front fender and the new 12 volt sealed-beam headlamp was mounted in a chrome-plated bezel. A front shock was now also optional.

From 1959, the 720s were available in two-tone color combinations of Charcoal Gray with Starmist White; either Huntsman Red or Cascade Blue could be added to create a tri-tone scheme.

Starting in October 1959, a 725 RoadKing two-speed 7.95hp scooter without bodywork was offered as an economy model.

Cushman's Eagle Series

Along with the introduction of the 60 Series in 1949, Cushman split its motorscooter production in two further directions that would continue until the company's demise in the 1960s. The traditional step-through scooter symbolized by the 62 and 64 were supplemented by the stripper Model 61 Highlander. The 61 would develop into the 700 Series Highlander, and 720 Series Pacemaker and RoadKing before Cushman switched to carry the Vespa line in 1961.

In 1949, Cushman also unveiled its new Eagle, a radical departure from the step-through design to a scooter reminiscent of the big-twin motorcycles of the time that ruled the American roads: a Harley–Davidson E Knucklehead or Indian Chief. As Robert H. Ammon recalled in 1992, "Somebody in our sales department wanted a scooter that looked like a motorcycle with gas tank between your legs. It turned out to be a hell of a good idea."

The Eagle was a motorcycle in miniature. It laughed at the scooter design set in stone by Salsbury nearly two decades earlier. In creating the Eagle, Ammon and Jesperson looked back to the Powell P-81 and the Mustang lines: the workings of the engine were proudly on display without engine covers and owners were not afraid to get their hands dirty working on these "real" machines. And these were machines for real men, riders who weren't afraid to swing their legs over the gas tank.

All in all, historical hindset has crowned the Eagle as the right scooter at the right time for the United States. Salsbury's 85 with its outrageous full bodywork died a quick death in the marketplace whereas the Eagle became the best-selling Cushman scooter ever.

Shriner Motor Corps Scooters

Shriners and motorscooters are made for each other. Beginning in the late 1950s, the fez-capped Shriners first took to two-wheelers, showing off their prowess by doing intricate figure-eight maneuvers in annual Fourth of July parades everywhere in the United States.

And just as a Harley is the motorcycle of choice for the Hell's Angels, the Cushman is the preferred ride for most Shriners. Sure, you may have seen them on a Vespa or Harley–Davidson Topper, but Cushman catered to the Shriner with an arm's-long list of optional goodies. And when OMC sold Vespas, it offered Shriner accessories for the Italian Hairdryer as well.

The Shriner fad for scooters started with Bob Ammon, Cushman's chief. Ammon was a long-standing Shriner, and offered Cushmans to his brethern at bargain prices.

In 1957, Cushman offered the following accessories and chrome trinkets to tantalize the Shriners: Buco black and white saddlebags complete with fringe and rivets; Buco fender flap with rivets and reflectors; Shriner emblems; speedometer; windshield; horns; flags; special paint jobs with lot prices; and of course chromed safety bars, fender tips, gas tank bands, locking gas caps, floorboards, stands, clutch arms, air shrouds, front seat rails, and rear seats with chromed seat rails.

765 Eagle Series I 1949–1954 ★★★★

The first Eagle was offered for sale by December 1949. It was a supreme example of styling selling the package. The mechanicals were largely carried over from the 60 Series scooters. It was the motorcycle look that sold the new product.

The frame was all new: a motorcycle-style tube frame with a rigid rear—hardtail in Harley-Davidson parlance. The front forks used the knee-action suspension of the 60 Series with barrel springs; the handlebars were welded to the fork tubes. Drum brakes were fitted to both the front and rear wheels.

Bodywork was at a minimum to show off the Husky's muscle. Front and rear fenders were curvaceous, continuing the lines of the motorcycle-style pea-shaped 2gal gas tank. The color was good old Farmall red. On the gas tank, a new decal had the Cushman script alongside the word Eagle superimposed over a bald eagle diving for prey.

The Eagle was powered by the round-barrel 5hp Husky engine with a chrome-plated exhaust pipe swooping down to the right. The two-speed transmission was operated by a handshift on the left side of the gas tank in the best Harley-Davidson tradition. Drive on the first 765 Eagles was shifted from the left side to the right, the opposite of all preceding Cushman scooters.

Cushman scooters were featured on the cover of *Business Week* on April 19, 1950, with a profile of Cushman's corporate expansion on the eve of the Korean War. "War talk has brought a sellers' market in automobiles, it had also started a boom in the motorscooter field," the magazine reported. Cushman production was going on a 48-hour six-day work week to meet demand; from 1936–1949, Cushman had made 200,000 scooters, and planned to build more than 10,000 scooters in 1950. Company President Robert Ammon stated that Cushman expected 1950 sales of $3.5 million—90 percent from scooters. And Ammon also boasted that Cushman controlled 90 percent of the United States' scooter market.

The debut of the Eagle was also the culmination of a three-year modernization effort within the Cushman factory. Ammon reported that efficiency was increased 50 percent by the new system of assembly-line production with roller conveyor belts and an overhead conveyor parts shipping from a central parts storeroom where one man supplied 165 machine-tool workers.

By November 1950, ads showed the "new" Eagle, now with a luggage rack over the rear fender. Cushman now listed three further colors for the Eagle: along with red, you could have light blue, green, or cream. The 1951 ads and brochures also announced a "new" Eagle for 1951 but the scooter had carried over from 1950 with no change except the price, up from $282.50 to $344.70.

In April 1952, the new square-barrel 5hp engine was added as an option. In addition, the new 7.3hp engine was available based on a 2 7/8in bore.

In 1952, black was also made available as a color option.

762 Eagle 1952–1954 ★★★

In 1952, Cushman offered a stripper economy model Eagle as the 762. And it was truly bare bones. The 762 lacked any sort of transmission, running the drive chain directly to the rear wheel on the right side of the scooter, as with the step-throughs. There was no rear luggage rack available and the seat was bare metal.

The 762 could be had with either the 4hp, 5hp, or 7.3hp engine.

The Model was rarely listed in Cushman advertising and was built in only limited numbers, according to Cushman archives. Still, with the addition of a transmission and other minor parts, the 762 could have been upgraded to a 765—or vice versa, as today a 762 is rarer and more valuable.

765 Eagle Series II 1955 ★★★★

Ads again promoted a "new" Eagle for 1955 but while changes were actually minimal, they were important. As the Eagle's model, the Harley-Davidson big twin, now offered its Hydra-Glide and its chief competitor, the Mustang, came with telescoping forks, Cushman had to have one, too.

Ads listed numerous updates for 1955: the use of ball bearings for the steering head; a new kickstarter design; a new front brake design; and a new front fender.

The Eagle's new "air-cushioned ride" had nothing to do with air; short coil springs were mounted on telescopic forks and covered by rubber boots just above the front axle. The forks and steering head were clothed by a sheetmetal apron with raised and painted Cushman script across the front; the headlamp mounted to a bracket above the logo.

Topping the fork apron was a small dash area for mounting the speedometer.

765 Eagle and 765-27 Series III 1956–1958 ★★★★

For 1956, two Eagle models were offered, the 765 DeLuxe with a new 7.95hp engine (often termed the 8hp) and the 765-27 Special with the old 2 5/8x2 3/4in 4.8hp engine. Top speed of the DeLuxe was 50mph and 40mph for the Special.

The new 7.95hp Husky was based on a 3x2 3/4in bore and stroke for 19.40ci and used a new high-lift cam. In a 1956 *Cycle* magazine test it achieved a quarter-mile dragstrip run in 24sec. As another Cushman ad stated, you could now soar with the "dynamic speed and power of the eagle itself."

In addition, all engines now came with a new cast-aluminum exhaust manifold with cooling ribs as well as a new chromed straight exhaust pipe and muffler with removable baffles. The styling of the new exhaust system prompted *Scoot* magazine to report that the "new Cushman is a snappy looker."

An Oil Airbath air cleaner also became available as an option. The oilbath mounted on the frame below the gas tank with a long rubber tube running back to the carburetor.

On May 10, 1957, the Ammons family sold Cushman to Outboard Marine Corporation (OMC), the long-time maker of Johnson and Evinrude outboard motors. Robert H. Ammon would stay on, working with Herb Jesperson, who would later head Cushman.

In 1958, a new two-speed transmission was made standard on the DeLuxe. The gearbox was smaller and allowed the Eagle to revert to the right-hand chain drive. As *Car Life* magazine reported, "Cushman's automatic clutch duplicates the driving ease of automatic transmission on Detroit's proudest iron."

And the Eagle continued to push the sales records. *Business Week,* on Valentine's Day, 1959, reported that Cushman was up from building 10,000 scooters in 1950, the year of the Eagle's debut, to 12,000 total scooters in 1954 and 25,600 in 1958.

Super Eagle 765-88 1959–1964
and 765-89 1959–1963 ★★★★

In 1959, Cushman gave the Eagle a facelift and produced a second line of Eagles, the Super Eagle 765-88 DeLuxe with 7.95hp engine and the Super Eagle 765-89 Special with 4.8hp engine.

Whereas the Series III Eagles had some of the brawn of a Harley-Davidson, the Super Eagle now took on the character of American car design of the late 1950s. Cushman once again called the new styling "streamlined," but that was just a stylish word at the time having little to do with aerodynamics; instead it stood for lots of bodywork and lots of shiny metalwork. The Supers were dressed up with a new fork apron featuring a polished aluminum nameplate with a large C and M logo.

But the main styling cue came at the tail end. A new squared-off fender rose from the wheel to hold the luggage rack. A scallop—also known among Detroit designers as blood trough in honor of a knife—ran along both sides with the exhaust fitting handily into the right side. A chrome tail

In 1959, Cushman created its Super Eagle with restyled front and rear ends. The telescopic forks had arrived in 1955 with the second series Eagles but the C and M logo on the front apron replaced a Cushman script logo. But the big news was the squared-off rear fender that denoted the Super Eagle. This 1959 model has the optional seat rail, passenger cushion, crash bars, windshield, and fender bumper; the chromed seat springs, wheels, and struts were nonoriginal. Owners: Keith and Kris Weeks.

panel was crowned by a taillight, and a clutch cover enclosed the engine.

In designer lingo, the Super Eagle was all styling pizzazz. But there were also substantial mechanical updates, the most important of which was the move to 12 volt electrics. In honor of the voltage upgrade, the headlamps were now sealed beam. The engine also now breathed through an air filter mounted in an oval canister directly on the carburetor.

Cushman brochures of the time were at a peak of buzzwords to back the solid sales the Eagle line was turning in. "Just to look at the brand new Super Eagle and Eagle is to feel an urge to take to the road. Why not yield to that urge? Swing into the saddle, ease open the throttle, and learn a new definition of fun." Why not indeed?

In 1960, the Eagle line was given a second mild "tuck" to update the 1959 facelift. The gas tank was squared off and fitted with plastic knee pads. The front fender rear stay was enlarged, probably more for styling than support.

The seat support, however, was upgraded for luxury with rubber bushing mounts. Brakes were also updated with the lining now on the shoes rather than on the inside of the drums; ads stated that this change tripled the braking power.

Ads now listed a choice of four colors for the Eagle line: Black, Huntsman Red, Cascade Blue, and Starmist White.

The 1961 models continued the lineage largely the same as the 1960.

Eagle Series IV 765 and 765-27 1959–1964 ★★★★

The 765 and 765-27 Eagles followed the updates of the new Super Eagle with exception of the rear bodywork. As the ads stated, it was a new era of "dynamic roadability."

Cushman's large brochure in the early 1960s listed a number of accessories for both the Eagle and Super models. A plastic windshield was available as well as chrome safety bars. A chrome fender tip could also be had along with a speedometer/odometer unit. At the rear, a dual exhaust pipe was offered to split and run mufflers along both sides of the rear fender for a "full-throated exhaust tone."

The ultimate option of the era had to be the leather saddle bag set complete with white fringe, chrome bangles, and locks. The ads promised "Lots of room."

With the arrival of the Silver Eagle in 1961, the 765 models were to be phased out, but when the Silver Eagle was pulled from production late in 1961, the 765s got a new lease on life. It was to last only until 1964 when the revived Silver Eagle finally spelled doom for the old Husky line.

Silver Eagle Series I 1961 ★★★★

In early 1961, Cushman began the quiet promotion of an all-new, all-aluminum OMC Super Husky engine to replace the long-lived Husky engine. The promotion was quiet because the new Silver Eagle was to be a 25th anniversary model for the 1962 celebration. To some Cushman fans it was a sad moment; to others the new engine was full of promise.

The Super Husky was a radical, modern engine that would be superior to scooter engines throughout the world. Made completely of die-cast aluminum alloy with a cast-iron cylinder liner, it featured a single cylinder angled forward with overhead valves and a new oiling system.

This 1960 Eagle was the first year for a new front fender with triangle-shaped bottom stay. Optional were the twin exhaust pipes and crashbars; customized pieces included the chromed seat springs and add-on lights. Owner:Ski. *Greg Field*

In early 1961, Cushman quietly added the all-new, all-aluminum OMC 9hp Super Husky engine to create the Silver Eagle, which was to be a 25th anniversary model for the 1962 celebration. But the new engine vibrated badly and destroyed the old Eagle frame, so the Silver Eagle was quietly sent back to the R&D shop. This 1961 Super Silver Eagle was a Shriner scooter hailing from Jamestown, North Dakota, and featured numerous options including the Folo-Thru Bendix turn-key electric starter. Owners: Keith and Kris Weeks.

The standard model was sparked by a flywheel magneto and kicked over by a side-mounted kick-starter.

Optional was a Cushman Permalite 12 volt alternator, rectifier, and 20 amp-hour battery, which powered the Folo-Thru Bendix turn-key electric starter.

The Super Husky was available in a 9hp version based on a 3 1/2x2 1/4 oversquare bore and stroke for 21.65ci. The engine created the 9 horses at 4000rpm and 15lb-ft of torque at 2500rpm. A restricted engine was optional with 6hp.

The Super Husky was to power a 1962 silver anniversary model to celebrate twenty-five years of Cushman scooters; the model would be named, not surprisingly, the Silver Eagle. But it was not to be.

The Super Husky came about as a cost-saving effort by OMC, which had closed Cushman's foundry in 1959 and brought the aluminum engine in to replace the old cast-iron one. The new OMC was originally a two-cylinder industrial powerplant but the scooter version would only have one lung—and the crankshaft was not counterbalanced to make up for the missing piston assembly.

Thus, the first Silver Eagles literally shook themselves apart. Held taut in the rigid Eagle frame, the new, out-of-balance engine vibrated until the frame's welds cracked. Cushman quickly halted production until a new frame could be designed and returned to the tried-and-true Husky in the old Eagle and Super Eagle models.

Silver Eagle Series II 1962–1965 ★★★

By 1962, the new Floating Power Chassis was developed with Power Frame rubber engine and transmission mounts to cope with a new Super Husky that included counterweights to balance vibrations.

The Floating Power Chassis was at times given to dealers to fulfill warranty claims against the Series I Silver Eagles, so it's possible to find Power Frames fitted with the first Super Huskys.

Four Eagles were offered as of 1964: manual- and electric-start Silver Eagles as well as manual- and electric-start Super Silver Eagles. Updates included a restyled tail for the Supers.

With the Silver Eagle in 1963 came a new line of accessories. The windshield and speedometer/odometer unit were still available. But now you could turn your scooter into a full dresser

In 1962, the Super Husky was refined and launched in a new Floating Power Chassis with rubber engine mounts. This 1963 Super Silver Eagle featured optional electric start, crashbars, fender tip, windshield, seat rail, passenger cushion, and more. Owners: Keith and Kris Weeks.

The end of a long line: this Super Silver Eagle was sold in 1965, although it may have been built earlier as Cushman's scooter assembly lines had largely closed down in 1965. This unrestored Eagle has less than 100 miles on the odometer and was originally owned by a funeral home—a sad irony to Cushman's demise. Owner: Jim Kilau.

47

with twin handlebar-mounted chrome mirrors, add-on white sidewalls, a chrome lean stand, chrome seat rail, chrome gas tank band, chrome battery cover, pillion cushion and foot pegs, as well as new fiberglass saddle bags. Cushman was truly "the big name in little wheels."

By late 1964, the Eagle was close to becoming extinct. In early 1965, production ceased.

Trailster 723 1960–1965 ★

Half motorscooter, half Jeep, the Trailster was an attempt to broaden Cushman's appeal. In the end, however, it would be the firm's last new scooter model.

Based on a 720 Series frame and front forks, the 723 used the 4.8hp Husky; by 1962, the 7.95hp engine was optional. The Trailster was driven by the two-speed sliding-gear transmission, which was parlayed in ads into a high-low range gearbox for 12.3mph and 6.9mph respectively. An optional sprocket kit converted it to street speeds.

Interesting features of the 723 included the "tractor tread" rear tire and two brake pedals for either the right or left foot, a safety feature. And instead of a luggage rack, a "game and gear" rack was made for the rear frame section.

Cushman's Demise

By the dawn of the 1960s, Cushman was facing hard times in scooter sales. The writing had been on the wall for several years. Cushman had largely owned the scooter market at the dawn of the 1950s. By 1958, Vespas and Lambrettas infiltrated one-third of the US market, counting for 20,000 of the 60,000 scooters sold in the United States.

And with the boom in scooter sales in the late 1950s came a legislative backlash of laws limiting the minimum age for scooter jockeys. In what had always been largely a youth market, the laws were a torniquet on sales. In Ohio alone, eleven deaths and 412 injuries were reported from scooter misadventures in 1958—although scooter industry spokesmen contended that twice as many youngsters had been killed on bicycles in the same year, according to *Business Week*.

In late 1960, a letter was mailed to dealers that sent a shock heard throughout the US scooter world: effective January 1, 1961, Cushman would distribute Vespa motorscooters across most of the United States. It was a move designed in one fell swoop to replace the aging 720 Series and cut manufacturing costs at the Lincoln works. Cushman would sell the Vespa 125, 150, and GS from 1961–1963, merely adding a Cushman nameplate to the legshield.

But most Cushman dealers didn't cotton to the Italian Vespa and many chose to drop Cushman and switch to the new rival, Honda. As Robert H. Ammon, who retired from Cushman in 1961, later said, "The Hondas were just frankly better machines than the Cushman Eagles—and they were cheaper." It was the end of an epoch.

It was not the end of Cushman, however. Throughout the 1950s, the firm had seen sales growth in a side market: its three-wheeled versions of scooters, and by 1957, the three-wheelers made up 16 percent of Cushman sales. With this data in the back of their minds, Cushman management prompted further production of the industrial Trucksters, Mailsters for the US Postal Service, and a new Golfster for the grown-up kids in kelly green who had once buzzed Main Street on an Auto-Glide and could now tour the links in a Cushman golf cart. It was the dawn of a new Golden Age for Cushman.

Custer USA ★★

Custer scooters were built in Dayton, Ohio, in the late 1930s in two-and three-wheel form. The US Army tested the Custer alongside the Cushman and Cooper when looking for a paratrooper scooter in 1944 but decided its 2.5hp engine was too weak-kneed. The name probably did not inspire much confidence either.

Cycle-Scoot USA ★

Cycle-Scoots were built in Rockford, Illinois, from 1953–1955 and fitted with Cushman Husky and Briggs & Stratton engines.

Cushman Three-Wheelers

Cushman offered its first three-wheeled scooter in 1939 as the Model 9 Package-Kar, which was an Auto-Glide Model 2 with a two-wheeled front axle holding a large box. In 1940, it was updated as the Model 19, becoming the Model 29 later that year.

From 1942–1945, the two-speed Model 39 and Floating Drive 39A in Package-Kar and Stake-Kar form were offered with many sales made to the military. These models were updated for 1946–1948 as the 59 with an automatic disc clutch and new sliding-gear transmission with two forward and one reverse gear.

With the 60 Series came the Models 69 and 69A Package-Kar and Stake-Kar with steering wheels instead of handlebars; an Ice Cream Special was also offered.

Later, Cushman three-wheelers included the Truckster line, Haulster, Trailster, Mailster, and finally the Golfster, which led Cushman into a new era of golf car construction. Today, OMC builds the three-wheeled police vehicles for giving parking tickets, which we all know and love.

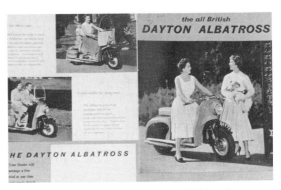

The Vespa looked like a wasp, the VW Beetle resembled an insect, but the Albatross looked nothing like a seagull even at top speed. The bad-luck image of the Albatross probably never helped sell a scooter either. Power came from a 224cc 1H Villiers two-stroke backed by a four-speed gearbox and riding on 4.00x6in tires. *Vittorio Tessera archives*

The Czeta brought speedboat styling to scooters. The 175 model was based on a 58x65mm 171.7cc engine breathing through the prestigious Kikov 2924 carburetor. During a road test by *Scooter* magazine in 1959, the tester reported the Czeta was "safe a speeds up to 60 mph" even though the test scooter's engine had siezed at 40mph. *Vittorio Tessera archives*

CZ Czechoslovakia ★★★

CZ stood for Ceská Zbrojovka, or Czech arms works, and began building motorcycles in 1932. After 1945, CZ was merged with Jawa under state control, and in 1946 was directed by the Communist board to build a scooter, which first appeared at the Prague Fair and was later distributed by Motokow with a 125cc engine and 16in wheels.

Three basic models were made after the original 1946 scooter, beginning with the Cezeta Bohème. Although Puccini would have rolled over in his grave at the sight of this bathosphere-styled scooter, the Bohème was propelled by a decadent 175cc engine.

The impressionists influenced the next Cezeta of 1958, reflected in the name Manet. The Parisian's scooter had more understandable lines, especially after moving the Molotov-cocktail-like gas tank from the front fender. The two-stroke

engine shrank to a 98cc producing 5.1hp. Finally in 1965, the Manet became the Tatran with a larger 125cc 7hp engine.

Dayton UK ★★

Dayton was a famous British manufacturer that decided to celebrate its fiftieth anniversary of bicycle building by offering a motorscooter, in 1955. The firm tempted fate in a volatile market by naming its scooter the Albatross; even if luck was with it, the name could not have been an effective marketing tool even to the most open-minded buyer.

Nevertheless, the Albatross was powered by a 224cc 1H Villiers two-stroke backed by a four-speed gearbox. The frame was of steel tubing with a rear swing arm, all covered by steel panels. But the bodywork ended abruptly below the steering head and front Earles forks were left bare-naked to fend for themselves.

In 1957, the Albatross Twin scooter was added with a two-cylinder 249cc Villiers 2T two-stroke. By 1958, Dayton designers finally admitted the error of their ways and covered the front forks.

Also in 1958, the model names were reworked: the Twin became the Empire, which was joined by a Continental Twin with new styling; and the single became the Single, now with a 246cc 2H. In 1959, the Single became the Continental Single and the Empire was available only on special order—and the Albatross name still remained as a prefix. In 1959, the line was joined by the Albatross Flamenco with a 174cc Villiers 2L engine. The frame and bodywork were shared in a joint venture with Panther and Sun.

DKR's Dove scooter was a warning: This is what happens when a scooter drinks too much beer. Nevermind the styling, the full front fender provided good rider protection against the elements, and that's what a scooter was all about. The Dove would be followed by the DKR Pegasus, Defiant, and Manx—inspiring names for scooters, but they still didn't help keep DKR in the market long. *Mick Walker archives*

By 1960, Dayton and the Albatross were no more.

Derbi Spain ★

Derbi's roots stretch back to 1922 when Simeon Rabasa Singla began building bicycles. In 1950, the firm showed its first motorcycle, named the Derbi, an acronym for Derivados de Bicicletus, or Derived from Bicycles. In 1953, the Masculino scooter was introduced, its name full of Spanish machismo—even with only 98cc. In 1955, a 125cc Masculino was added and both models continued until 1957.

In the 1960s, Derbi concentrated on two divergent markets: mopeds and Grand prix road racing. It was not until 1982 that another Derbi scooter was offered, the Scoot Derbi, with 12 volt electronic ignition firing a fan-cooled, reed-valve, near-horizontal engine with a torque converter transmission. From only 80cc, the Scoot Derbi produced 5.5hp at 7000rpm.

DKR UK ★★

DKR of Wolverhampton announced its Dove scooter in 1957 based on a 147cc Villiers 30C two-stroke with three speeds. The frame was of steel tubes with leading-link forks at the front. Wheels were 10in.

The Dove's styling was anything but avian; the front end had all the grace of a well-developed

The big catch here was the 1955 DKW Hobby Standard. The Hobby displayed all the beauty latent in pressed steel and the numerous air ducts and grilles were more than just styling gizmos—they were essential to prevent seizure of the two-stroke engine. The three-speed gearbox, 75cc engine, and large, spoked wheels resembled moped styling whereas the bodywork was unmistakably scooter. *Mick Walker archives*

beer belly. The tail section, on the other hand, was angular and awkward.

DKR launched two other scooters in 1958: the Pegasus with a 148cc 31C Villiers and three-speed gearbox and the Defiant with a 197cc 9E Villiers and four-speed. In 1959, the Manx joined the trio with a 249cc 2T Villiers, four-speed, and electric leg.

At the end of 1959, the Dove II replaced the original with a 148cc 31C engine. The Pegasus II was offered in 1960 with a 174cc 2L engine. In 1960, these two models were dropped to be replaced by the Capella, which ran on until DKR end in 1966.

DKW Germany

Choose your acronym for DKW and they're all correct: *Dampf Kraft Wagen* (for its first steam powered engine), *Der Knabische Wunische* (the Schoolboy's Dream—of DKW racing motorcycles), and *Das Kleine Wunder*, (the Little Miracle).

In 1919, DKW was founded by the Danish engineer Jorgen Skafte Rasmussen in the town of Zschopau originally named JS Rasmussen. DKW began making two-stroke motorcycles in 1920, and by 1921 released the 122cc Golem and the year after, the 142cc Lamos. Both of these were hybrid motorcycle/scooters boasting all the luxury of an armchair. Unfortunately, it was too much too early, and sales were meager.

By 1930, DKW was the largest motorcycle producer in the world, but over-extended itself and merged with three other manufacturers to remain solvent. DKW, Wanderer, Horch, and Audi joined to become Auto Union AG in 1932 with the symbol of four interlinked circles still used to this day by Audi. Under the union, DKW continued to make motorcycles as well as two-stroke cars.

During World War II, DKW changed production to assist the Third Reich and supply the Wehrmacht with the RT125, which was later copied by BSA, Triumph TEC, Harley-Davidson, and Yamaha. Following the war, the DKW plant ended up in the Russian sector, changing its name to Motorrad Zschopau or simply MZ, as the name of the town changed to Karl Marx to honor everyone's favorite Prussian.

The Auto Union, however, moved west, and DKW set up shop in Ingolstadt on the Danube and serviced old war vehicles until 1949.

Hobby Standard and Luxus 75 1954–1957 ★

The 74cc Hobby boasted an elaborate system of drive belts creating an automatic transmission with a clutch for disengaging the gears. The single cylinder was inclined forward for 47x45mm bore and stroke, while the electrics skipped a battery and stuck with the simple flywheel magneto, more eloquently known as the *Schwungradmagnetzünder*. Many scooter riders didn't like the motorcycle image of a kickstart, so DKW opted for the coveted lawn mower image, placing a pull-starter by the scooterist's left foot.

The Hobby's 3hp at 5000rpm achieved 40mph getting 139mpg (as opposed to some earlier DKW two-stroke motorcycles that got as low as 15mpg). An automatic gas-oil mixer and the large, 16in wheels provided smooth operation.

The Luxus version came with passenger handles on the rear cowling, a pillion seat, and deceptive go-fast horizontal chrome strips. Unfortunately, the added trim makes the rear section of the Hobby look suspiciously like a vacuum cleaner with seats.

In July 1956, an official DKW report stated "The DKW position is said to be far from happy." And so after producing approximately 40,000 Hobbys, DKW took it out of production. Then in November 1958, Mercedes-Benz gained control of the Auto Union and cut the number of DKW two-wheelers to three models, and by 1959 production halted altogether.

The Hobby lived on, however, being produced under license by the French company, Manurhin, and imported into England by AFN. Manurhin modified the styling, added wider tires, enlarged the engine, and improved the automatic gearchange resulting in the scooter's new name, the Beltomatic.

DMW UK ★

DMW built numerous lightweight motorcycles for the British market based usually on Villiers two-stroke engines, including the firm's Bambi scooter of 1957 with its 99cc 4F and two-speed gearbox.

The Bambi's chassis was made from steel pressings like the Vespa, with a triangulated front fork sprung by a spring within the steering column. The rear swing arm was also made of steel pressings, as were the wheels, which carried 2.50x7.5in tires.

In 1961, DMW offered its 249cc two-stroke Deemster scooter in Standard and De Luxe versions, the latter with electric start. The Deemster resembled a motorcycle converted into a scooter, retaining the motorcycle riding position and engine placement while adding full bodywork and small 12in diameter wheels. The Deemster defied categorization, which was a problem in the market. It lasted, however, until 1967.

Ducati Italy

Never mind horsepower ratings, power curves, or reliability, Ducati motorscooters were the only scooters blessed by the Pope.

The roots of Moto Ducati stretch back to 1922, when 19-year-old Bologonese finance student Adriano Cavalieri Ducati invented a radio transmitter, according to the family-written *Storia della Ducati*. He formed a company to make radio condensors, later branching into micro-spy cameras and Italy's first electric razor. During Benito Mussolini's rise, the Fascists charged Ducati to put a radio in every Italian house, the better to spread *Il Duce*'s word.

Meanwhile in Turin in 1943–1944, Aldo Farinelli created a 1hp 48cc clip-on engine for bicycles, which he named the *Cucciolo*, his puppy. Following the war, Farinelli's engine began limited production at Siata in Turin.

Ducati's Cruiser was one of the great scooters, a textbook case of too much scooter too early. Ducati reasoned in 1952 that its luxury Cruiser would win the market away from the no-frills Vespas and Lambrettas, but the Bolognese firm over-estimated the buyer. By the late 1950s, however, Piaggio and Innocenti launched their GS and TV luxury scooters and captured the market Ducati had sought. Owner: Vittorio Tessera. *Vittorio Tessera*

Postwar, Ducati's factory at Borgo Panigale was leveled and production halted. The Ducati family looked for a new product and was introduced to Siata via the Instituto per la Reconstruzione Industriale (IRI), a governmental rebuilding agency. The IRI invested in Ducati with other capital coming from Opus Dei, the Vatican's investment arm. Ducati began large-scale production and sales of the Cucciolo, which, along with other clip-on engines, was to become as important to Italy's postwar recovery as its contemporaries, the Vespa and Lambretta.

Cruiser 1952–1954 ★★★★★

Inspired by the scooter's success, Ducati launched its Cruiser scooter at the Milan Fiera Campionaria of 1952. The Cruiser featured a 7.5hp 175cc overhead-valve engine with the cylinder transverse in front of the rear wheel, 12 volt electrics, and electric start. Following the lead of the American scooters, the Ducati also had an automatic transmission based on a hydraulic torque converter. With the powerful four-stroke engine, the Cruiser had to be detuned to meet the Italian government's maximum scooter speed limit of 80km/h.

The front forks were telescopic with a hydraulic damper mounted at the hub. The rear wheel was held by the massive aluminum-alloy gearbox case that doubled as a swing arm with a hydraulic damper mounted horizontally below the engine.

The Cruiser was stylish, like a metallic sharkskin zoot suit on wheels. Its step-through chassis was clothed in elegant, flowing two-tone bodywork penned and produced by the celebrated Italian carrozzeria, Ghia. The long right side cover swung open effortlessly on a front-mounted hinge.

Ducati believed that by offering a luxurious four-stroke scooter, it would steal the thunder from Piaggio and Innocenti's two-strokes. Ducati was wrong. The Cruiser lasted until only 1954.

Brio 1964–1969 ★★

Ducati chose to concentrate instead on motorcycles, but built a second scooter series in 1964 that was what the Cruiser should have been for sales success.

In 1964, Ducati returned to the scooter fold with its Brio 48, based on a two-stroke 48cc engine pumping out 4.2hp. The Brio 100 used a two-stroke 94cc for 6hp at 5200rpm with ignition by flywheel magneto. To start either Brio, you were forced to a lowly kickstarter; to shift through the four gears, you had to use your hand. And the styling was as boxy as the Cruiser was sleek.

But the Brio was at least a limited success and continued in production until 1967 when it was superseded by the slightly updated Brio 50 and Brio 100/25 of 1968. By 1969, Ducati was moving from the two-stroke market, and the scooters were cancelled.

If Ducati's timing with the Cruiser had been different, the motorscooter world could have been changed dramatically. Instead, the Cruiser passed into history as a footnote.

Dürkopp Germany

Dürkopp called on the gods to assure its scooter's fortune and in honor of the goddess of forests, it named its two-wheeled temple the Diana.

Herr Nikolaus Dürkopp founded the company in 1867 as a bicycle manufacturer and by 1901 had designed its first motorcycle. After World War I, it produced clip-on bicycle motors and began making motorcycles again in 1949 after a thirty-five-year hiatus. In 1954, at the height of the scooter boom, it produced the attractive Diana scooter, which far surpassed the firm's motorcycle production.

Diana 1954–1959; Diana TS 175 and Diana TS 200 Sport 1959–1960 ★★★

The Diana's introduction was splashed across Dürkopp ads when Miss Germany 1954 "won" a Diana and posed on her beloved scooter for a photo op. The Diana had sleek lines, obviously borrowed from the Lambretta LD while making some notable updates such as the smooth side panel line, an enlarged engine, and the headlamp attached to the handlebars.

The first Diana's 9.5hp zoomed it to an 80km/h maximum speed. The later 194cc Sport and 171cc TS had 12hp for 100km/h and 10.8hp for 95km/h respectively. The four-speed Diana had a large 3liter gas tank and was a solid scooter made for long distances in spite of its smallish 10in wheels.

Dürkopp produced a total of 24,963 of the two-seated Dianas, a relatively high number for the small manufacturer.

Excelsior UK ★★★

Excelsior of Birmingham dated back to the 1870s when it began building bicycles. Through the prewar years, the firm sold large-bore motorcycles; following the war, it was reduced to churning out commuter machines.

The link between Excelsior's two periods was the Welbike, a lightweight, collapsible scooter built for the British World War II paratroopers. Harry Lester designed the scooter at a British Army R&D skunkworks, and the name came from the first prototype, built at Welwyn, England.

The 70lb Welbike was designed to fold into a canister to be dropped by parachute accompanying the British Red Berets into action. Based on a 98cc Villiers horizontal two-stroke that fit snuggly within the center of the scooter, its top speed was a poky 30mph.

According to English scooter historian Michael Webster, some 4,000 Welbikes were supplied to the British Army and used in Europe and the Orient as well as coming ashore at Normandy and braving the Eastern Front. After the war, the Welbike was civilized as the Corgi and produced by Brockhouse.

Excelsior returned to the scooter market in 1959 with its Monarch scooter, sharing body sheetmetal with the DKR and Sun scooters but fitted with a 147cc two-stroke Excelsior engine. The KS version had a kickstarter and the EL an electric. In 1960, the versions were renamed the MK1 and ME1 respectively.

Faka West Germany ★★

The Faka (short for Fahrzeugwerk Kannenberg) was built around one of the most stupendous of scooter styling cues: the rear section began with a jet turbine-styled intake surmounted by a huge—and solely ornamental—chrome bulb. Faka built three models: the Tourist 150 of 1953–1957, Tourist Commodore 175 of 1953–1957, and Tourist Commodore 200 1953–1957. The larger Com-

Eve, the apple, and a Dürkopp Diana: it was enough to tempt many a German scooter buyer in the late 1950s. The look of the Diana was sinfully stylish with lines borrowed from the Lambretta instead of the usual Teutonic tank- or zeppelin-inspired look of most German scooters.

Jetpod styling was all the rage for automobiles and scooter designers were easy victims to its lure. The Faka's phony turbine intake posed no danger for the scooterists' legs to get sucked into the nonexistent blades, but boy was it impressive.

modore weighed more (132kg.) than the Commodore 175 (126kg.) causing it to go 80km/h instead of 85km/h on its 8in wheels but with 9.6hp compared to 7.6hp. The smaller 148cc Tourist had 6.7hp for a top speed of 70km/h.

FB Mondial Italy ★★★

The Fratelli Boselli Mondial firm of Milan produced its first motorcycle in 1948, a four-stroke racer in a field of two-strokes. Like MV Agusta, Mondial always concentrated on competition motorcycles, creating some of the most famous Italian four-stroke small-bore racers of the postwar era and ruling the 125cc class for years.

Mondial built two scooter models that were as odd as its motorcycles were graceful. Introduced in 1952, the first Mondial scooter consisted of a steel-tube frame with bodywork covering all save the engine, a 125cc two-stroke. The front forks were telescopic, and a suspended swing arm cradled the rear wheel. But the Boselli brothers' souls were in racing, and the scooter was soon forgotten.

In 1959, Mondial tried again with its two-stroke 75cc Lady scooter and styling looking like the mirror image of the sleek Capri scooter. But once again, the Lady was in the competition machinery's shadow and quickly faded away.

Mondial also began to fade in the mid-1960s with the invasion of the Japanese two-stroke racers. Efforts to revive Mondial continue into the 1990s.

The FM T50 of 1951–1952 was bizarre, eccentric, innovative, and all those other things that make a scooter fascinating. The horizontal 125cc two-stroke engine and its gearbox were cast in unit with the rear swing-arm and pivoted from the frame. They were suspended along with the rear wheel by a shock absorber mounted below the chassis. Owner: Vittorio Tessera. *Vittorio Tessera*

Ferbedo Germany ★

In the style of certain American mail-order scooters, the Nürnberg-made Ferbedo R48 was an economical substitute for expensive larger scooters and a step up from bicycles "if you are tired of pedaling," according to its ads. In 1953, the R48 had such basic features as two barrel springs for the front suspension; it was discontinued by 1954. The 48cc Zündapp motor achieved 1.5hp for a maximum speed of 40km/h on this mini 32kg scooter.

Accessories included a luggage rack, a hand-powered rubber-bulb tooter, and what looked like a bird cage covering the engine to prevent burning flesh. As the ads advised, "Compare, choose judiciously and you can't help but become a happy owner of a Ferbedo."

FM Italy ★★

F. Molteni's FM Tipo 50 and 52 scooters were an interesting blend of scooter and motorcycle with styling similar to the Mustang and Powell scooters. First shown in 1951, the FM was powered by a horizontal-cylinder 125cc two-stroke of 5hp.

Foldmobile USA ★★

The Foldmobile was a license-built American version of the French Martin-Moulet Valmobile offered in the late 1950s and early 1960s with a 6hp engine.

Frera Italy ★

Frera of Milan was a long-established Italian make with roots stretching back to 1906. Following the war, Frera was reduced to building small-capacity two-stroke motorcycles and its 125cc Confort scooter. The Confort had a 52x58mm engine mounted in the center of the scooter creating 4.75hp at 5000rpm.

Frisoni Italy ★★

In 1952, Elettromeccanica Luigi Frisoni of Cedrate di Gallarate christened its 160cc Superba scooter at the Milan Fiera Campionaria based on an NSU 125cc engine with four speeds. Production started with a 160cc two-stroke engine of Frisoni's own making. Only a small number were produced.

Fuji Heavy Industries Japan ★★★

Fuji of Tokyo created Japan's first motorscooter, the Rabbit. Emerging from World War II, Japan was in ruin similar to Germany, and like the other European countries, economical transportation helped pull Japan out of the war's destruction. Fuji introduced the first Rabbit in

1946, the same year as the first Vespas went into production on the other side of the world. In that year, only eight Rabbits were built.

The Rabbit was a rustic little scooter, similar in style to prewar American models; Fuji had done its homework. A padded cushion provided seating and suspension; a luggage rack was mounted behind. The Rabbit was based on a 135cc four-stroke single of 57x55mm producing 2hp at 3000rpm. Top speed was 55km/h.

In 1950, the Rabbit was updated as the S-23 with luxury features: pillion pad seat, spare tire, and twin klaxon horns. Barrel-spring suspension was added front and rear.

Two new models were introduced in 1950. First came a 170cc Rabbit S-41 based on a larger bore for 61.5x57mm for 3hp at 3400rpm with 4.00x8in tires. Second was the Jack Rabbit S-31 based on a longer wheelbase and a Cushman-like tail with luggage compartment. The 270cc engine was a doubled-up 135cc Rabbit creating 4.5hp at 3500rpm.

The three models continued until 1954 when they were superseded by the restyled and more-powerful S-48 and S-61. The first was based on the S-41 but with a longer stroke, 61.5x67mm 200cc engine producing 5hp at 3600rpm. The S-61 was the luxury flagship featuring electric start on the 225cc engine, which produced 5.9hp at 4000rpm.

The styling was cutting edge Japanese design of the time, based on the philosophy of more is better. Thus, the Rabbit's flowing front apron was set against slab-faced legshields; the boxy tail was softened by adding multiple curved bodylines, contours, and air inlets. To make sure it all caught the eye, the whole affair was bejewelled by miles of trimwork and the debut of the circular chrome Rabbit logo.

In 1955, a small bare-bones 125cc S-71-I Rabbit was added to the line with a 52x58mm engine for 5hp at 5000rpm. The S-71 was updated as the Junior S-72 in 1957 with refined bodywork featuring even more chrome trimwork and air ducts on the side covers. In 1958, the S-82 arrived making 6.2hp at 5600rpm from its 125cc engine; this was updated in 1960 to the S-82S.

In 1957, the Rabbit Superflow S-101 replaced the luxury S-61. The Superflow featured a torque converter automatic transmission and a 250cc

The first Japanese scooter was this Fuji Rabbit of 1946, introduced in the same year as the Vespa but on the other side of the globe. The Rabbit was quaintly rustic with an agricultural frame and bodywork shaped more by a blacksmith than a designer. Yet its four-stroke 135cc engine did the job. Only eight Rabbits were built in 1946, but by 1947, Rabbit production was in full swing and soon followed about town by Mitsubishi's Pigeon scooter.

The Fuji Rabbit was one of the best scooters ever built in Japan. Its styling was also typically Japanese for the 1960s: chrome geejaws, grilles, and air ducts that made it look fast and purposeful like a jet fighter on wheels. *Classic Scooters Newsletter/Steven Zasueta*

engine of 68.5x67mm for 5.9hp at 4000rpm. Bells and whistles were everywhere on the Superflow: electric start, front and rear turn signals, instrument dashboard with gas gauge and warning light that lit at excessive riding speeds, parking brake, foot-operated headlamp dimmer, and stylish two-tone paint.

The Superflow was updated for 1959 as the S-101 D-2 with cleaner styling and 7hp at 4000rpm from 250cc. This was followed in 1961 by the 125cc S-300, which was redesigned in 1962 as the S-301 based on the Superflow styling. By 1965, the 125cc had matured to 150cc.

In 1961, Fuji introduced a 50cc Rabbit with a single seat and minimalist styling. Based on a square 40x40mm engine for 3hp at 6500rpm, the 50 rode on 3.00x10in tires.

Inspired by the success of Honda's Cub, Fuji began producing a series of 90cc moped-scooters in 1958, continuing through the 90cc S-202 of 1964, a dead ringer for the Honda.

The Nibbio predated the Vespa as the earliest Italian scooter. It could also conquer any mountain—at least in this artist's rendition of the balmy Italian Alps. One of two Nibbio designs, this version's stinging wasp abdomen probably influenced the Vespa. *Vittorio Tessera archives*

GAOMA Italy ★

Officine GAOMA of Milan created its Daino scooter in 1953. A lightweight scooter with 18in wheels, the Daino was powered by a two-stroke 65cc; later came a 75cc of 45x45mm delivering 2.5hp at 5500rpm via three speeds.

Gianca Italy ★★★★★

Gianca's Nibbio was the first Italian scooter. Built in Monza, the Nibbio used a standard tube frame covered by sheet steel bodywork with telescopic front forks. A swing arm was used at the rear with an avant garde monoshock mounted beneath the engine, as later developed by Harley-Davidson for its "revolutionary" Softtail.

The Gianca engine was a 98cc two-stroke of 48x54mm creating 2hp and cooled by flywheel fan. The multiplate clutch fed power to a two-speed gearbox, which was shifted by a heel-and-toe foot lever. Tires were 3.50x8in, and the Nibbio was available in dark green, dark red, or ivory.

In 1949, Nibbio construction was transferred to the San Cristoforo firm of Milan.

Gilera Italy ★★

In 1962, Gilera, one of the long-lived Italian motorcycle marques, decided to also enter the scooter fray. Gilera offered its G50 scooter based on bodywork and engine designs that were so similar to the Vespa it is surprising the scooters did not end up doing battle in court instead of in the marketplace.

But the Gilera G50 offered several differences and advantages over the 50cc Vespino that also appeared in 1962. The layout of the G50 engine was almost identical to the Vespa—except that it was mounted on the scooter's other side. And the G50 was a four-stroke with overhead valves.

The 50cc engine had a 38x44mm bore and stroke, creating 1.5hp at 4800rpm via three speeds shifted by a handtwist. In 1962, a 80cc G80 version was added with a square 46x46mm delivering 3.65hp at 6000rpm. Whereas the G50 had a sole saddle seat, the G80 had a two-person bench. Both models remained in production until 1966.

In 1969, Gilera was purchased by Piaggio.

Glas Germany ★★

Glas publicity read, "Everyone is amazed about the new Goggo," whether by its beauty or audacity is in the eye of the beholder. *Der Goggoroller* was in the style of the Maico and Bastert scooters except with the smaller 8in wheels typical of the Italian makes. Three models were offered: the Goggo 125 of 1951–1956, and Goggo 150 and 200 of 1952–1956.

The extended front fender was embellished with a front bumper and large winged Goggo label. The scooters were armed with 123cc, 148cc, or 197cc Ilo engines, to let you "go with the times" at a fast clip.

Globe USA ★★★

Globe Corporation of Joliet, Illinois, built two- and three-wheeled Globester scooters, beginning in 1948 and running into the early 1950s, based on a centrifugal clutch and "torque-shifting" V-belt Maximatic transmission. Power came from a Continental Red Seal 2hp four-stroke of 2 1/8x2in, sparked by a flywheel magento.

The Globe chassis was made of cast aluminum, which was considered a futuristic "miracle metal" at the time. A basket was mounted atop the fender, which held the 6in wheel.

Two models were offered: the solo Globester Runabout with a red body and gray "metallescent" frame and the Pick-up three-wheeler in red and grey or yellow and brown frame.

Göricke Germany ★

Göricke's Gö-Mo 100 of 1951 was less than glamorous with an unenclosed 98cc Ilo engine. The one-seated scooter appeared to borrow from the design of the early Lambrettas without the speed.

Although Göricke was one of the innovators of the German motorcycle industry, its Görette stadtroller (town scooter) of 1955–1956 was less than noteworthy. Available with either an Ilo 49cc or Sachs 47cc engine, the Görette sold at the same price for either motor.

Grasshopper USA ★

A Grasshopper scooter was tested by the US Army in 1944 as a possible paratrooper scooter.

Gritzner–Kayser Germany ★

Sewing machines, three-wheelers, an occasional motorcycle, and the KTM "Gritzner de Luxe Special" scooter was Gritzner–Kayser's renown. It built the excessively two-toned Austri-

Available on two or four wheels with similar styling, Glas offered the bulbous Goggo scooter as a cheap substitute for its Goggo Mobil micro car with suicide doors. The lux-ury scooter came in 125cc or 150cc, either of which were somewhat small for such a large amount of fender. *Roland Slabon archives*

an KTM scooter under license with the motor between the driver's feet. The white-walled tires and the sharp-but-tacky styling gave it the scooter-of-tomorrow look, yesterday.

Guizzo Italy ★

Guizzo was a moped builder that decided to make the step up to scooter production in the 1960s. It released a 150cc scooter in 1960s and sales plummeted, forcing the company to close.

Guzzi Italy ★★★

Moto Guzzi's roots stretch back to the 1920s. It remains in the market in the 1990s, one of the few motorcycle makers to survive the onslaught of Japan.

After decades of building sophisticated road and race motorcycles, Guzzi turned in 1950 to build a scooter, the Galletto, or Rooster. Just as Guzzi had bucked tradition in the design of its horizontal single-cylinder motorcycles, its scooter broke many of the established tenets and found a market niche that kept it alive until 1964, when many other scooters had long since come and gone.

The Globester Runabout and Pick-Up were typical US scooters of the 1930s and 1940s with their Maximatic automatic transmission and beer can-on-wheels styling. But the Globe Corporation added an unique feature: the frame of the Globesters was made of cast aluminum alloy, an untrusted miracle metal of the time. Rumi in Italy would later use a similar aluminum chassis. *Herb Singe archives*

The most striking feature of the Galletto was not its crude, agricultural bodywork; rather it was the large wheels, 17in—larger than the standard scooter's but at least an inch smaller than the smallest motorcycle's. These wheels, along with other motorcycle-type features such as the foot-operated gearbox and especially the taller stance, made it a "serious" scooter. It was almost an enclosed motorcycle and had the dignity of a motorcycle with the protection of a scooter; the Galletto was a scooter adults did not feel was beneath them to ride.

The prototype Galletto was based on a horizontal four-stroke 150cc engine, but production ran from 1950–1953 with a 160cc of 62x53mm for 6hp at 5200rpm via three speeds.

For 1953-1954, the Galletto was offered as a 175cc with a larger, 65mm bore and 7hp. More importantly, the gearbox now had four speeds.

In 1955, the stroke of the Galletto's engine was increased to 58mm giving 192cc and 7.5hp. The Galletto continued in production until 1964.

Hap Alzina USA–Germany ★

In the late 1950s, famed California Indian and West Coast BSA distributor Hap Alzina sold his Playboy scooter from his shop in Oakland. Made in Germany, the Playboy was powered by "the famed Pranafa" 1.5ci two-stroke, pumping out a whole 0.7hp. A 1956 Playboy flyer showed Junior

Moto Guzzi's Galletto was one the most long-lived of all motorscooter with a progressively larger engine year after year. Despite its styling—or lack thereof—the Galletto was exported throughout the world, imported into the United States by Berti. As this ad promised, the Rooster was "the scooter you'll ride with pride!" It had "real guts," no doubt due to its "sinewy" build—probably the only use of the word sinewy in any scooter, motorcycle, or automotive ad ever.

in the backyard with his diminutive scooter—"Small Fry's newest sport."

The flyer also assured Mom the Playboy was safe. As *Popular Science* noted in 1961, the "42-pound Alzina Playboy can be driven by a seven-year-old or a 200-pounder." Top speed was 15mph (presumably with the seven-year-old).

Harley-Davidson USA ★★★

The Harley-Davidson Topper was a Hell's Angels starter scooter—or at least a putt-putt for the crew-cut sons and daughters of Harley-Davidson motorcycle owners. But The Motor Company entered the scooter market just as Cushman, Mustang, and Lambretta were getting out—and getting out with reason. By 1960, the fad had largely faded in the United States, and the Topper would never sell to its potential.

The first Topper was released in 1960 to fanfare promoting it as "Tops in beauty and tops in performance." The Topper boasted a pull-start two-cycle 10ci (165cc) engine laying on its side with the 2.38x2.28in single cylinder facing to the front, which was supposed to eliminate the need for a cooling fan. Spark was by magneto with a generator supplying lighting.

Harley-Davidson got its two-stroke technology from the German DKW as the spoils of World War II. The Motor Company first used the DKW two-stroke in its S-125 and its Hummer models; the Topper's engine was largely new but the lineage was old.

The Scootaway automatic transmission used a centrifugal clutch and V-belt with final drive by chain. Ratios were "infinitely variable" from 18:1 in low to 6:1 in high range. With front and rear brakes, an Earles-style triangulated front fork, and 4.00x12in tires, the Topper was good for 45mph and 80mpg.

The Topper's frame was a standard tube chassis. The slab-sided body was made of fiberglass and even the two-tone paint scheme could not hide the scooter's mystifying resemblance to a refrigerator on wheels.

According to a June 1959 *Popular Science* preview, the Topper "has three main features that Harley-Davidson figures will appeal to American males: styling, automatic transmission, and those 12-inch wheels." The styling has already been discussed, the automatic transmission had its share of woes, but the 12 inchers were nice—2in more than the Vespas and Lambrettas of the day. The other feature *Popular Science* failed to mention was the Topper's parking brake. Why a scooter needed a parking brake was a question not worth asking.

The Topper's moment in the sun came when Ed "Kookie" Byrnes combed his hair and blasted away on his Topper in TV's "77 Sunset Strip." Promotional ads wheedled fans with "Advice to Teenagers: When it comes to combs and scooters, never a borrower or a lender be. Instead, start dropping hints to Mom and Dad about the new Topper."

From the start, two Topper models were available: the A was the 9.5hp standard and the AU was a de-tuned 5hp version with a carburetor restrictor to meet new state laws for minimum driving ages. In 1961, the models were upgraded: the A became the AH (touted in ads as simply the H) and the AU retained its designation. By 1962–1963, colors included Birch White, Tango Red, or Black with Birch White trim. The seat was made of fabulous Hypalon.

By the end of 1965, the Topper was but a memory. Harley-Davidson chose to follow the road traveled by Cushman in cancelling its scooter and shifting to golf carts.

The refrigerator-like Harley-Davidson Topper was for "fun-loving Jacks (and Jills, too)," according to this 1960 ad. Two models were available, the A (revised as the AH beginning in 1961) and the AU, both with the 10ci, 165cc engine but the AU was detuned for less than 5hp to suit state laws requiring a minimum driving age. The coveted pull-start was activated by the grip at the base of the seat section.

Harper UK ★★

Harper Aircraft in Exeter embarked on a scooter in 1954 based on a hefty tube frame covered by full fiberglass bodywork. The Scootmobile was first created with a 125cc Villiers and body styling that looked like a dustbin racing fairing in front with built-in panniers at the rear, copying the Maicomobil concept. Development continued through 1957 with a 197cc Villiers, but few production models were ever built.

Heinkel Germany

In 1922, Ernst Heinkel founded his company in Stuttgart and became one of the primary forces that helped Nazi Germany's Luftwaffe rise to be the world's most powerful air force at the time. Like many other German companies, Heinkel turned to two- and three-wheeled vehicles as they were forbidden to produce aircraft after the war. By 1965, after building 100,000 Tourist scooters, Heinkel returned to making solely airplanes.

Tourist 101 1953–1954; Tourist 102 and 103 1954–1965 ★★

As the scooter became more and more an instrument of teenagers, Heinkel thought the Tourist could appeal to both the youth and wannabe youth with slogans like "On two wheels you stay young" and "For young people who know what they want." Complete with front bumper, the Tourist was a reliable four-stroke scooter that was a common sight on German roads in the late 1950s. Even German police used Heinkels when law breakers were on scooters or micro cars, before they switched to Porsches to chase speeders on the autobahn.

For added incentive to drive a Tourist into the ground, Heinkel offered gold plaques to be mounted on the front fender if the scooter surpassed 100,000km. A silver plaque was awarded after 75,000km, and the bronze plaque was discontinued because every self-respecting Heinkel owner should be able to achieve 50,000km. The 150cc Tourist 101 had 7.2hp for 85km/h and the 175cc Tourist 102 and 103 had 9.2hp for 92km/h.

The Tourist scooter was so successful that Heinkel tried to pass off their three-wheeled, front-entrance car as a "cabin scooter" since one version had the 174cc Tourist engine. The "cabin scooter" was later produced in Ireland and imported to Britain under the name of Trojan.

Move out front with a

HEINKEL *Tourist*

The HEINKEL TOURIST is a completely new vehicle, offering all the comfort of a deluxe automobile. The HEINKEL's 4-stroke, overhead valve engine is quiet, reliable, more economical and longer wearing than 2-stroke engines, and requires no oil-gas mixture. The luxuriously styled TOURIST features single unit construction, 4-speed, hand operated gear box, 65 mph cruising speed, large brakes and wheels, 12-volt electrical system with electric starting. Ask your dealer for an amazing demonstration ride today or write.

Foreign Motorcycles Corp.

48-22 43RD AVE.   LONG ISLAND CITY 4, N.Y.

DEALERS: Attractive HEINKEL franchises for many key areas are still available. Write or wire today!

Heinkel used the scooter to keep afloat postwar during the imposed hiatus from aircraft manufacture. As with Piaggio, Heinkel applied its aviation technology to the creation and production of one of the most popular of German scooters.

Scooter Oddity Hall of Fame: Aqua Scoots Sail the High Seas

It was only a matter of time before motorscooters took to the open sea. Considering that the word scooter also means a small sailing boat and that present-day Jet Skis bear a striking resemblance to aquatic scooters, this should not be startling. But when one considers how it was done, it would make a land lubber out of the oldest salt.

In 1965 at the English Brighton motorcycle show, an aqua Lambretta aftermarket conversion kit with two pontoons on either side of the scooter sold for only £25. The kit came with a front end rudder and paddle blades that attached to the rear wheel. Not to be outdone, Piaggio then hooked up pontoons to the side of a Vespa with a propeller driven from the rear wheel. You merely kicked over your engine and set sail on the high seas.

One aqua scooter pilot, George Monneret, re-enacted William the Conquerer's 1066 invasion of England, setting off across the English Channel on his pontoon-equipped 125cc Vespa. He then removed the pontoons and raced to London on the scooter, receiving nothing less than a true hero's welcome.

In 1956, an English firm ventured to create its Amanda Water Scooter, a prop-driven midget speedboat powered by a Vincent industrial engine. But this pioneer aqua scoot had its share of woes due to its fiberglass hull, which constantly melted, slowing down its development. After one of the test drivers drowned during testing, interest in the Amanda sank as well. It took the Japanese several more decades to create successful Jet Ski water scooters.

In spite of such bold attempts, the Chunnel between Calais and Dover was built. Alas, Aqua scoots would have totaled a fraction of the Chunnel's cost without the worry of which side of the road to drive on within the tunnel.

The complete mechanical details of the Heinkel Tourist complete with admiring couple. This advertising poster was enough to convince any hesitant wannabe scooter owner to opt for Heinkel's best.

112 1957 and 150 1960–1965 ★★

The 125cc Heinkel 112 was one of the few scooters to ever have a model number less than the size of the engine. The 6.25hp Heinkel Roller 112 was an attractive scooter but unfortunately stayed in production for only one year. The 150, on the other hand, took a stab at new innovative scooter lines and failed miserably. The engine put out a decent 9hp for a maximum speed of 85km/h, but the lines and excessive two-tone make for a gaudy, at best, exterior.

Hercules Germany ★★

"You can fall in love with this scooter and every way you look at it, it's beautiful!" read a Hercules ad for the R200 of 1955–1960. Just as Triumph GB made a scooter with BSA, its owner at the time, so did German TWN Triumph produce a scooter with Hercules. The TWN Contessa and the Hercules R200 had nearly identical bodywork, used a four-speed 191cc Sachs with 10.2hp for a maximum velocity of 100km/h, and had different emblems on the paneling. Kieft of Britian announced the R200 under its own name for importation, but the project was quickly abandoned. Soon after, its name changed to Prior when the British BP Scooters of The Airport became the importer.

The later Hercules Roller 50 and 50S from 1964 were KTM scooters made under license. As with the Gritzner–Kayser scooter designed by KTM, the paint job displayed a garish two-color scheme.

Hirano Japan ★

Hirano made a series of two-stroke air-cooled mini-scooters primarily for the Japanese market in the 1950s and early 1960s.

Honda Japan

Siochiro Honda's story is classic Horatio Alger rags to riches. Born the son of the Komyo village blacksmith, he got his start producing a radical new piston ring pre-World War II. During

Not surprisingly, the Heinkel 150 made its debut in 1960, the decade when design and architecture went awry. Hoping to hit up the teen market, the firm's ad proclaimed, "The Heinkel 150 is the ideal companion for the young, the not so young, and the young in heart who know what they want." *Mick Walker archives*

the war, his fledgling company built wooden propellers for the Japanese air force. After the war, Honda turned his hand to designing economical motorbikes and scooters.

Honda first created a motorized bicycle, the Model A, in 1947 and built it in Honda's 12x18ft shed that housed thirteen employees. In 1953, the motorbike gave way to the first Cub clip-on motor, which developed into the Cub moped line that continued all the way into the 1980s as the Passport. By the end of its run, some 15 million Cubs had been built.

Juno KA 1954 ★★★

Inspired by the success of the major Japanese makers, Fuji with its Rabbit scooter and Mitsubishi with its Pigeon, Honda built its first scooter in 1954, the Juno KA. It was based on a 189cc overhead-valve engine measuring 65x57mm bore and stroke and creating 5hp at 4800rpm. The rear drive was by enclosed chain.

The Juno was available solely in metallic green—a color not far from the early Vespa green—and had two pad seats, enclosed handlebars, and a headlamp on the front apron. The styling of the Juno line would always be bizarre or futuristic, depending on your point of view. It continued the Japanese scooter design philosophy of more is better, and was dressed up with miles of molding running from the front turn signals to the rear turn signals.

Juno JB 1955 ★★★★

In 1955, the KB replaced the KA with a 220cc engine of 70x57mm for 9hp at 5500rpm riding on 5.00x9in tires. And the styling had grown even more outrageous.

M80 1960–1961 and M85 1962–1964 ★★★★

In 1960, Honda introduced a new scooter in its M80 based on a flat twin engine that was unique in the scooter universe. Each cylinder measured 43x43mm and together made 10hp at 9000rpm. The accessories followed the styling: turn signals, electric start, gas gauge, glovebox, and more.

The styling was again futuristic, but it was now minimalist or boxy, again depending on your viewpoint. The elements never quite fit together, looking like a toolroom special made up of not just Honda spare parts but parts from every other Japanese scooter make as well. Even the flashy two-tone paint could not save the lack of styling.

In 1962, Honda offered its M85 scooter powered by a 168.9cc overhead-valve flat twin engine of 50x43mm bore and stroke. Power was 12hp at 7600rpm riding atop 10in wheels. The M85's career lasted until only 1964, after which Honda concentrated on its Cub series and motorcycles.

The Elite for 1992 carried on Honda's long tradition of stylish and reliable scooters that began in 1954 with its amazing Juno series. The Elite was easy to operate yet still powerful and fun, making it ideal for the youth market Honda had set its sights on for scooter sales. *Honda*

Aero, Elite, Spree, and Helix ★

Twenty years later, Honda returned to the scooter fold, introducing its Aero series of 50cc and 80cc scooters in 1983 as well as an Aero 125cc in 1984. The Aero plastic scooters mimicked the styling of the Vespa Nuovo Linea, and were the first Honda scooters to be imported to the United States.

Simultaneously, Honda released its Spree 50cc line in 1984 as well as the modernistic Elite series with 125cc in 1984; 80, 150, and 250cc in 1985; and 50cc in 1987. In Italy, Honda sold its Vision scooter.

Whether you like the Helix or not, you must admit it carried on the tradition of radically bizarre styling that makes scooters so fascinating. Looking like a cross between a Barcalounger and a UFO, the 1992 Helix offered living-room comfort while traveling at warp speeds (compared to other scooters). *Honda*

In the 1990s, Honda created its line of CUV scooters, which stood for Clean Urban Vehicle and was based on an electric engine. The CUV-Canopy was a two-wheeler with a full bucket seat, protective rollbar canopy, and full windshield complete with wipers. The handlebars were pure Star Trek. A three-wheeled utility scooter was also offered, although as of 1993, the CUVs were sold only in Japan. *Honda*

In 1986, Honda created its Helix 250cc armchair motorscooter, a step back in time to the Ner-A-Car style. Based on a potent four-stroke liquid-cooled single-cylinder engine, the Helix looked like a cross between a Barcalounger and a UFO.

Horex Germany ★

Horex's motto was "Built by motorcyclists for motocyclists," so it's no wonder that in 1956 when it built its scooter it failed and ended up being a waste of time.

The powerful 16hp Rebell was so rebellious that Horex didn't sell a single one. Perhaps Horex mixed up the name of its scooter with one of its motorcycles, the Resident, which would seem much more appropriate for a scooter. Although not by any means a hideous scooter, the 249cc was a catastrophe for Horex.

Husqvarna Sweden ★★

Husqvarna is one of the grand old motorcycle makes, starting production in 1903. Through the years, it built myriad graceful large-bore motorcycles before concentrating on innovative motocrossers postwar.

In 1955, Husqvarna purchased a small number of scooter chassis from Parilla and fitted them with HVA engines and the Husqvarna crown nameplate. The 120cc HVA two-stroke engine created 4.3hp at 5000rpm. Riding atop 3.00x12in tires, top speed was 70km/h.

In 1958, Husqvarna developed its own scooter, the Corona Model 3842. Powered by Husqvarna's own two-stroke 0.8hp engine, it rode on 2.50x20in tires. In 1986, the Husqvarna motorcycle division was bought by Cagiva.

IFA East Germany ★

The IFA Rico-Roller was a spiritual predecessor of the great Trabant automobile. It was part motorcycle, part bicycle, and part scooter with its 19in wheels and springer rear suspension belying its heritage. But its 125cc engine covered by swooping sheet metal bodywork made one think of a motorscooter—or a medieval steed decked in jousting gear.

Indian USA ★★

In 1949, the famed Indian Motorcycle Company made several odd decisions. After decades of buildings its great V-twin motorcycles, it decided to develop vertical twins in the English style and sell motorscooters in the Cushman style. Both were ill-fated projects.

Indian contracted with Lowther to build its scooters; no less than twenty-four two- and three-wheeled solo and tandem scooters were offered. Among the array were the Spartan, Vagabond, and Stylemaster with varying degrees of bodywork from none to completely clothed, respectively. The styling left a lot to be desired; a kind word would be "agricultural."

Innocenti Italy

Ferdinando Innocenti was a plumber before starting his company in 1931 to produce steel plumbing pipes and tubing. From this background, it was thus no surprise that Innocenti's Lambretta scooter would be based on a tube frame versus the avant garde pressed-steel unit chassis of its chief rival, Piaggio's Vespa.

During World War II, Innocenti produced artillery shells and pontoon bridges, but following the Fascists' defeat, Innocenti and his general director, Giuseppe Lauro, looked for a way to turn swords into plowshares. They came upon the idea of building a scooter that all of Italy could afford to own and operate.

In 1945-1946, the duo assigned engineer Pierluigi Torre to create a scooter, which they named the Lambretta after the factory's site in the Lambrate quarter of Milan. The quarter was named for the bubbling brown Lambrate River that runs through the suburb, a river that is now one of the most polluted in all of Italy.

In 1958, the Lambretta Club of Milan celebrated Christmas bearing gifts of frankincense, myrrh, and a new Lambretta TV 175 Series 1. Although such offerings would appear to be blasphemy in Catholic Italy, it showed the reverence placed on scooters. *Innocenti*

Along with the ditty announcing the arrival of Innocenti's Lambretta A in 1947, this advertising image of the young cowboy in chaps and hat accompanied by his trusty terrier became famous throughout Italy.

Innocenti never restricted itself to just scooter production. Through the years it continued the production of steel tubing as well as making milling machines and presses. The Innocenti factory also manufactured parts for most Italian car makers as well as Ford of Europe and Volkswagen. In 1961, Innocenti began producing the British Austin cars under license.

Due to a decline in the scooter market, Innocenti ceased Lambretta production in 1971 after building some four million scooters. As a consequence of further financial problems, it fell into the hands of the Italian government in 1975. In 1975, Argentine-Italian magnate Alejandro de Tomaso added the Lambrate factory to his empire. The factory continues production to this day, including engines for the De Tomaso–owned Moto Guzzi.

Lambrettas had been built in Spain by Messrs Serveta Industrial SA (formerly Lambretta Locomociones SA) since 1954 and the Innocenti tooling was sold to Scooters India in 1972, both of which have kept the Lambretta in production into the 1990s.

Lambretta A 125 1947–1948 ★★★★★

The first Vespa was for sale in April 1946; by October 1947, the race with Piaggio was on as the first Lambretta scooter rolled off the production lines. Within a year, Innocenti would manufacture nearly 10,000 of its Model A.

The Lambretta's launch was preceded by months of advertising to ready the market for Innocenti's radical new vehicle. Italy's RAI radio played a Lambretta commercial day and night throughout 1947 with a ditty that became the Shave-and-a-haircut-two-bits of Italy, still subconsciously whistled by Italians.

The Lambretta was radical not in design but in its concept of providing inexpensive transportation with easy operation. The chassis was a traditional tube frame lacking bodywork. The frame was built in two sections: the front consisted of a pressed-steel main section connecting to the steering head, which held the front fork; the rear section consisted of two chrome tubes surrounding the gas tank and connecting to the pressed-steel toolbox.

The A lacked bodywork to cover the engine and had scanty legshields compared to its chief rival, but what it fell short of in covering, it made up for with a larger 125cc engine compared to its 98cc counterpart. The A's two-stroke, single-cylinder measured 52x58mm with its upright cylinder inclined slightly forward. A 16mm Dell'Orto carburetor fed the fuel, which was sparked by a Marelli flywheel magneto; power was 4.3hp at 4500rpm with a top speed of 65-70km/h or 40-44mph.

Drive to the rear wheel was via an enclosed shaft with bevel gears turning the axle. A foot-operated rocker pedal controlled the three-speed gearbox with an indicator on the inside right footboard to tell which gear had been selected.

Alongside the larger engine, the Lambretta's most important feature was a second seat for carrying a passenger, marking it in buyers' minds as a more social scooter than the more functional, one-seated 1946 Vespa. The front saddle seat sat above the gas tank with the rear pillion perched above the toolbox. The gas tank held 6 liters with 0.8 liter reserve for an incredible 300km on one tank of *miscela*.

The Model A was not received enthusiastically; buyers lacked confidence in the elfin 3.50x7in tires. Thus, in December 1948, Innocenti created a revised version of the A, called naturally enough, the B.

Lambretta B 125 1948–1950 ★★★★

The A evolved into the B with further comfort due to its larger, 3.50x8in wheels, a left-hand twist-grip gearchange using a push-pull cable system rather than a foot lever, and, in an effort to keep up with Vespa, rear suspension. The suspension worked by a swinging knuckle on the rear of the shaft drive case controlled by a coil-spring damper mounted horizontally under the engine. And the Lambretta was a hit; by 1950, Innocenti was building up to 100 scooters daily.

Lambretta C 125 and
LC 125 1950–1951 ★★★★

The new C was based on a completely redesigned chassis fitted with the tried-and-true 4.3hp shaft-drive engine. The A/B chassis with its twin-tube construction was replaced by a single large-diameter main tube wrapped around the engine and gas tank to support the two seats. Trailing-link front suspension eased the ride, and would become characteristic of almost all subsequent Lambrettas. Other features were updated as well: a horn was added above the redesigned front fender, which fit snugly inside the front forks; and the Lambretta decal was now affixed to the gas tank.

Even with its extra seat and more-powerful engine, the Lambretta trailed the Vespa in popularity, primarily due to Piaggio designer Corradino d'Ascanio's bodywork that saved riders from roadspray and engine grime. Innocenti finally recognized the importance of bodywork for a scooter and gave the public a choice of the "undressed" C or its new "dressed" LC, or Lusso C model, which

Restored 1948 Lambretta A 125 in light olive green. The long case housed the shaft drive and bevel gear set that drove the rear wheel. Cooling was by the passing air at the scooter's 65–70km/h top speed. Suspension was by the springs within the saddle seat. This scooter does not have the second, pillion seat mounted. Owner: Vittorio Tessera. *Vittorio Tessera*

Innocenti prototype for a collapsible military paratrooper scooter based on a C 125 engine. The frame was also influenced by the C's single large-diameter backbone tube but was shorter and lighter. Piaggio and Innocenti had originally been inspired to build scooters by the World War II Volugrafo Aeromoto paratroop scooter; with this scooter Innocenti had come full circle back to its roots. *Vittorio Tessera archives*

Restored 1949 Lambretta B 125 complete with the pillion seat that marked the Lambretta in people's minds as the more social scooter when compared with the no-frills functionality of the Vespa. This was the scooter to cruise the piazza on—and the second seat made it ideal for courting. The chrome Lambretta badge was affixed to the toolbox. Owner: Vittorio Tessera. *Vittorio Tessera*

In 1954, Innocenti manufactured its most powerful scooter to date, a 148cc based on a longer-stroke, 57x58mm D engine that created 6hp at 4750rpm via a more-powerful magneto of 36 watts compared to the 123cc model's 25 watts. Although the 150 added 5mph to its top speed, gas mileage dropped from 193mpg to 140mpg. And Piaggio quickly responded with its own 150cc model.

made its debut in April 1950 following the C's February arrival.

With the LC, Innocenti finally had a winning combination. Piaggio met the challenge by enlarging its engine to 125cc to compete.

On the now-covered Lambretta engine, meanwhile, a fan was added to the flywheel magneto to blow cooling air over the cylinder—a design that Vespa had perfected years earlier. The side panel also featured a door to allow access to the carburetor.

Lambretta D 125 and LD 125 1951–1956; D 150 1954–1956 and LD 150 1954-1957 ★★★

The D and LD sported a redesigned frame, front fork tubes that enclosed the front suspension springs, larger tires of 4.00x8in, and a new rear suspension setup, with the engine hung by pivoting links and suspended at the rear by a single damper. The unenclosed D was offered as an economy model alongside the Lusso LD.

The D engine measured 52x58mm, fathering 4.8hp at 4600rpm via a larger, 18mm Dell'Orto carburetor for a 45mph top speed. On the dressed LD, a two-piece sheet-steel housing was added to direct cooling air over the cylinder and head.

Restored 1954 Lambretta D 125 with the revamped frame based on a single, large-diameter tube. Along with the seat springs, the D now featured suspension at the front end via leading-link forks and rubber bushings. A Lambretta decal was now glued to the gas tank sides. Owner: Vittorio Tessera. *Vittorio Tessera*

Lambretta V-Twin Racing Motorcycle: Innocenti's Secret Weapon

In 1950–1951, Innocenti created its masterpiece: a 250cc double-overhead-cam V-twin racing motorcycle. Designed by Ing. Pierluigi Torre, who was responsible for the Lambretta scooter, and Ing. Salmaggi, responsible for the Gilera Saturno and Parilla dohc motorcycles, it was first shown to an awed public at the 1950 Salone di Milano.

The V of the engine ran transverse to the chassis in the style of Moto Guzzi's V-twins. Each cylinder measured square at 54x54mm. Originally beginning life with a single overhead cam on each cylinder, it was modified to dohc to produce 29hp at 9500rpm Drive to the rear wheel was via a shaft as used on the Innocenti scooters of the time.

Innocenti had aspirations of contesting the 250cc Grand Prix class, but in the end, the 250cc V-twin was run at only a handful of races during several years by factory rider Romolo Ferri and Nello Pagani. Its best showing came in August 1952 at the Locarno, where Ferri was running second to Fergus Anderson's Guzzi Gambalunghino before retiring.

So the Lambretta retreated without ever winning a race. Or did it? Perhaps it had won the most important race it could have competed in, that of showing the rest of the Italian industry that Innocenti could build a motorcycle to be reckoned with should any other maker ever think of building a scooter. In the end, the Lambretta 250cc V-twin was Innocenti's secret weapon.

Innocenti's 250cc dohc V-twin racer always wore the Lambretta scooter decal on its gas tank as a bold warning to other Italian motorcycle makers not to tread on the scooter builder or it would venture into motorcycles. The V-twin racer was a bold threat. Here, it was shown off by the Italian Lambretta club at a recent mostra scambio *at the Imola racetrack; it is currently housed at Vittorio Tessera's club museum in Rodano.* Tim Parker

The dual-porthole side panel trim of the LC was changed to a single oval grille on the LD. The access door to the carburetor, carried over from the LC model, continued for a short time on the first LDs.

As an added feature, electric-start LD 125 and LD 150 models were offered. These machines were not a great sales success as the cost of the starter raised the scooter's price above many buyers' means.

As a precursor to the primped scooters of the mods, Innocenti marketed extras for the LD including chrome trim pieces, extra driving lights, a clock, fuel gauge, and radio, all of which often ended up costing a scooterist more than the original scooter. The Lambretta was marketed in Britain as the "sports car on two wheels," and with all these luxurious extras, one need not have suffered any inconvenience while riding a Lambretta.

In 1956, Innocenti tallied $43 million of Lambretta sales, including 6,000 scooters shipped to the United States as well as additional exports to a total of ninety-six other countries.

Lambretta LD 125/57 1956–1958 and LD 150/57 1957–1958 ★★★★

Seated in Milan, Italy's fashion capital, Innocenti recognized the value of annual updates to keep its scooter *en vogue*. For 1957, the front area

Restored 1954 Lambretta D 125 factory racer painted in Italian *rosso corsa*. For races such as the French 24-hour Bol d'Or endurance race, the Milano–Taranto, or just backroad duels, this works racer featured the engine cooling shroud of the enclosed LD as well as a spare tire and large-capacity gas tank. Owner: Vittorio Tessera. *Vittorio Tessera*

was redesigned to add a sleek cowling over the handlebars that incorporated the speedometer/odometer and horn while leaving the headlamp on the front apron. An optional battery for the 125cc was available that sat alongside the gas tank. These two-tone luxury models with a grey and blue color scheme came in both the 125cc and the 150cc models.

Popular Science magazine in the United States got a chance to test one of the first 57 models and wrote of the Lambretta in July 1957 in purple prose that echoed Innocenti's own ads: "Once warm, its superb engine starts at first kick, responds jauntily to the throttle. Like other two-cycle power plants, it's fond of revs, and the constant-mesh three-speed transmission lets you take full advantage of this at all times."

The 6hp LD 150/57 came standard with such luxuries as a speedometer, pillion seat, white side-wall tires, and a mechanical marvel that made Italy great, according to *Popular Science*: "a clock that works." The 150 needed a 12volt battery to power all these appliances.

The Series IV LD was sold alongside the new TV and Li but was soon dated next to their advanced features.

Lambretta E 125 1953–1954 ★★★

The E for Economico was released as entry-level scooter with bare-bones features that were much simpler than the C or D. Since flashy fully enclosed scooters had become the rage, few scooterists wanted to be seen on this uncovered Lambretta; the E never sold well, was not exported to all markets, was only kept on the market for one year.

In spite of these checks against it, the larger-diameter frame tube of the E strengthened it far more than the other models, but added weight. The hand-recoil, cord-pull starter mounted in front of the engine near the magneto only added to the idea of this scooter as a working tool while the covered Lusso models gave the handsome appearance of a modern scooter in an age when people thought technology could actually alleviate all work.

The rear suspension equaled the D and LD, while the front suspension relied on elastic instead of the trailing-link of the C or the enclosed springs of the LD. The engine, with a gas tank of 6.7 liters, differed little from the D except for the prestigious pull start.

Lambretta F 125 and
F 125 Series II 1954–1955 ★★★

The F replaced the E with a kickstart replacing the pull start. Although this abolished the outboard motor look, top speed still kept well within trolling parameters.

The Innocenti sales flyer for the Lambretta LD 125 was aimed to women. Not only could you ride the scooter to market and keep your dress neat and tidy, but every eye in the market would follow you. The unwritten message was that the scooter was not only ideal transportation, it was also a fashion accessory. At the bottom of many of its brochures, Innocenti showed an aerial view of its Lambrate factory, promoting a cult of industrial might and power. *Innocenti*

Original 1959 Lambretta LD 125 Series IV with the horn mounted in the stylish handlebar cowling. The LD featured the oval side panel grilles, which replaced the twin portholes used on the LC. The pillion seat and spare tire mount were optional extras. Owner: Michael Dregni.

The F II updated the front forks and several other features but couldn't spark any further sales.

Lambretta TV 175 Series 1 1957–1958 ★★

In 1952, Ducati created its Cruiser, a luxurious four-stroke scooter with hydraulic suspension and all the accessories a rider could handle. Ducati believed its scooter would steal the thunder from Piaggio and Innocenti's no-frills two-strokes, but the Cruiser was too much too soon. Its price was too high for the floundering Italian economy and it was gone within two years. But the idea was sound.

By the mid-1950s, Italian automakers such as Ferrari and Maserati had created *gran turismo* cars that blended sport with luxury and began to sell to a new, more affluent class of Italians as well as to a strong export market.

Looking back to the Ducati Cruiser and at the new success of the GT cars, Piaggio decided in 1955 to create an upscale scooter with sports and touring features, the 150 GS, or Gran Sport. Locked horn to horn in battle for the scooter buyer, Innocenti responded in April 1957 with its TV 175.

TV stood for Turismo Veloce, or Touring Speed, a scaled-down translation of *gran turismo* into scooter-speak. Innocenti believed that while its earlier models had sold well as utilitarian workhorses, the times were changing; Italians now had some extra money in their pockets and the dawning of leisure time. That extra money could buy a more stylish scooter that could drive to work during the week and be loaded up for a trip to the sea or a picnic in the country on weekends.

The TV1 was a completely new design from the wheels up. The 170cc two-stroke engine mea-

Lambretta Production 1947–1971

From Innocenti archives, courtesy of Vittorio Tessera

Model Number	Production Run	Number Built
125 A	Oct. 1947–Oct. 1948	9,669
125 B	Nov. 1948–Jan. 1950	35,014
125 C	Feb. 1950–Nov. 1951	87,500
125 LC	Apr. 1950–Nov. 1951	42,500
125 D	Dec. 1951–Nov. 1956	123,141
125 LD	Dec. 1951–Nov. 1956	131,615
125 E	Apr. 1953–Feb. 1954	42,352
125 F	Mar. 1954–Apr. 1955	32,701
125 LD Elec Start	Feb. 1954–Dec. 1954	8,694
150 D	Oct. 1954–Dec. 1956	54,593
150 LD	Nov. 1954–Jan. 1957	109,344
150 LD Elec Start	Sept. 1955–Nov. 1956	2,020
48	Aug. 1955–Mar. 1961	63,223
125 LD/57	Dec. 1956–July 1958	44,665
125 LD/57 Elec Start	Dec. 1956–June 1957	52
150 LD/57	Jan. 1957–July 1958	113,853
150 LD/57 Elec Start	Apr. 1957–Dec. 1957	4,076
175 TV	Sept. 1957–Dec. 1958	10,089
125 Li	June 1958–Oct. 1959	47,747
150 Li	Apr. 1958–Oct. 1959	99,043
125 Li Series 2	Oct. 1959–Nov. 1961	111,087
150 Li Series 2	Oct. 1959–Nov. 1961	162,040
175 TV Series 2	Jan. 1959–Nov. 1961	43,700
125 Li Series 3 Slimline	Dec. 1961–Nov. 1967	146,734
150 Li Series 3 Slimline	Jan. 1962–May 1967	143,079
175 TV Series 3 Slimline	March 1962–Oct. 1965	37,794
200 TV	April 1963–Oct. 1965	14,982
150 Special	Sept. 1963–Oct. 1966	69,529
98 J	March 1964–Nov. 1965	17,642
125 J Three-speed	Sept. 1964–Sept. 1966	21,651
50 J 20/1	Oct. 1964–Jan. 1968	69,988
125 Special	Oct. 1965–Jan. 1969	29,841
125 J Four-speed	May 1966–Apr. 1969	16,052
200 X Special	Jan. 1966–Jan. 1969	11,712
150 X Special	Oct. 1966–Jan. 1969	31,238
39 Ciclomotore	Nov. 1966–Dec. 1967	15,676
48 Automatic	Oct. 1967–Nov. 1968	8,922
50 De Luxe	Jan. 1968–Oct. 1970	28,852
50 Lui	March 1968–June 1969	27,812
75 Lui	Aug. 1968–June 1969	8,840
125 DL	Jan. 1969–Apr. 1971	15,300
150 DL	Jan. 1969–Apr. 1971	20,048
200 DL	Jan. 1969–Apr. 1971	9,350
50 Special	April 1970–April 1971	13,599

This Lambretta TV 175 Series 1 was the first TV1 built by Innocenti, rolling off the assembly line in 1957. The goal was to offer an upscale sporting scooter that could take its owner touring on the weekends. The concept and timing were fine, but the TV1 was underdeveloped and plagued by reliability woes. Nevertheless, it was a vision of the scooter's future. Owner: Vittorio Tessera. *Vittorio Tessera*

sured 60x60mm and delivered a powerful 9hp, significantly more than any earlier Lambretta or Vespa.

The addition of a fourth gear to the transmission erased perhaps the LD's sole shortcoming. And the shaft-drive of all earlier Lambrettas was shelved in place of a radically modern enclosed duplex chain drive that required no adjustment, lubrication, or cleaning. Wheels were now 10in with 3.50x10in Pirelli tires.

The bodywork that was wrapped around the TV1 was like fluid metal. The curves followed the scooter's function with rich expanses of flowing steel that made the new Lambretta look more modern than Piaggio's GS, which only a trained eye could differentiate from the first Vespa of 1946.

A wider, fixed front fender shaped like a *zucchetto* replaced the pivoting fender of the LD, allowing the wheel to move independently. The headlamp was perched on the front apron with a peaked visor above it and the horn behind a grille just above the fender. The handlebars were covered by a cowling with the speedometer/odometer on top.

The Turismo Veloce concept was right, the timing was right, but Innocenti's execution was wrong. Whereas Piaggio's GS became its best scooter of the 1950s and 1960s, the first series Lambretta TV 175 was a dismal failure. It was underdeveloped and won a reputation for poor reliability that haunted Innocenti into the 1960s. Nevermind that in January 1959, the redesigned TV2 would be a worldbeater.

Lambretta Li 150 and Li 125 Series 1 1958–1959 ★★★

In early 1958, Innocenti launched its new Li line based on a completely new engine from the preceeding TV, although with similar bore and stroke dimensions to the old D. The Li featured a single horizontal cylinder with enclosed duplex chain drive to the rear wheel via a four-speed gearbox. The 148cc measured 57x58mm and created 6.5 hp; the 123cc was based on 52x58 mm for 5.2hp.

The Li Series 1 scooters were clothed by a body identical to the TV Series 1 with the apron-mounted headlamp and a small cover over the handlebars to dispel the bicycle look.

The Li was as a great a success as the TV1 was a failure. It was modern, powerful, and reliable whereas the TV1 was modern, powerful, and fragile. The Li line would dictate the direction of Lambretta scooters until 1971 when Innocenti halted production—and even then Serveta in Spain and Scooters India would continue building Li and Li-based models.

Lambretta TV 175 Series 2 1959–1961 ★★★★

Innocenti rushed to fix its TV and repair its image. After just sixteen months of production, the TV1 was pulled to be replaced by the TV2, which was a new scooter based not on the TV1 but on the successful Li line. The only items carried over from the TV1 were the name and the body style, which was also updated.

The new 175cc engine was a wider-bore version of the Li engine at 62x58mm, creating 8.6hp. Midway through TV2 production, the early 23mm Dell'Orto carburetor was swapped for a 21mm that provided for smoother performance throughout the powerband.

Betty Crocker goes Mod. Innocenti created its Li series in 1958 with both 125cc and 150cc versions of its new horizontal single-cylinder, ideal for a jaunt to Food Fair; the sunglasses and high heels were mandatory scooter-riding accessories. This was a Series 2 Li with the headlamp lifted from the front apron to the handlebars. As this dealer postcard invited, "See and judge for yourself the elegance of styling—the ease of handling—the perfect balance of this marvel of modern engineering." *Innocenti*

The ideal Mod hot-rod, the high-powered Lambretta TV 175 Series 2. Innocenti first offered its completely revamped TV2 in 1959 and this time the TV was a grand success. The new engine was not a reworking of the TV1 but an overbored version of the Li! The headlamp was also raised to the handlebars so it followed the front wheel's direction. This scooter has been retrofitted with a mechanical disc front brake from the later TV3. Owner: Tim Gartman.

Scooter Oddity Hall of Fame: Fuel Injection for Lambrettas

In the early 1960s, Great Britian discovered the performance latent in the Lambretta. Hot-rod components and overbore kits were marketed by dozens of firms, from the Rafferty Newman Wildcat Equipé kits to Amal carburetor conversions to the 1960s swapping of Japanese motorcycle cylinders and heads.

Among the most exotic and eccentric of hop-up kits was the British Wal Phillips fuel injection system for Li and TV series.

The Wal Phillips injection system was crude by today's terms but offered radical power for a tuned Lambretta to rattle the shop windows along Carnaby Street or scare away the Rockers at Brighton Beach in the 1960s.

The bodywork was redone with the headlamp moved to the handlebars and fitted beneath a streamlined cowling that also incorporated the speedometer unit.

With the TV2, Innocenti had its flagship sporting scooter that it should have had in the TV1.

Lambretta Li 150 and Li 125 Series 2 1959–1961 ★★★★

The Li line was modified in 1959 with the headlamp moved from the apron to the handlebars as on the TV2, creating a much more stylish scooter. The 125cc Series 2 engine breathed via an 18mm Dell'Orto whereas the 150 was fed through a 19mm carburetor. In addition, a wide variety of gear ratios were used to match the powerband of the 125cc versus the 150cc engine.

Lambretta Li 125 Series 3 Slimline 1961–1967, Li 150 Series 3 Slimline 1962–1967 ★★★

In 1961–1962, the bodywork of the Li and TV lines was redrawn. The new Slimline styling was sleek and angular with flash replacing the fleshy look of the earlier Lambrettas. The Slimline replaced the curvaceous Marilyn Monroe styling that characterized the 1950s Lambrettas with the thinner Twiggy look of the 1960s.

Power was now up as well: the 125 created 5.5hp whereas the 150 made 6.6.

Lambretta TV 175 Series 3 Slimline 1962–1965 ★★★★

The TV3 wore the the new go-fast Slimline styling over a high-perfomance 8.7hp engine and front hydraulic dampers for a smoother ride. With the TV3, a 20mm Dell'Orto replaced the late TV2's 21mm.

The TV3 dropped anchor with a mechanical disc front brake that pressed a full-circle pad against the rotor via the cable-operated hand lever. The rotor was prone to uneven wear or warping if heated by continual use.

The Lambretta's disc brake was an early use of what was considered a radically new—as well as complex and untrustworthy—braking system.

The first use of disc brakes on a motorcycle was on the 1957 Maserati motorcycle; the first use on a scooter was the optional disc brake offered in 1961 on the American-made Midget Motors Autocycle. Still, the TV3's disc brake was the best-known system and the most influential, leading the way for motorcycle and automakers in the mid-1960s.

Lambretta TV 200 (GT 200) 1963–1965 ★★★★★

The TV 200, aka GT 200 for Gran Turismo, was a TV3 hot-rodded with a 200cc engine with an overbore of 66x58mm fathering 12hp at 6200rpm and reaching a top speed of more than 70mph or113km/h. This high-performance TV was created for the large and enthusiastic British market, and specifically for the Isle of Man Scoot-

Mechanical cutaway of the new Lambretta Li series engine that would in turn become the layout for the new TV2. The horizontal cylinder was aimed to the front with the crankshaft transverse to the frame. The flywheel magneto and cooling fan were on the crankshaft's left side with the duplex chain drive to the gearbox and clutch on the right. The layout offered better balance within the wheelbase and to the sides than that of Piaggio's Vespa. *Innocenti*

For 1961, Innocenti restyled its scooter for an angular, modernistic look that followed the times when popular sentiment was moving from Marilyn Monroe's classical zaftig shapeliness to Twiggy's board-like lack of shape. Never mind what the trends did to feminine psyches, the style created the go-fast Lambretta Slimline. This Li 125 Series 3 was sold to the US market by Montgomery Ward, which named its Lambrettas Riversides. Owner: Eric Dregni.

Innocenti first offered its mechanical disc front brake on its TV 175 Series 3 Slimline of 1962–1965. It was not the first disc brake on a motorcycle or a scooter but it was the best and influenced the adoption of discs. This setup is retrofitted to a TV2.

er Rally, the most important scooter rally in Europe in the late 1950s.

The GT soon replaced the 175cc Lambretta in Britian, and was not initially available in any other market. It was built in relatively small numbers, only 14,982 units.

Lambretta 150 Li Special Pacemaker 1963–1966; 125 Li Special 1965–1969; 150 Special X (SX 150) and 200 Special X (SX 200) 1966–1969 ★★★

The Li Special and Special X Series were performance versions of the basic DL line that carried

on the hot image of the Turismo Veloce. In 1968, three Pacemakers, as the 7.1hp 150 Li Special was termed in Britian, swept first through third places in the Isle of Man Scooter Rally.

By 1969, the 125cc was up to 7.4hp, the updated 150cc was at 9.4hp, and the hot-rod 200 SX created 11hp. The SX series rode on 3.50x10in tires and the 200 SX featured a revised version of the TV3 mechanical front disc brake.

Lambretta DL 125, DL 150, and DL 200 1969–1971 ★★

The De Luxe Series updated the Li Series and soldiered on as Innocenti's no-frills commuter scooter. Power for the 125 was up to 7.4hp whereas the 150 created 9.4. The 200, meanwhile, had only 7.3hp but retained the disc brake and used electronic Ducati ignition.

With the DL, Innocenti created an updated bodywork styling with racing stripes on the side panels and a rectangular headlamp. The DL line continued through to Innocenti's decision to end scooter production in 1971.

Lambretta 50, Cento, J50 20/1, J98, and J125 1961–1966; J125 Star Stream 1966–1969 ★

At the 1961 Milan Show, Innocenti bowed a prototype 50cc economy scooter, which it followed with a 100cc production version, named the Cento, first shown at the 1961 Amsterdam Show. The line was based on a unitized steel monocoque chassis fitted with a vertical-cylinder engine, three-speed gearbox, and chain drive to the rear wheel. The Cento pumped out 4.7hp at 5300.

Later in 1961, the Cento gave way to the J, or Junior, Series with 49.8cc, 98cc, and 122.5cc versions. In 1966, the three-speed J125 was upgraded with a much-needed fourth gear and built primarily for export as the Star Stream.

Luna Series: Lui 50cc, Vega 75cc and Cometa 75cc 1968–1971 ★

The famous Italian designer Bertone slimmed the space-age lines on this new Innocenti series. In

Lambretta Three-Wheelers

Year	Model	Motor	Carrier Placement	Cabin
1949–1950	125 FB	Model B 125cc	Front	No
1950–1952	125 FC	Model C 125cc	Front	No
1952–1955	125 FD	Model D 125cc	Rear	No
1955–1959	150 FD	Model D 150cc	Rear	Yes
1957–1959	150 FDC	Model D 150cc	Rear	Yes
1959–1965	175 FLi	Li 175cc	Rear	Yes
1963–1965	200 Lambro	200cc	Rear	Yes
1967–1971	Lambro 500L, 500ML	175cc, 200cc	Rear	Yes
1965–1971	Lambro 550, 550N, 550A, 550M, 550V, 550ML	200cc	Rear	Yes
1970–1972	Lambro 600M, 600V	200cc	Rear	Yes

spite of other beautiful projects he accomplished, these scooters' design insulted the earlier classic Lambrettas. The 49.8cc Lui, meaning "he" in Italian, debuted in 1968 with 2.5hp. In the same year, the 75cc Vega was released with 5.2hp at 6000rpm and a top speed of 55mph (89km/h). Although not exceptionally attractive, the elevated body and fast engine rivaled the Vespa 90SS on the race track. The 75cc Cometa possessed a special feature called the Lubematic system, boasting a separate oil pump that automatically mixed the two-stroke oil with the gas..

The Martyrdom of Innocenti's Lambretta

In 1966, Innocenti produced a film to commemorate the death of its founder, Ferdinando Innocenti, who died shortly before. The film, *We Carry On*, idealized the massive Lambrate factory and its mechanized production lines, orchestrated to the sounds of Musique Concrète punctuated by blasts of industrial noise. The film was an odd blend of Futurism, Fascism, and Industrialism with the faceless, omnipresent narrator describing scooter construction with orgasmic delight: "the electro-magnetic test bed is the altar of destruction on which will be sacrificed the body of a Lambretta." It was enough to make your senses tingle, and the film won the nonfiction first prize at the Cannes festival.

But Ferdinando Innocenti's death and the late-1960s decline in scooter popularity were hurting Innocenti. By 1970, scooter sales had slackened

---

Scooters India Lambrettas

In 1972, the Indian government–run Scooters India bought Innocenti's DL scooter tooling and continued manufacturing late-1960 Lambretta models. The firm retained the DeLuxe Series tradition, making little change to the models besides adding turn signals and eventually making select body parts in plastic.

Scooters India offered three models: the 125 DL, 150 GP, and 200 GP. With a slightly higher compression ratio than the Innocenti-made SX 150 and SX 200, the Indian GP models were good for more horsepower and speed than their Italian counterparts. The 125 had 7.4hp for a 59mph top speed. The GP 150 (148cc at 57x58mm) ran to 7.8:1 and 9.3hp at 6300rpm for a 63mph top speed; by 1980, the GP 150 was breathing through a 22mm Dell'Orto SH with a cr at 8.25:1 for a stupendous 9.4hp still at 6300rpm. Fuel consumption was a mere 90mpg, but who cared anymore?

The GP 200 was an overbored 66x58mm version of the old Li Series engine fed via a 22mm Dell'Orto SH with an 8.2:1 cr fathering 12.4hp at 6300rpm. Top speed was a fleet-footed 71mph.

Badged as a Lambretta, the Grand Prix series was actually built by Scooters India and not Innocenti, which offered its SX series as competition. This GP 200 was exported throughout the world into the 1980s, offering a high-performance scooter in the best Lambretta tradition. The engine was based on the influential Li, now at 198cc and pumping out 12.4hp for an astonishing 71mph or 114km/h top speed. The racing stripes were essential at those speeds.

Serveta Lambrettas

In 1952, Lambretta Locomociones SA was founded in Eibar, outside of Bilbao in northern Spain, to import Italian-made scooters; the firm began licensed production in 1954. It later changed its name to Messrs Serveta Industrial SA, at which time the scooters were renamed Serveta scooters instead of Lambrettas.

The Servetas were rather crude with haphazard 6 volt electrics into the 1980s while competing scooters like the Vespa P200E boasted 12 volt, 100 watt electrics as well as electronic ignition. Serveta produced the Li 125 Slimline DL, 150 Special, and Jet 200. The 150 Special with Slimline styling had a bench seat above the side panels with a racing stripe interrupted by "150" numerals. Soon after, the Special had black trim and turn signals mounted with the new rectangular headlamps. This model was imported into the United States by Cosmopolitan Motors of Philadelphia.

The Jet 200, known as "la scooter que dura más" or the scooter that lasts longer, was equipped with a bench seat, racing stripes on the side panels (for added speed), and turn signals. The Jet 200 (a.k.a. the Lince 200 from 1975) was a hot scooter ideal for tuning and performance.

as buyers were stepping up to automobiles. By 1971, Innocenti halted its exalted scooter assembly lines and sold its equipment for building the DL Series to the Indian government.

In March 1993, the final nail was hammered home laying to rest the Italian Lambretta. In this day and age, it was probably inevitable: the old Lambrate factory was turned into a shopping mall. All things must pass.

Iso Italy

Iso's history followed the ups and downs of the Italian postwar economy in textbook fashion. Isothermos of Bresso near Milan—changed in 1948 to Iso Automotoviecoli SpA—entered the scooter market in 1948 with a background not in aviation, as did Piaggio, but in refrigerators.

Like Enrico Piaggio and Ferdinando Innocenti, Iso owner Renzo Rivolta saw the need for economical transportation. After the success of the Iso scooter and along with the country's gradual recovery, Iso developed the Isetta minicar—a stepping stone to a full-sized car such as the Fiat 500. The Isetta—which was truthfully inspired by a watermelon—was never a production success for Iso but was licensed throughout the world, including to its most famous maker, BMW.

With the Isetta royalties, Iso created a *gran turismo* car line—the Iso Rivolta, Grifo, Fidia, and Lele—to do battle with Ferrari. And at the company's zenith, it failed along with the economy in the mid-1970s recession.

Furetto 1948–1949 ★★

Iso's first scooter of 1948–1949 was the 65cc Furetto, which goes down in history as the scooter that so enraged Rivolta that he dug a big hole and buried his own Furetto as deep as possible. The Furetto inspired Rivolta to build a better scooter.

Isoscooter and Isomoto 1950–1956 ★★

In 1950, Iso baptized the Isoscooter and Isomoto, both sharing the same specifications of a 125cc two-stroke split-single-cylinder engine based on the Puch design. The engine had two bores of 38mm and a single stroke of 55mm creating 6.7hp at 5200rpm backed by three speeds. Despite its name, the Isomoto was half scooter,

Almost a mirror image of styling: an Iso Diva, left, parked next to a Lambretta TV 175 Series II outside the market of Salta, Argentina. Iso power came from a four-speed two-stroke 146cc single, a better design than the early split-singles that powered Iso's first Isoscooter. One-sided stub axles held the wheels front and rear; the engineering at front was obviously similar to that of Piaggio. An Argentine Siambretta LD 125 pulls in behind the Lambretta.

Iso's scooter masterpiece was its Diva, introduced in 1957 and known in some parts of the world as the Milano. Although largely forgotten today, in the 1950s Iso competed head on with Innocenti and Piaggio for the scooter buyer; as this 1959 ad noted, Iso had more than 2,500 concessionaires and scooter service stations in Italy and Europe. Iso had come a long way from making refrigerators.

half motorcycle with small, 3.00x12in tires and substantial bodywork. The Isoscooter was all scooter but with awkward, homely styling.

Iso Diva (Milano) 1957–1960 ★★★★

In 1957, Iso created its masterpiece, the Diva scooter, also known in export countries as the Milano. The styling was graceful with bodacious, flowing curves from the front fender to the side covers. The look was half Vespa, half Lambretta TV1; the effect was inspiring.

The Diva's engine was a two-stroke 146cc single of a square 57x57mm. With four speeds, 6.5hp at 5000rpm was possible. Like a Vespa, the Diva had one-sided lug axles holding the wheels and 3.50x10in tires.

Like the TV Lambretta, the Diva was a large-bore luxury scooter designed for touring. The scooter market had grown from basic, boring transportation to buyers with extra cash in their pockets and free time to spend; they wanted a scooter that could take them to the beach on holidays as well as about town. The Lambretta TV, Vespa GS, and the Iso Diva were the scooters of a new Italy.

Through the years, Iso played a key role in the postwar Italian recovery as one of the largest Italian scooter manufacturers, although its two-wheeled vehicles are virtually unknown in the rest of the world. But by the 1960s, Iso had foresaken the scooter market to concentrate on building *gran turismo* cars. It was a sad day for scooter aficionados.

Italjet Italy ★

The Italjet firm was formed in Bologna in 1966 by famed racer Leopoldo Tartarini. Besides building numerous racing and sports bikes, Italjet built the Pack-A-Way in the mid-1970s, a fold-up 50cc scooter. The Pack-A-Way was designed to be stowed away in the trunk of a car and unfolded for city driving.

In the late 1980s and into the 1990s, Italjet offered three plastic scooters for three different careers: the Shopping, Reporter, and Bazooka, all based on 49cc two-stroke engines.

At the 1992 Bologna show, Italjet announced a collaboration with Hyosung of Taiwan and displayed its Cruise scooter, a rolling sculpture of plastic.

James UK ★

James of Greet concentrated on building lightweight utility motorcycles, so it was only natural that the firm should try its hand at a scooter. James scooter debuted in 1960 based on an AMC 149cc two-stroke with a horizontal cylinder allowing it to be mounted directly under the floor-

JoeBe stood for Joe Berliner, who was standing on the left in this photo showing off his Ventruck model. Joe Berliner was one of the stalwarts of American motorcycling, importing Glas Goggo-Isaria and Zündapps for years to the United States. The Ventruck combined one of JoeBe's Goggo-Isaria scooters with an ice cream refrigerator on a two-wheel axle. What will they think of next?

Original, unrestored 1936 Keen Power Cycle powered by a 0.5hp Lauson engine with direct drive to the rear wheel without any of the hassles of a clutch. The engine exhaust was simply ported straight down through the chassis. Styling was purposeful or austere, depending on your point of view, but it did the job. Owner: Herb Singe. *Herb Singe*

The Keen Power Cycle was advertised in the back of *Popular Mechanics* magazines in the late 1930s. The world was a different place back then, and communications were not what they are today. *Popular Mechanics* was an ideal way for the scooter entrepreneur to reach a nationwide market. Dealer inquiries were always invited.

boards. This also placed the spark plug inches behind the front wheel and in a direct line for mud and water spray, symbolic of the James' troubleprone existence.

In 1963, the James scooter, designated the SC1, was updated to a four-speed gearbox, becoming the SC4. The scooter lasted until James' demise in 1966.

J. B. Volkscooter USA–Germany ★

The Volkscooter was planned as a two-wheeled version of the four-wheeled success of the 1960s, the Volkswagen. Two models were offered in 100cc and 125cc form. But part of the VW's success was due to Hitler's support; the

Original, unrestored 1940 Keen Power Cycle with obvious design roots stretching back to the Salsbury Motor Glide. This model was tested and procured by the US Army to help lead the fight during World War II. Owner: Herb Singe. *Herb Singe*

Volkscooter lacked Hitler's endorsement and never made a dent in the volks' market.

JoeBe USA–Germany ★

Joe Berliner's JoeBe line of scooters were actually Glas Goggo-Isaria scooters featuring the Glas emblem on the army-helmet-styled front fender and the JoeBe script emblem on the legshields.

Keen Power Cycle USA ★★★

The Keen Power Cycle was first offered by the Keen Manufacturing Company of Madison, Wisconsin, in 1936 as a basic step-through scooter following Salsbury's contagious design. Power was a 1/2hp Lauson engine with direct drive and no clutch. By 1939, four models were available based on a two-speed transmission. As a 1936 flyer asked, "Can you think of anything more thrilling?"

By the early 1940s, the manufacturing rights were sold to the J. A. Strimple Company of Janesville, Wisconsin, which carried on the legend.

To meet the onslaught of Nazi Germany's panzer divisions head on, the Strimple company created a military Keen Power Cycle. The Tiger tank had a 23,000cc twelve-cylinder engine and 88mm cannon; the Keen had a Lauson 8.9ci (146cc) single-cylinder engine and a bathtub-like sidecar to hide in.

Strimple's scooter still followed in the design style of the Motor Glide almost to a tee. But military requirements dictated aspects of the design, such as the 6x6in wheels, interchangeable with USAAF spotter aircraft. The US Army tested the Keen with sidecar in January 1944 and it was procured in limited numbers.

Kreidler Germany ★

Although little more than a moped, the Kreidler R50 was definitely "ein Roller mit Charme." Located in Kornwesteim, Kreidler at one time produced more motorcycles than any other company in Germany. In 1953, it grew into the scooter business after making the K50 and K51 mopeds. The Union of Bicycle and Motorcycle Industry (VFM) restricted the maximum speed to less than 25mph in 1955, so in 1956 Kreidler released the R50 scooter with the same 49cc two-speed engine as its moped. The scooter had 2.25hp for a top speed of 50km/h, but added a pillion seat, smaller 19in wheels, an enlarged rear fender, and an enclosed engine, thereby constituting a scooter.

According to publicity material from Kreidler, "Women prefer this scooter because it meets your wishes for a well-groomed, well-cultivated exterior without lacking a sporty, elegant feel. To go with this scooter gives one a feeling of being chic and charming."

Kroboth Germany ★★★

Second only to the Maico Mobil for outrageous design but unfortunately much less common, the Kroboth 100 of 1951–1955 was surrounded with a gigantic front fender and numerous air ducts in the paneling, giving it the appearance of a forklift with no lifting ability. The Kroboth had many attributes of an enclosed motorcycle, but it still had the small wheels, floorboard, and leg protection of scooters.

The Kroboth scooters all used Fichtel & Sachs engines, and the Truxa's 175cc motor was strong enough to carry a sidecar. The Truxa's style had 9hp for a top speed of 85km/h whereas the 100 achieved 3hp for 60km/h and the Cabrio of 1951–1955 upped it with 6.5hp for 75km/h. The design of the Truxa of 1953–1955 was considerably refined from the bare functionalism of the earlier Kroboth scooters.

LaRay USA ★★

LaRay Cycle of Los Angeles was a bicycle builder that decided to try its hand at the fledgling scooter market, offering its LaRay scooter in the late 1930s.

Laverda Italy ★★

The Laverda family began building agricultural engines and farm machinery in Breganze in the 1830s. Moto Laverda was formed in 1948 and established a distinguished motorcycle racing history.

The Laverda Mini-Scooter made its debut at the 1959 Milan Fiera Campionaria with a diminutive four-stroke 50cc engine measuring 40x39mm with a two-speed gearbox shifted by twistgrip. The Mini-Scooter was designed to meet a 1959 Italian regulation lifting taxes on one-rider 50cc mopeds and scooters that were a maximum of 1.5hp and 40km/h top speed. Ignition was by flywheel magneto and the scooter rode atop dwarf 2.75x9in tires.

Laverda followed Piaggio's lead in creating a unit body-chassis from stressed steel. The styling was simple; the scooter was so small there was little room for flourishes. A single saddle seat sat atop the engine and gas tank.

In 1962, Laverda decided its 40km/h top speed was not enough. A third gear was added to the transmission, and with tuning work to the 50cc engine, power was up to 2.5hp at 6000rpm for a top speed of 57km/h.

Along with the 50cc version, a 60cc model was added in 1962 based on a larger, 47mm bore

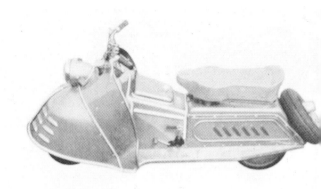

Sharing the dustbin styling of the Maico Mobil, the Kroboth Truxa was a rival for the ultimate touring vehicle. Still, the Truxa's lines can't help but be related to a two-wheeled Panzer tank. *Roland Slabon archives*

delivering 3hp at 6000rpm for a 65km/h top speed. The 60cc model was dressed up by a modern two-person bench seat with Wild West fringe around the edging, spare wheel with vinyl cover, and small luggage rack.

The Mini-Scooter never took Laverda far. Piaggio and Innocenti controlled the market and left little room for others. Laverda, however, struck an exportation deal to bring numbers of its scooter into Great Britian.

Ironically, the most successful Vespa of all time would be the 50cc Vespino, also introduced in 1962. Piaggio's might was far greater than Laverda's; it was a modern-day story of David and Goliath warring on motorscooters.

Lefol France ★

In 1954, La Société Lefol et Cie released its Scoot-Air as a civilian parachutist's fold-up scooter. Made of lightweight metal and moved by a 98cc Comet engine, the Scoot-Air dissembled into three pieces to make sky diving a snap.

LeJay USA ★★★

The LeJay Electric Rocket was the world's first electric motorscooter, arriving on the scene in 1939 from LeJay Manufacturing of Minneapolis, Minnesota. LeJay's kit added an electric motor to a Motor Glide-inspired scooter chassis that beat them all in economy of operation: 100 miles for 5 cents, according to ads. But there was no mention of how far the batteries would last.

Lenobile Belgium ★★

Lenobile had factories in Brussels and Charleroi where in 1952 it made its Kon-Tiki scooter, which goes down in history as the scooter

Laverda's Mini-Scooter was powered by the smallest four-stroke engine of any scooter: 49cc. Arriving on the scene in 1961, by 1962 a 60cc pushrod model was also available, both with unit steel chassis. But the Laverda had one problem: Vespa. Piaggio introduced its 50cc Vespino in 1962 and took over the market, controlling it even into the 1990s. *Tim Parker archives*

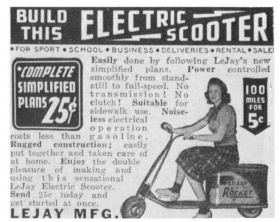
The LeJay Electric Rocket appeared in 1939, the first electric scooter in the world. But as this *Popular Mechanics* ad noted, it was "suitable for sidewalk use," which may have caused buyers hesitation before mailing LeJay their 25¢. The dream of an electric scooter has persisted to today; in 1992, Honda created its 1993 CUV electric scooters for the Japanese market.

with oddest name and silliest bodywork. Styling looked like a coffin on wheels with a headlamp and windshield on top; power was from a 150cc two-stroke Sachs engine and four-speed gearbox.

In 1953, Lenobile was back with its Phenix scooter with Sachs 150cc and 175cc engines offered.

Lohner Austria ★★

Lohner of Vienna showed its first scooter in 1951, the L98T with a 98cc Sachs two-stroke with two speeds. In 1953, it offered its Super-Roller L200 with a Rotax 199cc of 62x66mm creating 8.3hp at 5000rpm via a Famo four-speed gearbox and 4x10in tires.

Lohner continued in 1956 with its Rapid 125 and 200 based on a Sachs 125cc and a Ilo 200. A Rapid 200 was also offered with an integral sidecar that was built into the bodywork of the scooter.

In 1957, Lohner returned with its Sissy, a motorcycle in miniature with full bodywork and power from a Sachs 47cc and three speeds.

Lowther Manufacturing Company USA ★★

Lowther of Joliet, Illinois, built a wide range of motorscooters in the 1940s, which the company called "The 'Park Avenue' Scooter with the 'Main Street' price" in a 1948 flyer.

Lowther offered each model with a variety of "artistically created" body styles and a range of engine sizes, spawning a whole variety of scooters. The Stylemaster was a Art Deco vision on two wheels with red and black two-tone paint and a massive chrome Jet Age bumper on the rear that looked like a cowcatcher or 'roo bar gone wrong. It came in three bodies and with 3hp, 4hp, and 6hp.

The Lightin' was "as stylish as next year's fashion," according to a 1948 dealer letter. Power came from a Briggs & Stratton 4.5hp or 6.7hp engine; a rear hydraulic brake from a Plymouth car did the stopping. Two versions were available: the Model 600ZZ1-P Airflow and the 600ZZ2-P Playboy. A sidecar with 16cu-ft carrying capacity was optional. The three-wheeled Commercial came in an array of six bodies with 4, 6, and 8hp engines.

Lowther also sold its scooters to Indian, who rebadged them as its own line.

Lutz Germany ★

"Economical" described the Lutz R3 scooter of 1949–1954 since the 58cc Lutz engine had only 1hp and a top speed of 40km/h. Styling, if it can be called that, was definitely unique with a triangular front fender and wire-mesh side panels instead of typical molded sheet metal. Four exposed front cables added to the spaghetti design of the R3.

Lutz made up for lost ground, however, with the R175 of 1951–1954 with excessive rounded covering and dual seat, a design likely inspired by Dr. Seuss. The 174.3cc Lutz engine pumped out 6hp for a top speed of 75km/h on its petite 8in wheels.

Maico Germany

"In the shadow of the Wurmling Chapel, made famous by the well known song by Ludwig Unland, lies an extensive factory, animated by the spirit of progress, and staffed by men who take an intense pride in their work. This is the birthplace of Maico...."

—*1955 Maico Information Bulletin*

Maico's publicity made the factory seem godsent. And judging from the dustbin design of the Maicomobil, some paranormal influences had to be at work. During World War II, the Fatherland turned to Maisch & Co.'s (aka Maico) aviation expertise to supply the Luftwaffe, while DKW, BMW, and Zündapp were in charge of motorcycles. Following the conflict, the factory ended up in the French section of a divided Germany where manufacturing aircraft parts was banned, and so Maico began making children's toys. Maico soon relocated to Herrenburg in the American sector where tools and materials were readily available to again produce motorcycles.

Maico Mobil MB 150 1951–1953; MB 175 and MB 200 1954–1958 ★★★★★

Maico's own brochures said it best: "With its latest product, the Maico-Mobil, Maico have introduced a completely novel type of machine which lies mid-way between the conventional motor cycle and the scooter; it may be that this will prove to be the true touring machine of the future."

While the micro-car fad swept Germany, Maico believed it could convince the public that two wheels were better than three for a touring vehicle. At the Reulingen Show in June 1950, Maico introduced its "car on two wheels" with a

The Maicomobil 200 was a Volkswagen for the two-wheeled set. Replete with a windshield, turn signals, and luggage panniers as early as 1954, it was the coolest scooter on the strasse. *Mick Walker archives*

The Maicomobil, also known as the Maico Mobil, Maico-Mobil, or simply the Dustbin, topped the list of outrageous scooters. Underneath all that bodacious steel bodywork was a heavy-duty motorcycle frame, which required a subsection frame that extended out to support the enormous fenders. This was the 1954 175cc model. *Mick Walker archives*

tank-like frame to support the armorplated paneling, needed for weather protection and incorporated enough luggage space for a few suitcases. Its dashboard featured a speedometer that indicated the gear engaged, and a radio in the 1955 model.

Who wouldn't fall for the man riding a Maicoletta? Maico backtracked on its design of "the car on two wheels" in creating the Maicoletta, one of the fastest scooters ever built. Much as the Manhattan Project required absolute secrecy in the desert of Los Alamos, Maico kept development of its scooter project mum in the anonymity of its Herrenburg basement. *Mick Walker archives*

Underneath the bodywork, the Maico Mobil was more a motorcycle than scooter due to its 14in wheels, duplex-tube frame with a crossbar between the rider's legs, telescopic front forks, and its sheer size.

The first Maico Mobil of 1951 was powered by a 148cc single-cylinder engine. The air-cooled two-stroke measured 57x58mm and fathered 6.5hp at 4800rpm via a three-speed gearbox, which was not quite enough power to push along its 115kg or 253lb mass. In 1954, Maico updated the Mobil with two new models, a 173cc (61x59.5mm) and 197cc (65x59.5mm) for 8.5hp and 10.9hp respectively with a new four-speed.

The Mobil provided motorcycle handling with scooter performance and weather protection with styling like the Hindenberg zeppelin on wheels.

Maicoletta M175 1955–1966 and
Maicoletta M250 1956–1966 ★★★

The Maico design team of Pohl and Tetzlaff created the Maicoletta in secrecy in their basement away from the prying eyes of the cut-throat German scooter industry. It was unveiled at the 1955 Brussels Show, with classic scooter lines , although many of the Mobil's attributes carried over, such as the dashboard with an illuminated clock and the 14in wheels. Maico publicity bragged that "Even the most discerning rider will find that everything a modern scooter can offer in the way of comfort has been incorporated."

Although the Maicoletta's looks were undoubtedly scooterlike, several features such as the foot shifter, telescopic front forks, and hydraulic damping for the rear suspension gave it the advantages of a motorcycle. The powerful 174cc and 247cc engines gave 9hp and 14hp for top speeds of 85km/h and 105km/h. In autumn 1957, the Maicoletta was offered with a 277cc engine, one of the largest engines ever shoehorned into a scooter.

Maico underwent financial problems in 1987 from which even the shadow of the Wurmling Chapel couldn't protect it. By summer the factory was sold.

Mako Switzerland ★

In 1953, Mako offered its scooter with a Ilo 125cc and three speeds. Styling almost replicated the Lambretta LC—even down to the two portholes on the side cover.

Mammut Germany ★

In 1954, the 47kg Mammut Solo-Roller sported the coveted feature of wing bolts to hold on the side panels covering the 50cc Sachs or optional Ilo engine. Mammut-Vertriebsgeschaft of Bielefeld's scooter cruised to a 40km/h top speed on its 20in wheels.

Manurhin France ★★

Known for its production of munitions, pistols, and other weapons of destruction, Manufacture du Haut-Rhin began producing a two-wheeled weapon, the MR 75 scooter, in 1957. The MR 75 was a French version of the DKW Hobby scooter although many parts differed, such as the Gurtner carburetor instead of the German Bing, and a French Morel flywheel magneto, but the motor remained a 3hp DKW. In 1958, DKW joined the Zweirad Union at which time it gave up on the Hobby leaving Manurhin as the sole producer of the MR 75.

Martin-Moulet France ★★

The Martin–Moulet was the perfect briefcase for the commuter to work because thirty seconds later, *abracadabra!* it would transform into a scooter (albeit unattractive). Imagine carrying a small purse loaded with 25kg of gold bullion, now that's the Valmobile. The original prototype carried a 60cc Alter motor with a top speed of 50km/h on the miniscule wheels and by 1953 had changed to a 98cc British Villiers for 65km/h. A

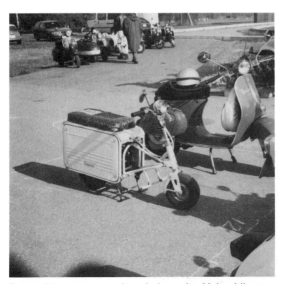

Depending on your point of view, the Valmobile was either a high-performance suitcase or a scooter complete with it own carrying case. This little mechanical abracadabra was originally created in France by Martin-Moulet; production was later licensed to create the American Foldmobile as well as British and Japanese Valmobiles. This Japanese model has add-on extras such as the mirror and airhorn. *Classic Scooters Newsletter/Steven Zasueta*

covered, large-fendered Valmobile made its debut at the Salon de Paris in 1955. The Valmobile's Parisian designer, M. Victor-Albert Bouffort, proved his scooters worth by traveling from Paris to Geneva in a day, and from Paris to Madrid in three days.

Production of the Valmobile was licensed to makers in the United States (called the Foldmobile), Japan, and Great Britain as well as tested by the French army for parachuting.

Mead Cycle Company USA ★★★

Mead of Chicago was established in 1889 by the Mead family and had long been famous for its balloon-tired Ranger bicycle, which went head-to-head against Chicago's Schwinn. When Schwinn turned to motorized bicycles with its Whizzer engine, the envious Mead firm followed suit.

Across town, Mead management had seen the Moto-Scoot of upstart manufacturer Norman Siegal. In 1938, Mead contracted with Siegal to build badge-engineered Moto-Scoots as the Mead Ranger scooter.

Throughout the Ranger's history, it would follow the style and specs of the Moto-Scoot, but sometimes with lesser features. The first Rangers of 1938 were basic step-through scooters with two speeds and 1hp engines good for 30mpg. Two models were initially offered: the basic 80-1 and the C-80-1, which added a clutch and kickstart.

The Ranger was available in the same variety of models as the Moto-Scoot from 1939 on but with different names. The 1 1/2hp Standard line

Mead Cycle Company was famous back to the turn of the century for its bicycles, but in the late 1930s, Mead foresaw motorscooters taking over pedal power and wanted in on the action. Mead contracted with nearby Moto-Scoot to provide it with Mead Ranger scooters, which were almost identical to the Moto-Scoot except for the paint scheme and decals. This May 1939 ad appeared in *Popular Mechanics*.

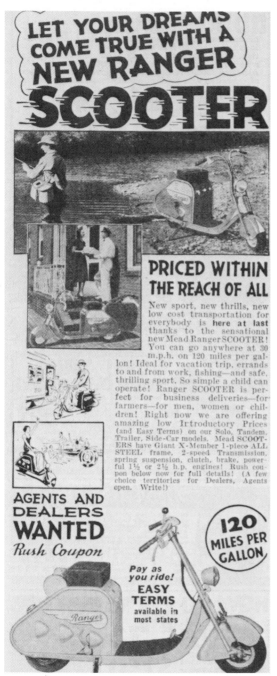

Your dreams came true with the 1939 Mead Ranger—depending on what your dreams were, of course. The first Ranger of 1938 was a no-frills scooter inspired by Salsbury's Motor Glide; the 1939 model added a full front fender and the cooling scoops to the sidepanels where the 1938 had merely a mesh screen. Mead continued to offer its badge-engineered Moto-Scoot into the 1950s.

included the Model 100 Solo and 101 Carrier. The 1 1/2hp De Luxe with Vari-Torque Drive featured the 103 Solo, 104 Carrier, and 105 Tandem. The 2 1/2hp Rocket line was the 106 Solo, 107 Carrier, and 108 Tandem. The Rocket Special added the Vari-Torque Drive to the Rockets and an S suffix to the model numbers. A Sidecar was advertised in *Popular Mechanics* ads as a three-wheel miniature auto.

Fuel consumption was always the key to 1930s scooter sales, and Mead ads usually headlined the figures. In 1938, the Ranger got 129mpg; by 1939, the Ranger was up to 130mpg, probably based on extensive engine reworking, or a reworking of arithmetic. As one Mead ad tantalized tourists: "Go across USA for $6.00 gas money!" There was no mention of how long the trip would take at 30mph top speed—never mind the Continental Divide.

Following World War II, the Ranger was extensively reworked along the lines of the new Moto-Scoot with a two-tiered rear bodywork design and a larger engine. By the 1950s, the Mead Rangers had ridden away into the sunset.

Mercury UK ★

Mercury of Birmingham was another British bicycle builder that decided to construct a scooter. At the 1956 Earl's Court Show, it unveiled its Dolphin scooter with a Villiers 98cc two-stroke of a modest 2.9hp with a two-speed gearbox riding atop 2.50x8in tires. In 1957, Mercury added its Pippin scooter with the same mechanicals as the Dolphin and a facelifted front fender.

Neither the Dolphin nor Pippin went far in the market, although attempts were made to export them to the United States.

Midget Motors Corporation USA ★

The aptly named Midget Motors built its Autocycle in the 1960s in Athens, Ohio. Styled like a Mustang or Cushman Eagle, power was 5hp from a four-stroke engine and two-speed gearbox with passing gear. Amazingly, disc brakes were optional on the Autocycle as early as 1961 as well as a 12 volt electrical system and electric starter.

Minerva–Van Hauwaert Belgium ★

The old Antwerp firm of Minerva was sold in the 1950s to Van Hauwaert of Brussels; the new firm offered its Minerva scooter in 1953 with a 150cc two-stroke of 9.5hp. At the same 1953 Brussels show, it also displayed a prototype "triscooter" based on the Minerva with two front wheels and two seats covered by bodywork. In 1954, the firm launched its Motoretta scooter with a Ilo 175cc two-stroke.

Minneapolis USA ★

The Minneapolis firm offered its 2.75hp Sportster scooter in the late 1950s.

Mitsubishi Japan ★★★

During World War II, Mitsubishi was one of several builders of the Zero-San for the Japanese air force. Like Piaggio, postwar Mitsubishi turned its talents in aircraft structural engineering to the field of motorscooters. Fuji had built Japan's first scooter in 1946 and Mitsubishi followed its lead, introducing its first in 1948. From the late 1940s and into the 1960s, Fuji and Mitsubishi would control the Japanese scooter market as a Far Eastern Piaggio–Innocenti zaibatsu duo.

The Japanese appetite for scooters was as strong as the Italians'. In 1946, only eight scooters were built in Japan, all by Fuji; by 1954, more than 450,000 scooters were on the road with the country's total production at 50,000 annually. By 1958, total annual production was 113,218.

Mitsubishi named its scooter "the Pigeon" from its debut in 1948 with the 115cc C-11 two-stroke. The styling was pure Motor Glide, following the design tenets set down by the Americans in 1936 almost to a tee. The engine was 57x44mm bore and stroke, creating 1.5hp at 3500rpm for a 50km/h top speed riding on diminutive 3.50x5in tires.

The Pigeon was updated in 1949 as the C-13 with a larger, dutiful headlamp and the Pigeon emblem on the front fork apron, a Nazi-esque symbol that would continue to be used into the 1950s. The overall styling was agricultural, shaped more by a blacksmith's hammer than a stylist's hand, a "look" the line would keep until the mid-1950s.

In the 1950s, the Pigeons began breeding off-spring models. The C-21 was introduced in 1950 with a 150cc engine of 57x58mm for 3hp at 3800rpm. It was available with a passenger or delivery sidecar, following the lineups of the American scooters once again. In 1951, the C-22 took over from the C-21 with even more bizarre styling featuring air ducts over almost every available space on the tailsection.

In 1953, the C-35 175cc Pigeon arrived with a four-stroke engine, three-speed transmission, and 4.00x8in tires. But the look was still blacksmith chic.

In 1954, the Pigeon got styling. A new 200cc C-57 model led the way with a 65x58mm four-cycle engine producing 4.3hp at 3800rpm with an automatic transmission and 4.00x8in tires. The design work was a blend of curves and slab sides that gave the scooter a weird elegance, all set off by the usual chrome trim, turn signals, covered

handlebars, and so many air ducts that you worried for the scooter's structural rigidity. A C-57 II arrived in 1956 with further chrome trim. In 1957, a new 200cc model bowed as the C-90 with sleeker, minimalist lines and 5.7hp from the same engine.

The small-bore Pigeon got styling in 1955 by copying the lines of the current Lambretta LC—even down to the Italian's three ports on the side covers, which must have impressed the Japanese by given their love for air ducts. This two-stroke 125cc C-70 was up to 3.6hp at 4200rpm with a new 55x52.5mm engine and 4.00x8in tires.

In 1958–1959, the C-73 took over from the C-70, retaining the Lambretta LC lines, and was followed by the 192cc four-stroke C-74. The four-stroke 125cc C-83 complemented the Standard C-73 with lines similar to the new Lambretta TV1!

Mitsubishi's fabulous Silver Pigeon line was imported into the United States by Rockford Scooter Company, which made certain it never mentioned the fact that the scooters were built by the Japanese firm that created the infamous Zero-San fighter. Anti-Japanese sentiment still ran high in the late 1950s and invoking memories of Pearl Harbor would not have sold scooters. Rockford did wholesale Silver Pigeons to Montgomery Ward, which sold them as Riversides.

Monark Skoterett

Monark Skoterett Modellnr. 901264	**Skärmar:** Sammanbyggda med chassiet	**Cylindervolym:** 48 cc	**Växellada:** 2-vaxlad fotmanövrerad
Ram: Pressad stålplåt	**Bromsar:** Total bromsarea 66 cm²	**Kompressionsförhållande:** 6.7:1	**Koppling:** Flerskiviy i oljebad
Framgaffel: Bottenlänkfjädring	**Bensintank:** Rymd 5 liter inbyggd under sadeln	**Effekt:** 1 hk vid 4500 v/min	**Belysning:** Huvudstrålkastare 6 V 15/15 W
Bakgaffel: Swingarm med stötdämpare	**Motor:** Husqvarna 1 cyl. 2-takt fläktkyld	**Förländning:** 2–2.5 mm	Bakljus 6 V 3 W. Bromsljus 6 V 5 W
Fälgar: Sammansvetsade stältallrikar	**Cylinderdiameter:** 39 mm	**Tändstift:** Bosch W 175 T 1	**Färger:** Metallblått och Bahamagult
Däckdimension: 3.00 × 10	**Slaglängd:** 40 mm	**Förgasare:** Bing 1/10/81	

Monark's Skoterett Model 901264 was powered by a 48cc two-stroke engine that pumped out a full 1hp. As Monark owned the Crescent firm, a Skoterett was also sold with the Crescent nameplate and the body painted a different color. *Gösta Karlsson archives*

Wishful thinking by Montesa: most Spanish post carriers were not young women in mini-skirts and high heels, and the Montesa 3hp 60cc Micro Scooter could probably not haul around the day's mail as well as a rider. The Micro was a Laverda overhead-valve four-stroke Mini Scooter built under license in Spain from 1962–1969. *Tim Parker archives*

The 5.5hp C-83 was nicknamed the Bobby De Luxe in a curious bit of Japanese-English. This was superseded by the four-stroke C-200 in 1960 as well as the C-90, which was advertized for the US market as being "heavy-duty, long-range luxury," as well as having "johnny-on-the-spot performance." Along with the Bobby De Luxe came the Peter De Luxe of 1959, a four-stroke 210cc luxury scooter.

In 1960, two new high-end models were unveiled with styling similar to the Maicomobil's dustbin front end. The C-110 was an overhead-valve 175cc good for 8.5hp; the C-111 was a larger-bore, 210cc version with 11.5hp and a 95km/h top speed.

In 1963, the 125cc was redesigned as the C-135 Silver Pigeon with curvaceous, multi-angled styling and 8hp from a small-bore version of the C-110 engine. In 1964, a facelift created the C-140 as well as the four-stroke 150cc C-240.

Beginning in the late 1950s, Pigeons were imported into the United States by Rockford

Scooter of Rockford, Illinois, which labeled the Rabbits as its own. Into the 1960s, Rockford imported the C-73, C-74, C-76, and C-90 models, which were wholesaled to Montgomery Ward and sold through its mail-order catalog as the Riverside.

Monark Sweden ★

Monark got its start in 1920 making bicycles but soon ventured into motorcycles from 49cc to a 998cc overhead-valve V-twin. In 1957, the firm ventured into the scooter market with its Monarscoot M33. Dressed in full bodywork, the M33 rode atop tall 20in wheels.

In the 1960s, Monark created its Skoterett Model 901264, powered by a 48cc Husqvarna two-stroke single of 39x40mm with 1hp at 4500rpm riding atop 3.00x10in tires. The bodywork styling was pure Lambretta Slimline. The fixed front fender and covered handlebars as well as the tail section belied the Innocenti influence. A scalloped section on the sidecover bore the Monark script in chrome.

Monark also developed a Honda Cub-style moped-scooter called simply enough the Skotermoped Model 901269 and powered by a two-stroke Sachs.

Monark purchased the Swedish Crescent firm and sold its Skoterett and Skotermoped under the Crescent name as well as its own. Today, Monark is owned by Volvo, the General Motors or Fiat of Scandinavia.

Monet–Goyon France ★★

As early as 1919, Monet et Goyon of Mâcon designed something of a scooter called the Vélauto with a 147cc 2hp Villiers engine and a Super-Vélauto run by a 270cc Villiers. It built these scooter-like mobiles until 1925.

The firm began making scooters again in 1953, twenty-four years after taking over Koehler–Escoffier from Lyon. Monet et Goyon produced the 52GDC Starlett with a 98cc Villiers MK1F engine with 2.9hp. Later models were the S2s and S2L Luxe and Grand Luxe, keeping the same design of a covered bicycle with paneling giving away the location of the chain.

In 1956, Monet–Goyon produced two evolved prototype Starletts called the Starlett Record 53R as well as Le Dolina painted in Eiffel Tower gray.

Montesa Spain ★★

Montesa began building small commuter motorcycles in the years following World War II under the guidance of co-founders Pedro Permanyer and Francisco Bulto and under the watch-

The SC Mobyscoot made by Motobécane added fancy reverse hand levers for one of the sportiest French scooters by a company known more for their mopeds than their limited engagement in the world of putt-putts. *Vittorio Tessera archives*

ful gaze of Fascist "El Caudillo" Generalissimo Francisco Franco.

Montesa built a strong racing reputation but by 1958, the founders split apart: Permanyer sought to return Montesa to building commuter cycles; Bulto wanted to continue racing, and left to start Bultaco. Later that year, Montesa's first scooter was unveiled.

The Montesa scooter was an oddity in a scooter market full of oddities. Instead of a step-through design as with Derbi's Masculino scooter, Montesa opted for more of a motorcycle-like design with two seats atop the fiberglass bodywork. The end effect was a scooter that looked like a two-wheeled car.

The seats and luggage rack were mounted on rails and could be adjusted fore and aft. It was an interesting feature on a scooter that lacked many normal features that buyers expected. Production started in 1959 and ended in 1960.

For 1962–1965, Montesa returned to scooters, building its version of the Laverda Mini Scooter as the Montesa Micro Scooter. With a three-speed gearbox and 60cc four-stroke engine, it was the sole four-stroke Montesa ever built. Riding atop 2.75x9in tires, the diminutive overhead-valve engine pumped out 3hp at 6000rpm. From 1966–1969, the Montesa's scooter was called the Micro 66.

Motobecane/Motoconfort France SCC/STC 1951 ★★

Géo Ham designed the first Motobecane/Motoconfort scooter, which was shown at the Salon de Paris in 1951 with a four-stroke 125cc engine for 5hp at 5000rpm. The Motobecane version came under the name of SCC and the Moto-

Restored 1936 Moto-Scoot: if you didn't look closely, you might have missed the engine and taken it for a child's push scooter. Like the Vespa of ten years later, the 0.5hp Lauson engine sat on the right side of the rear wheel but with a shaft transfering chain drive to the left side. The seat really was held aloft by just the one bit of tubing, which also hung the gas tank for gravity feed. Owner Herb Singe believes this scooter may have been a preproduction prototype built for use in Chesterfield cigarette ads of late 1936–1937. *Herb Singe*

Moto-Scoot's first production model was this 1937 model equipped with a 0.5hp Lauson engine with direct drive to the rear wheel sans clutch. This was possibly the first scooter to mount the headlamp at handlebar height, the funky casting looking like a submarine periscope. Owner: Herb Singe. *Herb Singe*

confort was the STC, but all their scooters were affectionately known as "Mobyscoots."

SB/SV 1954–1956 ★★

The SB/SV (again SB=Motobecane, SV=Motoconfort) was a French version of the "undressed" Lambrettas as opposed to the "dressed" SCC/STC. This latest Mobyscoot had an air-cooled engine producing 5hp on 10in wheels up from the SCC/STC's 8in wheels.

SBH/SVH 1956 and SBS/SVS 1957 ★★

Following Innocenti's lead, the Mobyscoot went back to "dressed" scooters with the SBH/SVH and SBS/SVS, the "grand luxe" versions of the SCC/STC four-strokes. Updates were made in the engine including a fan-cooled engine and the rubber "Flexi-bloc" suspension to eliminate vibrations. The SBS/SVS were the latest Moby-Montagne versions with two-tone paint jobs. In 1959, Motobecane's naming changed again to M Montagne-Standard and M Montagne-Lux (substitute and O for the M to get the Moto-confort name).

Motobi Italy ★★

Moto B was formed in Pesaro when one of the six Benelli brothers, Giuseppe, left the Benelli firm in 1952; by 1955, the new firm's name had been settled as Motobi.

Wasting no time, in 1956, Motobi displayed a scooter prototype at the Milan Show based on a tube-frame chassis covered by sheet steel bodywork. By 1957, Motobi had entered into production with a full line of scooters based on the one prototype and 3.50x12in tires: the Ardizio with 125cc and 150cc two-strokes; the Imperiale with 125cc four-stroke delivering 5.5hp; and the Catria with a 175cc four-stroke giving 11hp.

The Catria was a stylish scooter along the lines of the Lambretta LD, with two saddles and full bodywork. As the Motobi flyer stated of the Catria, it was "Lo scooter per l'intenditore"—the scooter for the one who understood.

In 1959, Motobi introduced a scooter-moped called the Pic-nic with a 75cc four-stroke engine; by 1963, the Pic-nic was available at 125cc.

Moto-Scoot Manufacturing USA ★★★★★

In 1936, 27-year-old Norman A. Siegal grew tired of racing Fronty-Fords on the dirt track chitlin circuit, reformed his ways, and rolled the dice to go for broke where he envisioned the big money was: motorscooters. Siegal sold his share in a Chicago Loop garage for $1,090, hired three workman, rolled up his sleeves, and set to work constructing the Moto-Scoot in the corner of a West Side Chicago factory.

Siegal had obviously done his homework and studied E. Foster Salsbury's Motor Glide when he designed—and named—his scooter. The first model of 1936 used a 1 1/2hp Lauson engine with direct drive and no clutch, all mounted on a step-through chassis. Suspension was by a padded seat at the rear. Lighting and a rear drum brake were standard as was a spiffy two-tone paint job.

By 1937, the headlamp had been built into the handlebars. In 1938, the engine was enclosed by a Space Age, rounded cover set off by two-tone lines.

By 1939, Moto-Scoot offered several lines: the De Luxe line was powered by a 1 1/2hp Briggs & Stratton and included the basic Solo, Delivery, and Tandem. The upgraded Century line with 1 1/2hp and Vari-Torque Drive in Solo, Delivery, Tandem, and Side-Car models. The ultimate Moto-Scoots were the Imperial line with a 2 1/2hp engine in Solo, Tandem, Delivery, and Side-Car models. As a 1939 brochure warned, the Century and Imperial models were identical in outward appearance. A Moto-Scoot Trailer was available for all Solo models.

An early brochure promised, "The 1939 Moto-Scoot is the sensation of the highways." Top speed was 30mph but more importantly—and probably the source of the scooter's sensation versus its speed—was the fuel consumption: 120mpg.

Siegal began advertising his wares in back-of-the-book one-column *Popular Mechanics* ads—the nationwide sales tool for motorscooter upstarts of the 1930s and 1940s. Here, the Moto-Scoot did battle for the techno-minded reader's eye with the Rock-Ola, Zipscoot, Constructa-Scoot, Trotwood, and others long lost to the junkyards of America. Siegal persevered.

On April 3, 1939, *Time* magazine did a profile of Siegal and the motorscooter mogul's success. The article offers a list of production figures, presumably from Siegal's mouth: In 1936, the first year of production, 186 Moto-Scoots were built and sold; in 1937, 2,700; and in 1938, 4,500. For 1939, Siegal had high hopes of selling 10,000 Moto-Scoots from his new factory at 8428 South Chicago Avenue where he then had seventy-five workers. According to the magazine, Moto-Skoot (sic) was the largest American scooter maker in 1939, which may or may not have been true. Regardless, *Time* crowned Siegal "the Henry Ford of the scooter business."

Part of Siegal's success was due to the badge-engineered scooter he built for Mead Cycle Company of Chicago, long famous for its Mead Ranger bicycles. Mead had seen the potential of the scooter and contracted Siegal to build Mead Ranger

Following World War II, Siegal renamed his firm American Moto-Scoot and created this late 1940s scooter with a humpbacked design hiding the gas tank and a cramped luggage compartment. The styling was suddenly old-fashioned with the arrival of the new Salsbury Model 85 and the coming invasion of Vespa. This was an original, unrestored Moto-Scoot. Owner: Jim Kilau.

scooters beginning in 1938 and lasting until World War II.

With the start of World War II, Siegal turned his manufacturing expertise to war materiel, but postwar a redesigned scooter appeared. Now called the American Moto-Scoot, it had stylish new bodywork wrapped around a Lauson engine in a two-tiered affair punctuated by rows of louvers. The rear end now rose up to enclose the gas tank and offer a small luggage compartment as well.

By the 1950s, the Moto-Scoot was but a memory.

Mustang USA

The story of the Mustang began in the garage of a budding young engineer named Howard Forrest. Growing up in southern California, Forrest loved to race anything with an engine. In the early 1930s, he built and ran midget sprint cars, which formed the source of two mainstays of Mustang design: powerful small-bore engines and small wheels.

Forrest loved small wheels. Midgets typically raced on dwarf wheels, and under Forrest's hand Mustangs would keep to 8in and 12in wheels through thick and thin. It was to be one of their great features, making them competitive in Class C dirt-track racing against Harley-Davidsons and Indians. It was also one of the reasons for the firm's eventual undoing; the small wheel always denoted a motorscooter rather than a motorcycle.

Much of the background information here comes from Michael Gerald's excellent self-published history, *Mustang: A Different Breed of Steed*.

Howard Forrest Four-Cylinder Motorcycle

Forrest built one of the first ten or twelve midget cars on the West Coast, according to his son and keeper of the flame, Jim Forrest. His midget was powered by an Ace motorcycle four-cylinder with his own homebuilt water-jacket for cooling. But in the 1930s, Forrest was also bitten by the motorcycling bug; he acquired an Indian big twin and later a Salsbury Motor Glide. The Motor Glide had small wheels but its engine, while small, was not powerful. Forrest began work.

In 1936, Forrest, then 22, fabricated his own in-line four-cylinder engine to power a midget, but as these things always happen, he eventually stuffed it into the modified chassis of his Motor Glide, building his own version of what a motorcycle should be.

The Forrest four-cylinder bore looked like a miniature version of the famous Offenhauser engine that ruled sprint car racing and the Indy 500. Forrest's 19ci or 311cc engine breathed through a single carburetor mounted on the right side and run via an overhead camshaft. Forrest machined the crankshaft himself from billet, as well as the connecting rods, camshaft, and pistons. As Jim Forrest told *Classic Cycle Review* mag-

Flyer for the 1956 Colt, which revived the lineage of the first Mustang production model of 1945–1947. The new Colt was to be an economy model complimenting the Model 4 and used the Bumble Bee side-valve engine detuned to only 8hp; a 5hp throttle governor could also be ordered. The paint scheme was Silver Grey (sic) wheels with Banner Green forks, fenders, gas tank, and frame. The second Colt continued until 1959. *Michael Gerald archives*

azine, "The only things he didn't build on that engine were the spark plugs and the carburetor."

Stuffed into the light-duty Motor Glide chassis, Forrest's four was cramped. In 1940–1941, he built his own frame by hand, as well as his own two-speed gearbox, a right-angle bevel-drive unit. Since a suitable radiator was not at hand, Forrest bought a car radiator and a new saw. And the wheels were small, 8in whitewalls.

Just before World War II, Forrest was hired on as an engineer at Gladden Products based at 635 West Colorado Boulevard in Glendale, California. John N. Gladden started the firm with backing from the Los Angeles Turf Club to manufacture small airplane parts, a business that boomed with the coming war.

Forrest commuted to work on his four-cylinder scooter and on lunch hour it was a conversation piece; one day, John Gladden saw the scooter and was amazed to learn that Forrest had built it himself. The scooter sparked the development of a Gladden motorcycle.

Mustang Colt 1945–1947 ★★★★

John Gladden was far-sighted. He knew of the success of the Motor Glide and other scooters conceived as alternatives to a second car for working families during the hard times that led up to the war. With Gladden's wartime business devoted solely to government contracts, he wisely was scanning the scenery for postwar success. In 1944, Gladden set up a motorscooter skunkworks with Forrest and fellow engineer Chuck Gardner.

Walt Fulton, who later started as a Mustang dealer in Kansas City, Missouri, and eventually became a Mustang sales rep and racer, remembered the inner workings at Mustang in a 1992 interview for this book. "Howard Forrest was very capable, very imaginative, and he did not hesitate to experiment. He was energetic, completely dedicated, and an enthusiast."

By 1945, Forrest and Gardner built five different prototype scooters on 12in wheels and powered by English prewar Villiers single-cylinder two-stroke engines. Based on a 59x72mm bore and stroke, the engine breathed through a rear-facing Amal carburetor and exhausted through twin ports with exhaust pipes running out along both sides of the frame to end in distinctive English-style mufflers of the time. The engine was built in unit with an integral Villiers three-speed gearbox shifted by a long-throw "suicide" hand shifter.

Photos of the prototypes show a simple scaled-down motorcycle chassis similar in lines to Forrest's homemade chassis for his four-cylinder. The tail was rigid but the front used a short-throw leading-link suspension with long coil springs running up both sides of the front forks all the way to the headlamp bracket. A single saddle seat was placed behind the pea-shaped gas tank.

The invention was to be named the Mustang after the P-51 Mustang fighter that had proven itself during World War II and for which Gladden had supplied landing struts. And it was to be called a motorcycle, not a motorscooter.

In late 1945, Gladden ordered 100 Villiers 197cc engines but the English firm had been bombed during the war; only a limited supply of its small vertical single 122cc engine was available. Gladden requested the shipment and a scaled-down Mustang was readied for production using the 122cc and 8in wheels.

The smaller Villiers two-stroke was a truly prehistoric design dating back to 1937. Overall, it was similar to the 197cc with twin exhaust ports, a rear-facing Amal carb, and Villiers unit three-speed gearbox. But the 50x62mm bore and stroke was based on a built-up crankshaft riding on a roller-bearing big end and firing through a cast-iron barrel; power was only 4hp, barely half that of the 197cc.

The Colt carried the styling of the final prototypes with the addition of stylish fishtail mufflers and a Mustang script decal on the gas tank. Lighting was blamed on Lucas, the infamous English electrical system manufacturer disdainfully nicknamed the Prince of Darkness.

For the name of the first model, Gladden added the wild horse Mustang image, calling it the Colt as plans for larger machines were in the works.

The first series of Colts were largely hand-built. The first production Colts are believed to have been sold in 1946 and continued through early 1947 when the supply of engines dried up. Between 235 and 237 Colts were believed to have been built, depending on different sources.

Model 2 1947–1950 ★★★★

In the postwar years, Gladden bought the local Kinner Motors Company, which had built a radial five-cylinder Army Air Corps training engine and before running into financial trouble, switched to producing a 19.4ci or 317.6cc single-cylinder side-valve industrial engine quaintly named the Bumble Bee, previously used to power airborne generator units.

America was the land of four-stroke engines; two-strokes were for lawn mowers, and the two-stroke Villiers never satisfied Forrest. With some modifications, the four-stroke Bumble Bee became

---

Scooter Oddity Hall of Fame: Mustang Hot-Rod Specials

The Mustangs of Howard Forrest started life as hot rods and the hot-rodding tradition never ended.

Forrest's four-cylinder motorcycle that sparked the creation of the Mustang goes down in American motorcycle history as one of the all-time unqiue creations—albeit little known among most motorcyclists who look on small wheels as toys.

While the Mustang was in production, Forrest tinkered. The list of his own Mustang specials is a long lineage:

• With aid of a sharp saw, he cut a Triumph twin-cylinder head in half and fit it to a Mustang Bumble Bee. The overhead valvetrain made for a formidable race engine.

• Always a fan of four-cylinder engines from his days racing his own Ace four-powered midget sprints, Forrest acquired a 1931 597cc Ariel Square Four engine and shoehorned it into a slightly modified Mustang chassis. This Mustang-Ariel became Forrest's own favorite commuter for several years.

• With little surgery, Forrest and partner-in-crime Chuck Gardner replaced a Bumble Bee with a BSA 350cc Gold Star engine. This hot rod became Gardner's main ride.

The Mustang's race successes caught the fancy of other hot-rodders as well. In some people's eyes, it was a cycle made to be customized. One of the remaining specials built by an unknown hand is a Thoroughbred fitted with a 500cc Matchless thumper, discovered by James M. Chappell.

Right side of the Gladden-built Bumble Bee side-valve engine mated to a separate Burman four-speed gearbox. This factory photo showed the engine as mounted in a Model 5 Delivercycle, as noted by the reinforcing down tube at left. *Michael Gerald archives*

Mfg. By – MUSTANG MOTOR PRODUCTS CORP.
Glendale, Calif.

GENERAL SPECIFICATIONS

WHEEL BASE:	50 inches	LENGTH OVERALL:	72-1/2 inches
TIRE SIZE:	4:00 x 12	HEIGHT OVERALL:	41 inches
SEAT HEIGHT:	27-1/2 inches	WIDTH AT HANDLEBAR:	28 inches
ENGINE:	Single cylinder, 4-cycle L head	BRAKES:	Rear wheel, internal expanding, foot operated.
BORE:	2 7/8 inches		Front wheel, internal
STROKE:	3 inches		expanding, hand operated.
PISTON DISPLACEMENT:	19.4 cubic inches	FRONT FORKS:	Telescopic, with hard
COMPRESSION RATIO:	7:1		chrome plated and polished
CARBURETOR:	Amal, 7/8 inch bore		actuating tubes.
IGNITION:	Flywheel, incased magneto	POWER OUTPUT:	10.5 horsepower @5000 RPM
LIGHTING:	Flywheel, incased generator	MAXIMUM SPEED:	70 - 72 MPH
TRANSMISSION:	Burman, 3-speed, toe shift, enclosed kickstarter	GROUND CLEARANCE:	5-1/2 inches
		FUEL CAPACITY:	2.4 gallons
CLUTCH:	Multi-cork plate type, oil mist, enclosed in primary case, hand operated.	OIL CAPACITY:	3 pints
		GAS MILEAGE:	70 miles per gallon

The Mustang Model 4 Special of 1957 added features to the Standard to make it truly gallop. These included a front brake, higher, 7.0:1 compression cylinder head, and high-lift camshaft as well as a high-level exhaust pipe and higher price. The Special breathed through an Amal 7/8in carburetor and produced 10.5hp at 5000rpm. As famed Mustang racer Walt Fulton recalled in 1992, "The Mustang was far superior to anything else available at that time in the lightweight motorcycle or scooter class." *Michael Gerald archives*

the new powerplant for a revised version of the Mustang Colt, called the Model 2 with the engine and other changes.

The Bumble Bee cranked out 9.5hp, which was much more "American." Bore and stroke measured 2 7/8x3in.

The engine still breathed through a British-made Amal carburetor and an English Burman three-speed gearbox now with a foot-change backed up the engine and housed the kickstart; early Burmans had exposed lever return springs until this was changed on the Model 4 Mustang. For ignition and lighting, a Wico generator was driven by a belt from the exposed flywheel.

In 1947, the Mustang became the first American motorcycle to use telescopic forks. Walt Fulton was kind in calling the forks "unsophisticated," but they did the job, and the Mustang now rode on 4.00x12in disc wheels.

Ads of the time from the factory and its major distributor, Johnson Motors of Los Angeles (which was the West Coast Triumph importer), reflected the two-faced image of the Mustang. On one hand, the firm promoted the 70mpg fuel efficiency; on the other, it promoted the 9.5hp and a top speed of more than 60mph.

With the success of the motorcycles, Gladden separated Mustang as a division with Forrest as chief engineer and Chuck Gardner as production manager.

Model 3 Delivercycle 1949 and
Model 5 1950–1956, 1963–1965 ★★

Salsbury had its Cycletow, but this was only an adaption—"training wheels"—added to the basic two wheeler. In the world of big motorcycles, Harley-Davidson built its three-wheeler Servi-Car and Indian its DispatchTow, both of which fit the market better and sold well for years. Thus it was little surprise when Mustang followed suit with a tricycle-chassis delivery scooter.

With the addition of trunk and a Crosley miniature automobile rear end, the Model 3 became a commercial delivery machine; a tow bar attachment allowed auto dealerships to deliver cars with the Model 3 in tow and then have their drivers return on three wheels. They were hardy enough that oil well service companies also used them.

The Model 5 updated the Model 3, soon with a Burman four-speed gearbox to handle the heavier loads. A later option was electric starting, which was never offered on the Mustang cycles.

By 1956, Delivercycle production was discontinued. But in 1963, new Mustang management revived the Model 5 and continued to build it until Mustang's last days.

Model 4 Standard and
Special 75 1950–1958 ★★★

The Model 2 was updated in 1950 as the Model 4 and offered in a Standard and Special model.

The chief modification marking the Model 4 was the reversal of the Bumble Bee engine in the frame, placing the intake and exhaust manifolds to the front of the chassis. This promoted airflow to the carburetor and cooling air for the exhuast manifold.

In addition, the exposed flywheel was now enclosed as a flywheel magneto replaced the belt-driven generator. The clutch was a multi-cork plate type lubricated by engine oil mist. The Burman three-speed gearbox mounting was also changed, bolting directly to the engine versus to the frame—a change that shaved 15lb from the cycle, according to Michael Gerald's history. The four-speed Burman that had been used to handle the extra workload of the Model 5 was soon to be optionally available on the Special.

The gas tank capacity was enlarged to 2.4gal by converting to two tank sections in the style of the Harley-Davidson and Indian big twins of the time.

The Model 4 Special added features to the Standard, including a front brake, higher, 7.0:1 compression cylinder head, and high-lift camshaft as well as a high-level exhaust pipe and higher price. The Special breathed through an Amal 7/8in carburetor and produced 10.5hp at 5000rpm.

With this "speed equipment," a Model 4 Special could truly gallop. The power-to-weight ratio for a 215lb cycle with a 19.4ci engine was pure hot rod. The acceleration made you hold onto the reins, and while the hardtail and early telescopic forks didn't always hold the road, it was a spirited beast. Top speed was advertised at 70–72mph.

Fulton began racing a Model 4 Special in the late 1940s and lauded its handling and ride. "The frame was designed for stability. Early on we had problems with the frame breaking but that was fixed with the tube framing. Everything worked in harmony and the engine was well placed in the chassis. It didn't have the comfort of the big motorcycles but it was adequate for its size, power, and the types of riders.

"The Mustang was far superior to anything else available at that time in the lightweight motorcycle or scooter class."

Model 8 Special 1957 ★★★★

The Model 8 was a short-lived Special based on the Model 4 Special with the same 10.5hp 19.4ci engine but with a cast-aluminum primary case. The 8 added the heavy-duty four-speed

Walt Fulton and the Mustang Racers: So Fast They Were Outlawed

One of Mustang's first great race victories came at the hands of Walt Fulton on September 3, 1950, as Mustang was proud to advertise in a 1950 dealer poster. Fulton rode a showroom demonstrator Model 4 Special with a high-compression cylinder head and 20 percent lower gear ratio to win a Tulsa, Oklahoma, endurance run of 225 miles. Fulton's Mustang beat out sixty-four entries, with second going to an Indian Scout and third to a Harley–Davidson. The race was sponsored by the Midwest Harley–Davidson Dealers' Association, and it was the first of many humblings the big twins were to endure.

In 1951, Fulton led a factory team to the Catalina Grand Prix, the famous island race that blended city streets, dirt roads, and mountain passes into a gruelling race that simulated the Isle of Man Tourist Trophy. Fulton led the Lightweight Class by 2 1/2 minutes until the head gasket blew, but Mustang rider Tommy Bizzari took second.

The 1952 Catalina saw Fulton sidelined as well, but in 1953, he was determined to win the 100-miler. Running a bored and stroked 497cc Bumble Bee in Open Class, Fulton picked up seventy positions in the four laps his Mustang survived. "The reason it broke was that it had been prepared too quickly," Fulton recalled in 1992.

"They literally rolled it off the ferry boat, I got on, and the race started."

At the same time, Mustangs were challenging the big twins in desert racing, scrambles, and TTs. Howard Forrest's son, Jim, said he believed the small wheels gave the Mustangs an advantage with less of a gyroscopic effect than the large 20-inchers that were used on the big bikes. In addition, the power-to-weight ratio of a 240lb cycle with a 375cc race engine was all a rider could wish for.

Fulton also lauded the small wheels. "The Mustang could out-perform all the other big motorcycles through its handling. It was not horsepower, although the engine was torquey because of the big bore. The small wheels required less motion to get the motorcycle to perform. Coming into a turn with a big motorcycle, you had to brake and set yourself up to slide through it. It was full throttle with the Mustang; you just turned it sideways and went."

Fulton listed three items that made the Mustang a race winner: good handling, low-end torque, and "My determination to go where I wanted to go." And as he taunted in 1992, "In those days, I would have pitted the Mustang against anything that came along."

Fulton once raced his Mustang on Harley–Davidson's home turf in Milwaukee and the race came down to the Mustang versus a

Salesman-turned-racer Walt Fulton at 100mph on a souped-up Mustang hot rod at Rosamond dry lake in California. Fulton's flat-out style would later be copied by rider Rollie Free on a Vincent Black Lightning when he rode in only a bathing suit to beat Harley–Davidson's speed record. But Fulton eschewed the big motorcycles as competition for the Mustang: "I could have been riding it hands off at 100mph." Michael Gerald archives

Harley. "It was just me versus Carroll Resweber on a factory Harley–Davidson—a beautiful factory bike. We went around and around trading the lead until he finally quit. He came in with blood running down his hands."

Fulton was a well-respected competitor; he and his son went on to race for Harley–Davidson. After the Mustang years, Fulton worked 8 1/2 years for Triumph before going to Japan to help Honda set up its US operation. He later did the same for Suzuki.

Mustang also mounted a five-year attack on speed records. In 1947, a souped-up Forrest Mustang hit 62mph on the flats of the Rosamond dry lake in California. In 1948, it was up to 77mph, 86.12mph in 1950, and 90mph in 1951. In April 1952, Forrest and Fulton combined efforts to hit a 100.0mph average in four runs at Rosamond. Fulton remembered the day well, commenting on the Mustang's inherent stability at speed, "I could have been riding it hands off at 100mph."

Following the 1953 Catalina, Harley–Davidson, Indian, and Triumph browbeat the American Motorcyclist Association into ruling cycles with wheels smaller than 16in out of Class C racing. The Mustang was so fast it was outlawed.

Mustang Model 8 Special flyer from 1957. Powered by the Model 4 Special's 10.5hp 19.4ci engine, the 8 added a cast-aluminum primary case and heavy-duty four-speed gearbox as well as a deluxe color scheme. The flipside of this flyer hinted at the arrival of a Model 8 Standard, but alas, it was never built. *Michael Gerald archives*

gearbox of the Model 5 Deliverycycle in place of the three-speed Burman of the 4, which was a great advantage.

The 8 was also finished in a deluxe color scheme. The frame and forks were Lustre Black while the fenders were black with white striping, and the gas tank was black with a red panel outlined in white. The Mustang decal was gold and black.

A Mustang Model 8 flyer promised the future arrival of a Model 8 Standard with the same paint scheme but using a low pipe, standard cylinder head, and without the front brake. The 8 Standard never went into production as such.

Colt 1956–1958 ★★★

With the Model 4 as the deluxe model, Mustang decided to create scaled-down economy cycle and chose to look back to its beginnings and named it the Colt.

This new Colt continued with the Bumble Bee side-valve engine but detuned to 8hp; a 5hp throttle governor could also be specified, making the Colt legal for young riders in certain states.

Instead of the standard clutch, an automatic centrifugal clutch was used as on the Cushman automatics. Use of this clutch was possible as the new Colt eschewed a gearbox for economy of production and lower sales prices.

The new model featured a new traingulated Earles-type front end, similar to that used on the Cushmans of the time with a lever-action linkage that had a longer reach than that used on the first Colts. A spring damped the forks.

The new Colt was available in two-tone Banner Green and Silver Grey.

The package was aimed at kids. Ads read, "Hit the Trail! . . . to school, paper route or just good fun."

Pony 1959–1965 ★★

In 1959, Mustang reorganized its lineup giving equine names to variations on the old Model 4 versions. The Model 4 Standard became the Pony with the base 9.5hp engine and three-speed gearbox.

By 1960, the complete line would shelve the old Amal carburetors and switch to Italian-made Dell'Ortos, which were more easily adjusted and longer lasting than the older English units.

Mustang began offering a full line of accessories to keep its cycles as well dressed as Cushman's new line of Super Eagles. Options included a chrome luggage rack, crash bars, folding kickstart lever, speedometer, and high-level exhaust system. A 5hp engine conversion was also option-

Consider the odds of reaching your destination alive, and you'll realize Magellan was a wimp. Scooter explorers and conquistadors headed off for the four corners of the globe with full fuel tanks and extra inner tubes. American Dick Miller rode this Mustang around the world in 1954, which was probably one of the bravest things for any human being to ever attempt. *Michael Gerald archives*

al, replacing the old throttle governor; the special engine was fitted with a sleeve and new pistons to decrease the bore, giving a 14.7ci displacement.

Bronco 1959–1965 ★★★

With the change in 1959 model changes, the Bronco was created as deluxe edition of the Pony, with a 10.5hp engine and the three-speed.

Ads in 1959, show the complete line riding on the old disc wheels, but soon after only the Pony kept the discs as the Bronco came with new Italian-made 12in spoked wheels and full-hub-width brakes.

Stallion 1959–1965 ★★★★

The Stallion replaced the former Model 4 Special, riding now on spoked wheels and using the Burman four-speed transmission that had originally been used in the Model 5 Delivercycle. In addition, the Stallion lived up to its name with a special high-lift camshaft creating a 12hp, high-torque Bumble Bee engine featuring a chrome-plated flywheel.

Thoroughbred 1960–1965 ★★★

Harley-Davidson had followed Mustang's lead in the use of telescopic forks; now Mustang followed The Motor Company in moving away from the rigid hardtail and developing a new frame with a rear swing-arm suspended by dual shock absorbers. Walt Fulton led the way, adding a swing-arm and suspensions to the tail of one of his racing creations, as he recalled; Mustang's new chief engineer Chuck Gardner added the swing-arm to create the new Thoroughbred that became Mustang's top of the line model in 1960.

The Thoroughbred used the 12hp Bumble Bee of the Stallion and the new wire-laced wheels. But the new frame design allowed for the addition of a two-person bench seat with an optional toolbox hidden below.

Trail Machine 1962–1965 ★

In 1962, Gladden stockholders voted in a new general manager at Mustang, Ralph L. Coson. In the next few years, the company was shook up as John Gladden and Chuck Gardner resigned, followed by many other key personnel. Times were tough and the market was taking its toll.

In 1965, Coson supervised the production of the Mustang Trail Machine as an attempt to take back market share. The off-road mini-bike seemed to be the hot item in the US market; Cushman had recently offered its Trailster, and Mustang was not to be outdone.

The Trail Machine had been Gardner's last design for Mustang. It used a Briggs & Stratton engine in a basic, no-frills frame. Two models were offered: the Rigid Frame Model and the Rear Suspension Model with their differences readily apparent.

The Trail Machine took Mustang off the right track. The firm's specialty had been in building a unique motorcycle cum scooter, and the monies paid to developing the Trail Machine ultimately spurred on Mustang's demise.

Mustang's Demise

Just as availability of the English-made Villiers engine had stumbled the Mustang at its birth, availability of the English Burman gearbox spelled its doom twenty years later. The English motorcycle marques such as Matchless that had used the Burman boxes shifted to redesigned unit engines; suddenly the Burman was obsolete.

And then came Honda. The new line of inexpensive and reliable Japanese motorcycles hobbled Mustang where it hurt most: sales. Buyers needed to lay out $500 for a Mustang and Honda undercut them.

The year 1965 was a sad one for American motorscooters. Cushman curtailed production on its Silver Eagle line, and Mustang production was limited in 1965. In 1966, production ceased, with the new owners continuing to stock Mustang replacement parts.

Fulton remembered Mustang's last days: "John Gladden was purely a business man. He expanded his company into something that was totally foreign to his main line of building industrial engine and airplane hydraulics, and he got in over his head.

"I contend to this day that if Gladden had both pulled the plug on Mustang Motorcycles and Forrest had been allowed to use his imagination,

Mustang could have cornered the whole light-weight motorcycle market."

It was not to be.

Don Orr Stallions ★★★★

In 1971, Los Angeles chopper customizer Don Orr bought the rights to the Mustang name and began production of custom-built Mustangs. He named his new creation the Stallion, but while it used many original parts, it also differed from the original Mustang Stallion—and differed from unit to unit due to parts availability. Many had extended chopper forks. During the one year, Orr was estimated to have built between thirty to fifty Stallions, according to Michael Gerald; others state that less than a dozen were made.

By the end of the year, Orr's Mustangs were mavericks, according to the California DMV. Orr ran onto the wrong side of the law's paperwork beauracracy; his new Stallions failed to meet legal lighting requirements and so he did not have proper ownership titles for the cycles when they were sold.

As quickly as he had arrived on the scene, Orr was gone. But a few of his rare custom-built Stallions have survived, a collectible blend of exclusivity and outlaw history.

They Shoot Horses—Or Do They?

In 1972, Circle Industries of El Monte, California, bought the Mustang rights with plans to revive the old warhorse. But the plans failed to materialize into motorcycles, and Circle soon auctioned off more than 20 tons of components to former Mustang dealer Roy Stone of Waco, Texas.

Stone has done more than anyone in carrying on the Mustang heritage. He continued to supply replacement parts into the 1990s. Stone sold the frame-making jigs to Alan Wenzel of Dallas, Texas, who manufactures replacement Stallion frames. Other parts suppliers have also continued the Mustang tradition to this day.

MV Agusta Italy

In 1945, an odd scenario was unfolding. At the Piaggio factory, Enrico Piaggio was turning from wartime aviation production to a novel peacetime venture: a motorscooter to be called the Vespa. At the same time at the new MV Agusta firm, Sicilian aristocrat Count Domenico Agusta was switching from his aviation love to a novel peacetime creation: an economical, basic motorcycle to be called the Vespa.

MV, soon to be called MV Agusta, stood for Meccanica Verghera, the latter being the name of the factory site near Milan. MV's Vespa was based on a 98cc two-stroke single, wet clutch, unit construction, and two-speed gearbox. The specifications could have easily been for the Piaggio Vespa.

MV Agusta always concentrated its energy on racing motorcycles and built scooters and road bikes just to fund the factory race team. The racing was not in vain, but MV's scooter designs left little reason for vanity. This original Model B from 1949 was MV's first scooter effort, fitted with a two-stroke 123cc engine in a Vespa-influenced pressed-steel unit chassis and carrying its wheels on single-sided stub axles. By 1950, the B was replaced by the tube frame C. Owner: Vittorio Tessera.

But Piaggio registered the name first, and Agusta's cycle went on the market as the MV 98. And the two went their divergent ways from there: Piaggio to fame with the Vespa scooter; and MV to fame with its numerous racing motorcycles that would win thirty-seven manufacturers' world championships. Alongside its racing motorcycles, MV always produced street bikes as a way to finance Count Agusta's love of competition—much like Enzo Ferrari did.

Model B 1949 ★★★★

After developing a prototype Model A scooter, MV introduced its Model B 125cc scooter in 1949 with full monocoque bodywork and one-side front and rear lug axles—again, specifications shared with the Vespa scooter.

The engine was a two-stroke single of 53x56mm creating 5hp at 4800rpm. Cooling was by fan with a flywheel magneto giving spark; a wet multiplate clutch connected to the four-speed gearbox. The tires were 3.50x10in.

Popolare, Normale, and CGT 1950–1952 ★★

In 1950, the B was accompanied by the Popolare scooter, a bare-bones economy scooter that looked like a Lambretta from the seat backward and a Vespa from the seat forward. Renamed the Normale, by 1951 it was renamed again as the CGT, or C Gran Turismo; in 1952, the CGT was available in 150cc form.

While MV's first scooter followed the Vespa, its second scooter design, this restored CGT, was influenced by the Lambretta. The open bodywork and single large-diameter backbone frame all spoke of the Lambretta C. But while Innocenti had made its name with scooters, MV never became a dominant force in the field. Owner: Vittorio Tessera.

Model C, and CSL 1950–1951 ★★★

Also in 1950, the Model C replaced the B with a tube-steel chassis covered by unstressed bodywork bearing similar styling. In 1951, the CSL, or C Super Lusso, was offered. Production was halted by the end of 1951.

Ovunque 1952–1954 ★★

In 1951, the CGT was replaced by the Ovunque, translated as Everywhere. Using a tube frame, portions of the body were still uncovered. And while the engine was the same as the CGT, the gearbox was a three-speed. The first model, the Ovunque Tipo 51 for 1951, had one exhaust pipe; it was followed by the Ovunque Tipo 52 from 1952 with twin pipes. Production ended in 1954.

Chicco 1960–1964 ★★

MV held itself back from the scooter market until 1959 when it showed the Bik and Chicco scooters. The Bik had a four-stroke 166cc with semi-hydraulic tappets, but unfortunately never went into production.

The Chicco was built from 1960–1964 with steel monocoque bodywork that was easily mistaken for a Vespa but with a Lambretta's fixed front fender. The horizontal two-stroke 155cc engine created 5.8hp at 5200rpm with a four-speed gearbox and 3.50x10in tires. The Chicco was widely exported, coming to the United States via Cosmopolitan Motors, the Parilla importer.

MV's scooters, while interesting, were always second place to the Vespa, Lambretta, and Iso.

Early 1951 flyer for the new MV Agusta Model C scooter showed the little boys watching the big boys doing the real thing: the Milano–Taranto road race, contested by MV. The message was obvious: scooters were for children; racing was for adults. This focus would always hurt the development and marketing of MV's scooters. *Vittorio Tessera archives*

The firm's winning motorcycles meanwhile command monstrous prices and the scooters are often weighted down under price tags that are proportionally high due to the name recognition.

Neue Amag Switzerland ★★

Sited at Baden, the firm offered its Piccolo, or Small, scooter in 1950, a miniature scooter motorcycle in the style of the American Mustang. In 1951, the Piccolo was renamed the Ami, or Friend, and was fitted with a Sachs 98cc. Also in 1951, the Ami A3 was launched with full bodywork, a two-person bench seat, and 150cc Sachs.

In 1953, the Ami Achilles A6 was offered as a Sport model with full bodywork; a 175cc Sachs was optional.

NSU Germany

The history of NSU dates back to April Fool's Day, 1880, when Christian Schmidt founded a company to build *strickmaschinen*—sewing machines. The firm was soon set up in the village of Neckarsulm in the Baden–Württemberg region of Germany. The name NSU stood for Neckarsulm Strickmaschinen Union. In 1887, a new owner, Schmidt's brother-in-law Gottlieb Benzhoff, took the reins and started production of bicycles. By 1901, NSU expanded to construct its first small motorcycles powered by Swiss-made 234cc Zédel engines. By 1955, NSU was the largest motorcycle maker in Germany.

During World War II, NSU built its amazing HK101 Kettenkrad tank-tread motorcycles for the Wehrmacht. After the war, Germany was in need of economical lightweight transportation, the fertile breeding ground for motorscooters the world over. Italy had gone through a similar history but had recovered more quickly than Germany postwar, so it was a far-thinking NSU that approached Innocenti to build Lambrettas under license.

NSU-Lambretta 125 1950–1954 and 150 1954–1956 ★★★

In 1950, NSU began fabricating Lambrettas in Neckarsulm under a five-year contract. The first NSU scooters used Innocenti C/LC engines shipped from the Lambrate works; bodywork was stamped out at the nearby Volkswagen factory.

The Lambretta C/LC 125 engine had a 52x58mm bore and stroke for 123cc. Running through a three-speed gearbox and shaft drive, the 125 was good for 4.5hp at 4500rpm and a top speed of 73km/h.

But the Germans had no patience for certain features of the Lambretta that they found lacking in good teutonic over-engineering. Soon, NSU was building the majority of components for its scooters, and the NSU models surpassed the Innocenti Lambretta in the quality of brakes, Bosch 6 volt horn, Magura seats, and higher-output, 30 watt flywheel magneto at a time when the Lam-

The first MV Chicco imported into the United States, pictured in front of the Cosmpolitan Motors showroom in 1960. The Chicco's horizontal two-stroke 155cc engine created 5.8hp at 5200rpm with a four-speed gearbox. The 10in wheels were carried on stub axles.

bretta LC had only 25 watts. The Germans also added a glovebox behind the legshield topped by a small dash featuring the ignition switch, speedometer with odometer, choke, and a handy clock.

The styling of the NSU retained the lines of the LC with open handlebars. On the left legshield, NSU added its logo above the Lambretta nameplate. Colors available were beige, mittelgrau und hellblau.

At the 1953 Frankfurt Motorcycle Show, NSU unveiled a new 12 volt electric-start scooter powered by two 6 volt batteries wire in series; ignition remained 6 volt. This Luxus-Lambretta also included parking lights!

In 1954, NSU introduced a 150cc version with 6.2hp at 5200rpm. Top speed was 81km/h but the scooter retained the three-speed gearbox when a four-speed would have done it well.

In 1950, only 743 NSU-Lambrettas were built; in 1951, a mere 1,100. By the end of its life, however, production of the NSU Lambretta in all versions was prolific—117,045 units—but never approached the success of Innocenti's original.

Prima D 1956–1958 ★★★

The NSU-Innocenti contract expired in 1955 and was not renewed. Instead, in 1956, NSU introduced a Lambretta that was not a Lambretta; this was NSU's version of what a Lambretta should be.

Always competitive and class-conscious, NSU chose to call its new scooter the Prima, Italian for First.

The styling of the Prima D belied its Lambretta LC heritage but it was masqued beneath gaudy chromework, including side-cover trim, a single-piece headlamp/horn bezel, and a bulbous front fender bumper. The handlebars were now covered in a sheetmetal sleeve and electric start was standard. Colors included jade green, wine, polar blue, and several two-tone schemes: green and black, and ivory white paired with turquoise or racing red.

The engine was NSU's version of the shaft-drive Lambretta LC, still producing 6.2hp at 5200rpm with the one-cylinder two-stroke engine of 57x58mm bore and stroke. With a three-speed transmission, the Prima ran on 4.00x8in wheels and tipped the scales at 123kg.

The only substantial difference between the Prima D and the new Lambretta LD of 1954 was in NSU's use of pressed-steel front forks versus Innocenti's tried-and-true steel-tube forks.

KÖNIGLICH
freut sich Deutschlands Schönheitskönigin 1950. Susanne Erichsen. Das kann sie auch, denn für die elegante Dame ist die elegante NSU-Lambretta die eleganteste Lösung.

"Mommy Dearest" rode a Lambretta, in this case an NSU 125 with bodywork courtesy of the Volkswagen factory. If Hoffman's Vespa presided as the queen of the German scooter world, NSU's Lambretta kept the Bismarck lineage and reigned as the king of Deutschland's scooter empire.

Scooter Oddity Hall of Fame: NSU Double-Scooter Car

In 1953, NSU cobbled up a prototype car made from two NSU-Lambretta 125 scooters welded together side by side. Bathtub-like rear bodywork was added on to allow for four saddle seats. The handlebars on the left-side scooter had a bar running across to the steering rod of the right-side scooter so the two front wheels could be controlled by the one set of handlebars. To complete the automobile styling, a single chrome front bumper stretched across both front fenders, presumably with a pivot system to allow it to move with the wheels as they leaned into turns.

A photo from the NSU archives shows a beaming family of four out for a spin in the NSU-Werbeabteilung with a Volkswagen Bug in the background; presumably this was the family's second car, a "convertible" for Sunday putt-putting along the autobahn.

The world remains a poorer place as the NSU-Werbeabteilung never went into production.

The Prima D was only planned as a stopgap scooter to serve NSU's faithful during the year when the contract with Lambretta was finished and a new NSU scooter could be made ready.

Prima Fünfstern 1957–1960 ★★★★

In 1957, NSU created an original scooter, the Prima Fünfstern, known variously throughout the world as the Five Star or by the roman numeral, V.

NSU engineers were schooled in Lambretta design, and the Prima V carried on with a central large-gauge tube frame covered by sheetmetal bodywork; the old Lambretta LC styling was still visible underneath the new, smoothed-out lines. Chrome hid the similarities along with a bulbous new front fender that was derisively said to be styled from a leftover Wehrmacht army helmet—which was in truth being kind.

The most fascinating feature of the new NSU was its exotic engine design. It was still a one-cylinder two-stroke but the cylinder was horizontal and transverse to the chassis. The flywheel magneto was at the front of the engine with the new four-speed gearbox to the rear of the crankshaft with a single-plate clutch mediating between the two. Final drive was via bevel gears.

The complete engine unit was suspended from the frame by a front pivoting mount and damped at the rear by a shock absorber with well-cushioned preload to handle the best German beer drinker. In an ironic twist of NSU and Innocenti's interwoven fates, the Italians would later use a similar design with their 125 Li Series of 1958.

The electric-start Prima V engine was of 174cc from an oversquare design of 62x57.6mm and a four-speed gearbox. Power was now 9.5hp, all electrics were 12 volts, and the wheels had finally grown to 3.50x10in but with an overall weight of 138kg, top speed had climbed to only 90km/h.

Much of that weight was due to the luxury equipment. Along with speedometer, horn, and electric start, the V also had an electric fuel gauge and foglight.

The Prima V was exported worldwide and imported into the United States by Butler & Smith, Inc. of New York City, which also imported the later Prima III as the Deluxe. Butler & Smith was a renowned promoter, also carrying the BMW line—it even got a Prima V on the "Price is Right" TV game show in June 1959. The correct, winning price was $555.

Friendship knows no boundaries when a chrome-ladened NSU Prima V compliments the scene. This scene of the pastoral German countryside predates the eventual outlawing of scooters from the autobahn, which led to their decline as a serious form of transportation for Germans.

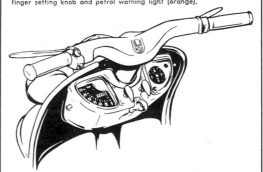

The Instrument Panel

Here are located the speedometer, knob for the starting device, the ignition lock for the starter-ignition-lighting switch, the lighting switch for fog lamp, the dynamo charging light (red) the clock with finger setting knob and petrol warning light (orange).

With a dashboard often more intricate than cars of the time, the NSU Prima wowed riders with an array of gauges, knobs, and buttons that would make a jet fighter pilot green with envy. Technology of this kind marked the Funfstern as one of the fanciest scooters of its day. *Deutsches Motorräd Register/W. Conway Link archives*

Five stars was recognized worldwide as the highest rating; the Prima Fünfstern was NSU's two-wheeled answer to Mercedes–Benz. This was the scooter that the good German plutocrat could love, a blend of world-class engineering, luxury features, and power.

Prima III K 1958–1960 and KL 1959–1960 ★★★

The Prima III was a simplified, democratic version of the V with two stars-worth of features deleted. This included a smaller, 57mm bore engine of 146cc producing 7.4hp and a top speed of 84km/h. The bodywork was also revised with a new, modernistic rear-end treatment. And of course, the III cost less.

The standard K model featured bare-bones trimwork, black saddle seats, and any color of paint as long as it was ivory. The K stood for "mit Kickstarter," according to the ads.

In 1959, the Luxus version was offered with electric start, chromed trim, two-tone color scheme, and an optional dual bench seat.

Maxima Prototype 1960 ★★★★

In 1960, NSU engineers began work on a prototype of the ultimate scooter, the Maxima. Designed as an alternative to the high-class Heinkel Tourist and Maicomobil, its name reflected its quality as the top-of-the-line Prima model, blending the words Maxi and Prima.

The Maxima was powered by NSU's exotic Prima V engine still at 175cc but now producing 10.5hp for a 95km/h top speed.

Instead of going ahead with the Maxima, NSU curtailed scooter production in 1960. By the end of its production life, some 69,000 Prima V and III units had been constructed. NSU now chose to concentrate on building automobiles using the avant garde Wankel rotary engine

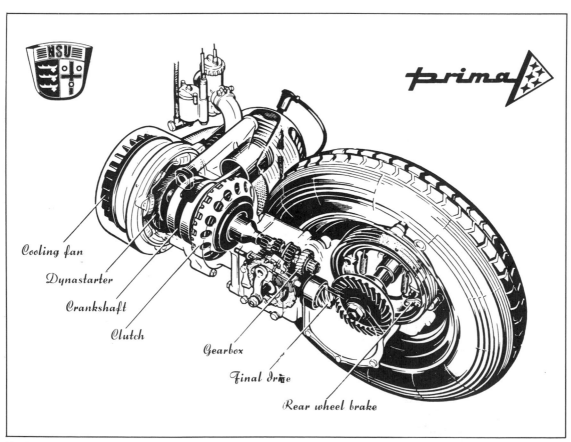

Cooling fan
Dynastarter
Crankshaft
Clutch
Gearbox
Final drive
Rear wheel brake

Mechanical cutaway from the NSU instruction book of the fascinating and innovative Prima V and III engine. The horizontal cylinder moved transversely to the chassis with the cooling fan, flywheel magneto, and electric starter at the front side of the crankshaft. The gearbox drove direct to the rear wheel via bevel gears. *Deutsches Motorräd Register/W. Conway Link archives*

instead of motorscooters as the German economy had rebounded figuratively from two wheels to four.

Oscar UK ★★

The Oscar scooter was created by Projects and Development Ltd of Blackburn. It appeared as a startling prototype at the 1953 London Show; yet while production was promised for several years, the Oscar ended its life in prototype limbo.

OLD France ★

Age had nothing to do with the name, although the OLD's Miniscoot could hardly be called modern. The Levallois-based company was known more for its luggage racks than mobiles, and its 75cc miniscoot bore a striking resemblance to a ski rack with a pull-start engine.

Pannonia Hungary ★

Pannonia motorcycles and scooters were built at the Mogürt factory in Budapest, sharing the assembly lines with the Czepel Danuvia motorcycles—and often design and parts. Pannonia's Panni R50 scooter was powered by a 48cc two-stroke of 38x42mm giving 1.8hp.

Panther UK ★★

The famous Panther works in Cleckheaton dated back to the pioneer days of motorcycling. In 1959, it released its Princess scooter based on a 174cc Villiers 2L engine with either kickstart or optional electric leg.

By 1961, the Princess was available in four models: 174cc kickstart and electric start versions and 197cc kickstart and electric start. The Princess lasted until 1963, by which time Panther was in receivership.

Parilla Italy

Moto Parilla was created in the back of a truck diesel-injector repair shop on the outskirts of Milan in 1946. Whereas most of the immediate postwar motorcycle firms built scooters and small

The Panther Princess of 1959 bore more than a passing resemblance to Innocenti's new TV1. It was powered by a 174cc Villiers 2L engine with either kickstart or optional electric leg. The frame was a conventional tube affair covered by bodywork shared with Dayton and Sun. *Mick Walker archives*

cycles to capitalize on the need for economical transportation, founder Giovanni Parrilla went with his heart. He began by handcrafting a limited series of beautiful 250cc overhead-cam racing motorcycles; only later did he mass-produce motorscooters and then merely to provide funding for his racing effort.

At one time in the 1950s, Moto Parilla was one of the major Italian makes, ranking fourth behind Piaggio, Innocenti, and Gilera in production. Founder Giovanni Parrilla opted to drop one *r* from his Spanish name for easier Italian pronouncation of the motorcycle marque. But like Iso, which produced thousands of scooters in its time, Parilla has largely been forgotten in this age of Honda and Yamaha.

Levriere (Greyhound) 125 and 150 1952–1959 ★★★

Moto Parilla's motorscooter was introduced in January 1952 at the Milan Fiera Campioniara. As Parilla's logo was a racing greyhound, the scooter was named the Levriere or "Greyhound."

Giovanni Parrilla chose to give the scooter buyer the option of a more refined scooter with a powerful engine, telescopic forks, large, 12in wheels, and stylish bodywork. The Levriere was built in large numbers and sold well through its history, but it never challenged the inexpensively efficient Vespas and Lambrettas.

The chassis was primarily that of a motorcycle with a central duplex tube frame covered by sheetmetal bodywork. The bodywork was used not only to shield rider from the engine and road grime but also for aerodynamics: the central step-through section channelled cool air from behind the front wheel back to the engine and transmission and then out through side vents.

The first Levriere was offered with a single-cylinder two-stroke 125cc with square internal measurements of 54x54mm. A three-speed gearbox was shifted by a twist grip. Secondary drive was to be chain.

A unique feature of the Greyhound was its 3.00x12in wheels, which were again of motorcycle design featuring Borrani aluminum-alloy rims laced to 112mm hubs with drum brakes front and rear.

In 1953, a 150cc version was offered based on a large, 60mm bore engine capable of producing 7hp at 5700rpm. The 150 model ran via a four-

Parilla's Levriere, or Greyhound (never mind the misspelling on this ad), scooter was not pretty but it was functional and reliable. It created a whole family tree of Levriere copies: Sweden's Husqvarna bought Parilla chassis in 1955 and mounted HVA engines; Germany's Victoria Peggy was a Levriere in disguise; and in addition, the Levriere was the major influence behind Zündapp's first Bella. The Parilla was prolific, being sold around the world throughout Europe, the United States, and as far east as Vietnam.

The Slughi offered all of the advantages of a scooter to motorcyclists. The pressed-steel bodywork covered the tube frame and all the potentially dirty parts, such as the engine, chain, and rear wheel. Legshields, windshield, and saddlebags were also available. Like Parilla's Levriere, the Slughi had a long career, being sold throughout Europe, into the United States as the Ramjet, and even being copied by a Japanese maker. *Moto Parilla archives*

Peugeot got it right the first time with its stylish line of scooters. Although primarily sold in France, some models were exported to neighboring countries as well as the United States. With a glowing ivory paint job and dapper whitewalls, this 1955 Peugeot scooter was perfect for cruising the Parisian sidewalk cafés and asphyxiating the hordes of expatriates with two-stroke exhaust. *Deutsches Motorräd Register/W. Conway Link archives*

speed gearbox but all other features were identical. Top speed was advertised at 85km/h.

Slughi (Ramjet) 1959–1961 ★★★

In 1957, Parilla showed its new Slughi 99 at the Milan Show. Unorthodoxy prevailed: the backbone of the Slughi—named for a breed of desert racing greyhounds—was of pressed steel with other sheet steel body panels covering the engine and much of the 2.75x17in rear wheel. The Deluxe version had legshields, panniers, and windshield.

Original plans called for a horizontal single-cylinder 98cc overhead-valve four-stroke but production finally commenced in 1959 with a 125cc two- and four-stroke offered.

All things considered, the Slughi was a motorcycle version of the Vespa. And while it never sold as well as the scooter, the poor sales were due more to Parilla's financial health at the time than to the Slughi's failure.

Imported into the United States, the Slughi was renamed the Ramjet and fitted with a jet ornament launching from the front fender. A copy of the Slughi was also sold on the Japanese market beginning in 1959.

Oscar Prototype 1960 ★★★★★

Moto Parilla created one of the most fascinating scooter prototypes in 1960, but like the Rumi prototypes of the same year, the Oscar was fated to prototype limbo.

The bodywork of the Oscar was sleek and stylish, like a refined Lambretta. But it was the engine that was the most unique.

While Rumi was looking at a V-twin, Parilla created a horizontal two-stroke twin similar in layout—but little else—to Rumi's classic powerplant. The electric-start Parilla engine displaced 160cc and featured double cooling fans drawing air through channels between the inner and outer walls of the crankcase. Backed by a four-speed transmission, the motor-gearbox unit pivoted on a front mount and was suspended at the rear by shock absorbers. Primary drive was by duplex chain, whereas secondary drive was by gears to the rear hub.

Development of the promising Oscar came at the wrong time for Parilla. In 1961, Giovanni Parilla was forced to sell out to a holding company, SIL, to avoid bankruptcy. Moto Parilla soldiered on for two more years but its soul was gone.

Parillas were imported into the United Kingdom and the United States through much of their run. The US importer, Cosmopolitan Motors of Hatboro, Pennsylvania, even purchased the factory's stock in 1963 and continued limited Parilla assembly in the United States until 1967.

Peripoli Italy ★★

In 1961, Peripoli introduced its Giulietta scooter named for Romeo's better half. The scooter was a jolly blend of fanciful styling, brilliant color, and chrome jewelery.

The Giulietta was powered by a Morini two-stroke motor of 125cc with 38x42mm and 2.8hp at 7200rpm. Top speed on the dwark 3.25x8in tires was 80km/h.

Peugeot France

Peugeot threw caution to the wind in breaking from the other large European automakers that were monomaniacally focusing on cars and risked a scooter.

S.55 1953, S.57 1954, S.57 AL 1955 and S.157 1955 ★★★

Unlike many French scooter makers, Peugeot got it right the first time with a classic design and optional 125cc or 150cc engines atop 8in wheels. The enlarged front fender borrowed directly from the bizarre Scootavia, this time actually using the space for storage and space on top it for strapping down extra luggage. Although protruding luggage space off the front didn't detract from the lines, one can't help make a correlation to a hinged toilet seat.

Two brave air force quarter marshalls trusted their Peugeot scooters enough to venture from Saigon to Paris, leaving April 21, 1956, and arriving August 25, 1956. After traversing eleven countries, their beat up Peugeots were displayed at the Salon de Paris in 1956.

S.57B 1956 and S.57C 1957 ★★★

With a new day dawning, Peugeot updated its earlier scooters, the C with larger 10in wheels and 5.1hp, up from the 4.6hp of the B.

Peugeot scooters were also sold under the name of Griffon/FMC with only different labels and names. The S.55 was the S.555, the S.57 the S.5577, and the S.157 became the S.657.

Peugeot returned to building scooters in the 1980s and 1990s, offering a variety of modern plastic scooters, including its basic ST50L and SC50L Metropolis models as well as its Rapido with red and white two-tone graphics that made up for its lack of rapid speed. At the 1992 Bologna show, Peugeot displayed its Fox 50 scooter with Buck Rogers styling, a large purposeful-looking muffler, and neon graphics.

PGO Italy–Taiwan ★

The PGO Star 50 scooter was made in Taiwan in the 1990s and imported into Italy by Rimoto of Palermo, Sicily. PGO was an obvious takeoff on Piaggio; its scooters also paid homage to the Piaggio line. With a 49.4cc engine of 40x39.3mm, the PGO was a typical modern-day plastic scooter of sharp-angled design.

Phoenix UK ★★

The H. B. Engineering firm arose from the ashes of Tottenham, London post World War II with its Phoenix scooter. Spearheaded by Ernie Barrett, the company concentrated on a line of scooters with different-size Villiers two-strokes in a common chassis with similar bodywork.

In 1956, the first model was launched at the Earl's Court Show with a 147cc 30C backed by a three-speed gearbox in a standard tubular frame with a swing-arm rear and leading-link front forks holding 3.50x8in tires. The bodywork was svelte and stylish, jewelled by chrome trim. In 1958, the range expanded to Standard and De Luxe 147cc versions.

In May 1958, the four new models were launched with facelifted styling and a fiberglass rear body section. New models included the Standard 100; 150 Super de Luxe with the kickstart 147cc 30C and dressed up by whitewall tires; the S150 with electric-start 148cc 31C; the S200 with electric-start 197cc 9E; the T250 with the Villiers 249cc 2T twin-cylinder engine with electric start and 10in wheels; and the gussied-up 250 Super de Luxe.

In 1959, the range was further expanded to fourteen models with the S prefix denoting single-cylinder and T marking the twins. The 150 De Luxe was dropped, but sidecars were available for the other three 150cc models.

New T325 and fancy 325 Super de Luxe models were offered with an electric-start 324cc Villiers 3T twin with 17hp at 5800rpm. The large-bore models were designed as mules to pull sidecars. As the 325 models' flyer promised, "The Phoenix Scooter is an accumulation of the best ideas and suggestions of a great number of people in the trade and also scooter owners themselves, and we feel sure that many happy and safe miles will be covered by the proud owners of this very British product."

In 1960, three new models were added: the Standard 200 with kickstart and the kickstart Standard 175 and the electric-start S175 both with the 174cc 2L. For 1960, the 150 Super de Luxe was upgraded to the 31C engine.

Production continued until 1964, when the Phoenix scooter died.

Piaggio Italy

Throughout the world, scooter is synonymous with Vespa. In many European countries, the names are interchangeable: in Paris, parking signs refer to all scooters as Vespas; in Italian, there is even a verb meaning "to acquire a Vespa," *vespizzare*.

Piaggio named its scooter the Vespa not for the ancient Roman emperor Titus Flavius Sabinis Vespasianus, but rather for the buzzing of its two-stroke engine that sounds like a wasp, or *vespa* in Italian. The styling of the scooter's tail also bears an odd resemblance to the wasp's abdomen.

Piaggio's scooter began its career in 1946 as the two-wheeled "car" upon which the Italian postwar recovery rode. By the 1950s, the Vespa brought freedom of mobility to large sectors of the population—and became a symbol of Italy in many foreign minds. And by the 1960s, the Vespa, along with Innocenti's Lambretta, had become a counterculture statement.

The changing image of the Vespa was chronicled in film. The 1953 William Wyler movie, *Roman Holiday,* starred Audrey Hepburn as an Italian princess who escaped the humdrum royal life of the palazzo to cavort about fairy-tale Rome on a Vespa with dashing American journalist Gregory Peck. The Who film, *Quadrophenia,* told the tale of the Mod-Rocker wars of 1960s Great Britian; the subtext was a scooter-motorcycle war, although both vehicles stood for the same thing: rebellion.

By 1993, Piaggio had built 10 million of the archetypal scooters worldwide, millions more than its closest rival, Innocenti's 4 million Lambrettas. Besides merely creating an industry, the omnipresent and omnipotent Vespa created a youth culture that was, to rework John Lennon's words, more popular than Jesus Christ or The Beatles combined.

Società Anonima Piaggio factory was founded in 1884 by Rinaldo Piaggio in Genoa, Italy, to make wood-working machinery and later, railroad cars. In 1915, Piaggio delved into aviation, developing such innovations as cabin pressurization. The firm also built a remarkable aviation engine that set twenty world records; in the 1920s, Piaggio constucted a series of remarkable racing seaplane prototypes in hope of contesting the Schneider Trophy. Rinaldo Piaggio died in 1938, leaving the factory to his sons Enrico, born in 1905, and Armando.

During World War II, Piaggio produced Fascist Italy's only heavy bomber, the P108B, which killed Benito Mussolini's son, Bruno, during a test flight crash. In the waning years of the war, the Piaggio factory at Pontedera was bombed and destroyed by the Allies; the remaining machine tools were confiscated by the Nazis. The factory was rebuilt after the end of hostilities, and Piaggio began looking for a new product to construct and sell.

Enrico Piaggio described those immediate postwar days to *American Mercury* magazine in 1957: "Our over 10,000 employees were thrown out of work by the bombings and by the fact that, as soon as the war was over, our production fell to zero. In fact, we were prohibited from making airplanes by the peace treaty. So you see it was

Holy Vespa

Enrico Piaggio professed to a "profound religious faith that guides and inspires me," as he told American Mercury in 1957. Although the Vatican didn't financially support the Vespa as it did Moto Ducati, 30,850 Italian priests did invest in scooters (most of them Vespas) in the 1950s, *Time* magazine reported in 1956. By traveling on scooters, the priests had increased the Church's religious proficiency by 3,000 percent.

But all were not equal in the eyes of the Lord. With only some of God's messengers on motorized wheels it led to "the decline of the more introverted Benedictines and foot-slogging Franciscans in favor of the fast-moving Jesuits, whose high-octane practicality thrives on the motor-scooter age," according to *Time.*

Much as the Vatican recanted its condemnation of Galileo's theories, Pope Pius XII became an avid believer in automation in the 1950s. Perhaps the Church's motorization via Vespas was an offer of apology to Piaggio for the Vatican's partisan support of Ducati in the high-stakes world of scooter politics, as His Holiness called for "greater and greater speed to the glory of God."

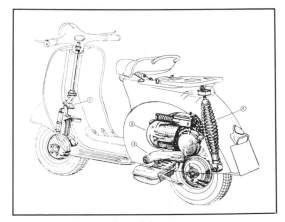

From 1946–1951, Vespa gearchange was controlled by an intricate and fastidious rod linkage that was old-fashioned and better left to primitive bicycles. In 1952, cables replaced the rods, and the Vespa finally entered the 20th century. This factory cutaway drawing shows the new cable system as well as the compact and innovative mechanical layout of the scooter. *Piaggio*

The Paperino, or Donald Duck, was the first Piaggio scooter ever built, even though Enrico Piaggio recognized it as "a horrible looking thing." Only one Paperino prototype was built before Piaggio sent designer Corradino d'Ascanio back to the drawing board, where he penned the Vespa. The bridge between the rider's legs was removed for the Vespa since Piaggio wanted to make the scooter easier for women to ride, which the firm saw as its main audience. The Paperino prototype survives in Italy.

essential that we find a new peacetime product for the sake of the Piaggio Company and our employees."

Enrico Piaggio had witnessed the lightweight Aeromoto paratrooper scooter built for the Italian Army in World War II by Volugrafo, and believed that there might be a market for a civilized version of such a scooter to provide transportation, primarily for women. He instructed his chief designer, Corradino d'Ascanio, to begin work.

The abruzzese engineer d'Ascanio led the firm's aeronautics division and was an authority on helicopter design, aircraft engines, and stressed-skin bodywork where the body was designed to serve double duty as the frame in a monocoque unitized design. Such advanced monocoque structures had been used on airplanes prewar, but their adaption to scooters was indeed cutting edge; today this design is used throughout the world in automobiles.

After a false start with a first prototype, called the Paperino, d'Ascanio created the Vespa, which

made its debut in 1946. D'Ascanio's Vespa was truly revolutionary, incorporating features of motorcycles (two wheels, easy-to-use handlebar-mounted controls, and saddle seats), airplanes (monocoque unit design and single-sided stub axles), and automobiles (protective bodywork, covered motor, and floorboards). After a rocky introduction, the scooter won acceptance, and soon Vespas were everywhere.

Since the majority of Italians couldn't afford a motorcycle, let alone a car, most of them had to settle for a "two-wheeled car," as Piaggio promoted its scooter in the postwar years. And they soon came to love the wasp. It was ideal for driving down the narrow Italian streets in cities and hill-towns from Genoa to Palermo where cars could not fit. For personal transportation, the scooter was ideal. "I'd give up my car, only the Vespa won't hold my trombone," quipped American dixieland jazz artist Wilbur de Paris to *The New Yorker* in 1956.

Because of its small, 8in wheels, the first Vespas were not designed for touring any significant distance, but competition for the scooter came not from the motorcycle companies as much as from the car manufacturers who were producing three wheelers and micro cars, such as Iso's Isetta and Fiat's revived prewar 500 Topolino. Piaggio's marketing focused on the working class, who needed inexpensive transportation; according to a poll of the Italian market by *Business Week* in 1956,

"2% of all Vespa owners are priests, 2% doctors, 3% students, 7% other professionals, 10% skilled laborers, 16% merchants, 30% white-collar workers, and 30% laborers."

Enrico Piaggio confessed that the success of the Vespa was due to its affordablity. "Just like Henry Ford put the workers on wheels in America," he told *Newsweek* in 1956, "we put automotive transport within the reach of people who never expected to travel that way." Scooters were available, affordable, operable, and desirable to everyone—even the Duke of Edinburgh had an affection for Vespas and ordered a fleet in 1956 to cruise the grounds of Buckingham Palace.

Paperino 1945 ★★★★

Fiat called its 500cc midget car the Topolino, or Mickey Mouse, so d'Ascanio's first creation was nicknamed the Paperino, or Donald Duck, trading on the Italian love for Walt Disney's cartoon characters, which are almost as popular as images of the Madonna in Italy.

The Paperino was powered by a single-cylinder 98cc two-stroke engine of Piaggio design mounted alongside the rear wheel with direct drive via the in-unit gearbox. The gearbox was shifted by rod linkage from the left twistgrip; the throttle was cable-operated from the right twistgrip. This basic engine-gearbox-controls layout would carry over to the Vespa.

The Paperino's body design foreshadowed that of the Vespa. A central tunnel housing ran from steering head back to the engine cover, which would have made it difficult for Piaggio's female target audience to straddle the scooter. This, along with other details, doomed the Paperino. "Admittedly," Piaggio said, "the first motor scooter was a horrible looking thing, and people ridiculed us to our faces."

After creating the single Paperino prototype, it was back to the drawing board for d'Ascanio.

Vespa 98cc 1946–1948 ★★★★★

In creating the Vespa, d'Ascanio refined many of the ideas set forth by the Paperino. He outlined his parameters in creating the scooter to an Italian magazine: "Having seen motorcyclists stuck at the side of the road many times with a punctured tire, I decided that one of the most important things to solve was that a flat should no longer be a large problem just like it wasn't for automobiles.

"Another problem to resolve was that of simplifying the steering, especially in city driving. To help this, the control of the gearshifting was placed on the handlebars for easy shifting without abandoning manueverabilty making its use intuitive for the novice.

"Another large inconvenience with traditional motorcycles was oil spraying on clothes, so I thought of moving the engine far from the 'pilot,' covering it with a fairing, and abolishing the open chain with a cover placing the wheel right next to the gearchange.

"Some solutions came from aeronautical technology, with which Piaggio was obviously familiar, such as the rear tubular wheel holder borrowed directly from the undercarriage of airplanes. The single shell frame surpassed even the most modern automobile design since the stamped bodywork of strengthened steel was a rarity."

The Vespa prototype was first shown to the public at the 1946 Turin Show, and 100 pre-production prototypes were built before the production lines started rolling.

A mere 100 specimens of the Vespa prototype were built prior to starting the production lines rolling in 1946. These first Vespas came under considerable criticism in the Italian motoring press due to a perceived lack of safety. Enrico Piaggio dismissed the unkind words as irrelevant since the Vespa was designed for just short trips around the city. The prototypes were changed only in minor detail before entering production. D'Ascanio became an Italian hero, and after his death in 1981, a plaque was mounted above the door of his house commemorating his achievement. Several of the Vespa prototypes survive in Italy.

Early Piaggio Production 1945–1950

Year	Model	Number Built
1945	Paperino	1
1945–1946	Vespa 98cc Prototype	100
1946	Vespa 98cc	2,484
1947	Vespa 98cc	10,535
1948	Vespa 125cc	19,822
1949	Vespa 125cc	35,578
1950	Vespa 125cc	61,881
1952–1954	Vespa 125 U	ca. 7,000

The Vespa was powered by the single-cylinder 98cc two-stroke measuring 50x50mm bore and stroke. A cable-operated throttle controlled the Dell'Orto T2 16/17mm carburetor. Cooling was by ambient airflow. The engine was backed by a three-speed gearbox with rod gearchange controls that provided direct drive to the rear wheel. The single-sided stub axles held the bolted-up stamped-steel wheels fitted with 3.50x8in Pirelli tires; the wheels were interchangeable front to rear.

Power from the little engine was 3.3hp at 4500rpm, enough to propel the Vespa to a 60km/h or 35mph top speed and still return 100mpg, according to *Moto Revue* magazine of July 1946.

The early Vespa featured its headlamp mounted on the front fender and was typically painted in Piaggio's classic metallic green, which became the quintessential Vespa color even though other colors were available such as a dark maroon. The metallic green is believed to have been a war surplus rustproofing industrial paint. Piaggio added an extra seat on its scooter to compete with Innocenti's A 125 two seater, but the added weight of a second rider required an increase in engine displacement to 125cc in 1951. Owner: Vittorio Tessera.

As on the Paperino, d'Ascanio opted for handlebar-mounted controls for the gearchange, throttle, clutch, and brakes, making it easier for the uninitiated rider than the foot levers of motorcycle; he left the handlebars uncovered to give them the look of being taken from a bicycle and therefore familiar and easy to ride.

In 1946, the Vespa's styling was strikingly modernistic—almost to the point of exaggeration. Prior to World War II, the Italian Futurist movement lead by poet and gourmand Filippo Tommaso Marinetti preached a philosophy of cleansing society through speed, power, and war. After Italy's defeat, war was no longer so appetizing, but speed and power still reigned to mobilize the people. Inevitably, Piaggio was influenced by the Futurists since the smooth, streamlined design of the wasp gave the (mistaken) image of a super-fast scooter.

The most unique feature of the scooter was the step-through frame, flat footboards, and full bodywork to protect the rider from the elements. The large front fender carried the headlamp and turned in unison with the wheel that it all but covered.

The Vespa boasted a toolbox that was housed within the body under the curve of the single saddle seat; a luggage rack rode behind the seat. The left sidecover housed a glovebox by the spare tire which balanced the right leaning motor leaning off to the right. The interchangeable spare and the muffler exiting on the left didn't weigh as much as the motor on the right, forcing Vespisti to learn to lean to the left to compensate, which became a characteristic trait and you could spot the arrival of a Vespa from afar by the silhouette.

The Vespa was immediately derided by the Italian motorcycle industry. Pundits put down the scooter's near-vertical front fork and elfin, 8in wheels, insinuating for all potential buyers to hear that the setup made for a dangerous ride on Italy's wartorn roads and that it was unsafe on wet cobblestones. The front knee-action suspension was criticized as being too soft, forcing the scooter to dive frontward under even the lightest braking. In the end, the erratic sparking and the simple pump lubrication caused motorcycle companies to dismiss the scooter on the grounds of engineering faults.

Piaggio rebutted these attacks, claiming that the Vespa was not a small cousin of the motorcycle, but rather an entirely novel form of transportation made for slower speeds and short distances. In the end, the Vespa proved Piaggio and d'Ascanio's concept was a success.

By 1948, the front fender was redesigned to allow the wheel to be more easily removed. A fan was introduced to cool the engine; a horn was added on the front apron.

Vespa 125cc 1948–1950 ★★★★

In 1948, after less than two full years of production, the Vespa was updated. Innocenti had introduced its Lambretta scooter in 1947, and the firms would be locked in competition until 1971, when Innocenti finally threw in the towel. In the intervening thirty-four years, updates and changes—as well as completely new models— would be added to both firms' lines largely in response to real or imagined threats from the other maker.

The Lambretta was powered by a brawny (in relative terms) 125cc engine, so Piaggio quickly created its own 125cc, which bowed in 1948 to replace the original 98cc. The 125cc measured 56.5x49.8mm and created 5hp at 4500rpm via a new Dell'Orto TA 17 versus the 3.2hp of the smaller Vespa engine and the Lambretta's 4.3 at 4000rpm. The top speed of the 125cc scooter reached a full 70km/h or 44mph.

Hoffman Vespas

Hoffman was licensed in mid-1949 to begin production of the Vespa 125, which the firm called Die Konigin, or the Queen, for the German market. The 124.7cc Hoffman Vespa A had 4.6hp at 4900rpm, 0.6hp more than the Italian 125 at the time. The Hoffman was also 5km/h faster, which Piaggio matched the following year and surpassed in horsepower. In 1951, Hoffman offered an official Vespa sidecar with a windshield as well as floorboards. By 1953, some 1,800 Konigin Vespas were manufactured monthly.

In 1954, the Vespa Die Konigin was replaced by the Vespa 54, which had 5hp. On some of the Hoffman models a second, larger headlamp was mounted on the bicycle-style handlebars for extra safety.

By 1955, Hoffman was looking to switch from scooters to motorcycles and cars, and so the Piaggio–Hoffman license was cancelled.

Even though the Vespa was dubbed the "Queen of Motorscooters," Hoffmann's ads still put the man in the driver's seat and the woman rode in ridiculous side-saddle fashion as the couple meandered through the Schwarzwald.

The other major change to the Vespa in 1948 was the redesigned suspension, giving a smoother ride and combating the front braking squat.

In 1949, the old-fashioned, though functional rod control system was updated to become more flexible. In 1950, the rear body was redesigned with an added egg-shaped muffler.

Vespa 125 '51 1951–1952 ★★★★

In 1951, the Vespa's cable gearchange control was finally replaced by cables; Innocenti had always used cables—as did most other manufacturer in the world—and Piaggio's stubborn refusal to use cables had probably cost them some sales.

By 1951, the right sidecover was hinged upward with a catch (that inevitably broke) to hold it for easy engine access. Unlike the Lambretta with its glovebox under the seat, the Vespa's glovebox was a small panel on the left sidecover, and the panel under the seat accessed the carburetor. The carb's long manifold routed the fuel on a long path through the monocoque bodywork.

The gearbox still had only three speeds but the direct gear final drive of the first models was replaced by a chain secondary drive. The updated

The Vespa revolutionized transportation in postwar Italy: these two Indians from the city of Turin were modernizing from horse to the steel steed, according to a 1952 Vespa Club d'Italia newsletter. The Vespa in question was one of the new 125 '51 models.

112

rear suspension with hydraulic damper also smoothed the ride. The handlebars remained essentially the same with the 150mm headlamp still perched on the front fender; the '51 boasted a new rectangular taillamp.

Vespa 125 U 1953 ★★★★

In 1953, Vespa unveiled its 125 U, or Utilitaria, economy model with the headlamp now mounted on the handlebars, which were partly covered by a steel cowling. The headlamp's ascension was due to laws that regulated its height; Vespas made in other countries followed suit, although some makers waited until 1955 before making the change, as with England's Douglas.

The single-saddled Utilitaria (also know as the Vespa Junior) was exhibited at the 1952 Milan Show but did not go into production until 1953, priced below the Normale model to combat the (unsuccessful) Lambretta E and F economy models. The Utilitaria had front suspension harking back to the simplicity of the early models as well as a bare-bones front fender. Piaggio cut out the baggage compartment on the top of the left side cover and exposed part of the engine on the other side with a cutaway around the top of the fan.

Vespa 125 1953–1957 ★★★

In 1953, the 125cc engine was upgraded with a revised cylinder head and barrel with twin transfer ports to feed the fuel-oil mix. The compression ratio was now at 6.4:1 fed by a Dell'Orto TA 18mm carburetor; power was up to 5hp at 4500rpm. The gas tank was enlarged to 5.25 liters and by 1946, it would be at 8.2 liters; meanwhile the wheels remained 8in with 3.50x8in tires.

While the headlamp was moved to the handlebars on the 125 U for safety concerns, the Normale retained the fender-mounted light—and it had been switched to a smaller, 130mm diameter.

The Vespa's front fender was redesigned, however, bearing a bulge to clear the right-side forks and shock. Piaggio cut out the baggage compartment on the top of the left sidecover and exposed part of the engine on the other side with a cutaway around the top of the fan.

In 1953, the classic metallic gray-green of the Vespa was changed to a new nonmetallic gray-

Vespa and *la bella donna*. Motorcycles lacked the curvaceous beauty of scooters, but motorscooters had style in abundance: voluptuous legshields, buxom front fenders, slim Coke-bottle waist, and a sensuous rear. Piaggio originally targeted its Vespa to female buyers but always promoted its scooters in ads and calendars with beautiful women. The Italians understood the double entendre: sex sold scooters to both men and women. The model wooed men but also showed women that they could be beautiful and drive a Vespa, too. Here, American movie starlet Raquel Welch stands by her Vespa.

Sears and the Allstate Cruisaire

Sears, Roebuck and Co. was famous for selling everything under the sun, so it decided to order 1,000 Vespas in 1951 as an experiment. It offered them throughout the United States via its mail-order catalog as its top-of-the-line Cruisaire scooter accompanying the Cushman-produced Allstates. The $279.95 Vespas sold so fast that Sears placed a rush order for 5,000 more by September 1951, and planned to buy up to 2,000 more every month thereafter, reported *Time* magazine in 1952.

Sears always sold the 125cc Vespa with the sole change being the addition of an Allstate emblem to the left legshield. The Allstate model was always priced $10 below the cheapest 5hp Lambretta sold by Montgomery Ward. Sears also offered sidecars and a wide range of accessories.

As a 1957 Sears ad stated, "The Allstate Cruisaire is the smartest scooter we've ever built [sic]—smart in the advanced brilliance of styling and power—smarter still in the bedrock economy of operation." And as an enthusiastic Sears executive told *American Mercury* magazine in 1957, "The day may come when a swarm of the minute 6hp Vespas will proudly share the American highways with large 300hp sedans."

That day never came to pass, but Sears did import tens of thousands of Vespas into the United States in the years 1951–1963.

Douglas Vespa

The English Douglas firm bore a long lineage of elegant flat-twin motorcycles stretching back to motorcycling's pioneer days. But in 1948, Douglas chief Claude McCormack got religion. While vacationing in Italy, he was amazed by the Vespas and other scooters buzzing through the streets like insects. Douglas envisioned a business venture, contacted Piaggio, and first showed an imported Piaggio Vespa with Douglas Vespa nameplate on the front legshield at the 1949 Earls Court Show in London. Plans were announced to build 10,000 Vespas in England.

Douglas launched its Vespa line on March 15, 1951. Built under Piaggio license at the Douglas factory on Hanham Road, Bristol, the first Douglas Vespa was almost a carbon copy of the current 125cc rod-control Vespa; Douglas termed its model the 2L2 with the major difference being that the headlamp was placed on the front apron just below the handlebars to meet British headlamp height laws.

Beyond the headlamp, Douglas followed Piaggio even down to the same metallic industrial green paint. But as they were made in Britian, many of the components were sourced in the UK, such as the Amal carburetors, Lucas electrics, Milverton saddles, British-made Michelin tires, and BTH magnetos.

In 1953, Douglas upgraded its Vespa with Piaggio's new cable-control gearshift; the new Douglas was termed the G. In 1954, Douglas again followed the leader, introducing its GL2 based on a new engine with revised cylinder head and barrel with twin transfer ports to feed the oil-fuel mix. The engine also had a new full flywheel and a square 54x54mm bore and stroke. A dual bench seat was optional.

In February 1955, Douglas announced its 42L2 Vespa, following Piaggio's lead in mounting the headlamp on the handlebars, where it was backed by a speedometer. The cooling cutaway on the engine sidecover was redone with simple louvers and a hydraulic damper was added to the front suspension.

In 1955, Douglas also offered a new model, the Piaggio Vespa 150 GS, or Gran Sport, which Douglas named the VS1 for Vespa Sports. With a 145cc tuned engine of 57x57mm and a four-speed gearbox, the GS represented a new stage in scooters. With the recovery advancing, buyers had extra money in their pockets and vacation time on their work timecards; the GS, like Innocenti's TV, were sporty, higher-speed touring models designed to meet this new, developing market.

Douglas' VS model designation was updated annually: the 1955 was termed the VS1; the 1956 was the VS2; 1957, the VS3; 1958, the VS4; 1959, the VS5. But oddly, while Douglas was building the 125cc Vespas, it only imported and never built the Piaggio GS, rebadging it as a Douglas model. The reason for this lay in the firm's growing financial troubles.

Despite the sales success of the Vespa line, Douglas was purchased by Westinghouse Brake and Signal. In 1955, the 42L2 was termed the Standard version and was joined by the Magna and Ultra versions with further options. In February 1959, the 42L2 was replaced by the 152L2. Later, the 125cc 232L2 and 150cc 312L2 rotary-valve models were produced.

British production of Vespas ended in 1963–1964, after which Douglas continued to import Piaggio models. Douglas had built a total of 126,230 Vespas.

Douglas Vespa Model Nomenclature

Year	Piaggio Model Name	Douglas Model Name
1951–1953	125cc (Rod control)	2L2
1953	125cc (Cable control)	G
1954	125cc (Twin-transfer-port)	GL2 2/1955–2/1959
	125cc	42L2
2/1959	125cc	152L2
1955	150 GS (Gran Sport)	VS1 (Vespa Sports)
1956	150 GS	VS2
1957	150 GS	VS3
1958	150 GS	VS4
1959	150 GS	VS5
1960	150 GS	VS
1961	150 GS	VS
1962–1964	160 GS	160 GS

Douglas Rotary-Valve Models 1959–1977

Piaggio Model Name	Douglas Model Name
125	232L2
125	VMA1
125 Primavera	VMA2
90	V9A1
90SS	V9SS1
90 Racer	V9SS2
150 Sportique	312L2
150 Super	VBC1
150 GL	VLA1
150 Sprint	VLB1
180 Rally	VSD1
Rally 200 Electronic	VSE1

114

green, although other colors were still available, albeit rare. In 1955, a light gray color was added to the Vespa line as well as stronger front suspension and the saddle pushed forward to allow easier access to the gas cap.

In 1954, a sidecover made its debut that completely covered the fan and flywheel magneto, approaching the definitive Vespa design used on all future models.

In describing the Vespa 125, Piaggio ads proclaimed that the "Vespa's Always In Style—the basic design of this handsome machine doesn't change from year to year. This means that your Vespa will be slow to depreciate, will never become obsolete." Unfortunately, the conformity of style aged the newest Vespas and no matter how hard Piaggio tried to promote its scooter, the new model looked much the same as the old one.

Vespa 150 1954–1958 ★ ★ ★

A new 150cc Vespa made its debut in 1954 based on a square 57x57mm engine that fathered 5.7hp. Not surprisingly, Innocenti had introduced its LD 150 in 1954 as well. The very first Vespa 150s didn't have a battery to support the electrics, but this soon became a standard feature. The headlamp followed the Utilitario model's lead with the placement on the handlebars, which were updated in 1957 with an entirely enclosed handshifter.

The American Popular Science magazine tested a 150 in 1957, commenting on its "horn like a Model T's with a foreign accent." The threat of Vespas becoming widespread in the United States led to a media assault on the loud noise of the scooters' two-stroke engines—there was no qualms about the four-stroke noise of the American-made Cushmans—and later to exaggerated claims against their safety. *Popular Science* described a new Vespa's sound in 1957 as a "vacuum cleaner" with "a polite but busy whisper," while a 1956 *Fortune* article claimed it was "the sound of riveting guns."

Piaggio claimed the Vespa had the lowest decibel level of all scooters—except when Italian hot-rodders sawed off an inch or more of the muffler for better gas mileage and about a 10 percent power increase, essential for piazza cruising. Piaggio, however didn't condone the decibel increasing muffler adjustment, but still got blasted in the American press for the noise when Vespas were first sold in the United States. *Fortune* reported, "Not content with making the Italian night hideous, Piaggio & Co. of Genoa, which manufactures one of Italy's most popular scooters, the Vespa, has launched a determined assault on the American market."

Piaggio had designs on creating a sporting scooter as early as 1949 when it developed this Sport prototype. The Sport never went into production as Piaggio chose instead to perfect its Vespa into a sport model, which made its debut in 1954 as the Gran Sport. The Sport prototype survives in Italy.

In April 1956, the one-millionth Vespa was produced worldwide, combining the production of all factories in France, England, Germany, and elsewhere that were building Vespas under license. A celebration was held in Pontedera and Vespa Day was declared throughout Italy with festivities held in fifteen Italian cities, including a convoy of 2,000 Vespas traveling en masse through Rome and halting all traffic. The Piaggio factory in Italy now manufactured 500 scooters a day, and by this time, the French Vespa firm, ACMA, had produced a total of 100,000 Vespas.

At least once a year, the Vespa Club of Europe sponsored tours of the continent in which the traveling groups would meet up with local Vespa clubs in each country and wax poetic on the merits of their machines. Annual Vespa rallies in a lucky European city would attract as many as 30,000 scooterists. For these large meets, clubs would present pageants, often with hundreds of folk dressed in traditional customes in each show displaying the folklore of their respective country, all on the essential medium, the Vespa. The spectacle included large groups of scooterists straining to sing national songs over the harmony of hundreds of buzzing Vespas. Never to be outdone, an Italian Vespa club tried to dance the tarantella while driving their scooters. They failed miserably.

This English Douglas ad from 1955 portrayed the Vespa GS, top, which cost considerably more than the Vespa 125cc, below, but was worth every shilling. In the Gran Sport, Piaggio created its *capolavoro*, and the model sold well into the 1960s. Douglas built its own versions of the small-bore Vespas but imported the GS model, naming it the VS for Vespa Sports.

In 1956, French and Italian scooter acrobat groups dressed up in matching outfits to perform daredevil stunts on Vespas, and in Spain and Portugal, scooters were used in comic bullfights during an intermission from the main attraction.

Vespa 150 GS 1955–1961 and 160 GS 1962–1964 ★★★★

Beginning in 1949, Piaggio created a series of sport, racing, and speed-record prototypes and factory works machines. Piaggio saw winning races and setting speed and endurance records as a way to prove its product and sell more machines.

In 1949, the firm built a special prototype for a Sport scooter backed by a belief that as the economy recovered, there would be demand for a high-performance sporting model. The Sport was based on the 125cc model but bore a radically

reworked body. An enlarged front fender covered most of the wheel to provide better aerodynamics; a slotted vertical opening on either side allowed cooling airflow to the brake. The legshield was narrowed, again to cut wind resistance, and no horn or headlamp was fitted. The right sidecover was cut away from the engine even more than standard to let in more cooling air. A gas tank was mounted between the rider's legs to form a bridge to the handlebars; a pad was strapped to the gas tank's top so the rider could lean on its for long-distance races.

The timing of the Sport was too early, but the idea was sound, and Piaggio would return to the sporting theme six years later in creating its Gran Sport model. Some of the Sport prototype's features would be used in designing the GS, while others would carry over to the later 90 SS.

By 1954, the time was right. Italians had extra money in their pockets to buy an upscale scooter that offered extra power and luxurious accessories. Piaggio beat Innocenti to the punch in creating a *gran turismo* scooter in the image of the Ferrari GT cars of the same era, albeit on a different scale.

The 150 GS first appeared at the Salone di Milano in late 1954. The GS design stunned all;

Italian design was on the cutting edge and recognized throughout the world, with the Vespa scooter upheld as a quintessential example alongside Olivetti typewriters, espresso *màcchinetti*, and the wares of Milan's fashion industry. Renowned car designer Giorgetto Giugiaro even created his own signature *radiatore* pasta. The inspired attention to design detail on Piaggio's scooters was exemplified by the flashy taillight used on the GS, a piece of functional beauty. This ad from *Motociclismo* in 1960 was run by taillight maker Mabo SpA.

The Vespa GS was the mod hot rod of choice. The Gran Sport quickly took the mantle as the quintessential performance scooter, overshadowing Innocenti's TV, which had established the market. And it seemed that Piaggio had thought ahead: the glovebox was ideal for mounting stereo speakers for blasting out the latest R&B. The flywheel magneto was not powerful enough to run more than about six headlamps, however, so more juice needed to be added. This GS 160 has a funky aftermarket rear railing/bumper, complete with heraldry shield. Owner: Sam Pitmon.

Piaggio had refined and perfected its scooter into a high-performance touring and sporting model. The engine was a square 57x57mm with a compression ratio of 6.7:1, pumping out 8hp at 7500rpm via a UB 23 S 3 Dell'Orto carburetor. Backed by a four-speed gearbox, the GS reached 100km/h or 62mph on the new 3.50x10in wheels.

The 150 GS came with a bench seat for two people and was available exclusively in metallic grey. On early models, the spare tire was mounted on top of the central tunnel behind the legshields as the left sidecover now housed a luggage trunk.

In 1958, the 150 GS featured a new speedometer as well as wheel and saddle design. Although the GS reigned as the most powerful Vespa, its lack of fuel efficiency compared to the other Vespas was criticized. To put these worries to rest,

Joan Short and Tommy Behan of the Vespa Club of Britian loaded up their GS with a mere £1 worth of gas and rode all the way from London to Paris in 1959.

In 1957, Innocenti responded to the Gran Sport by offering its Lambretta TV 175. With a 175cc competitor threatening to steal the thunder created by the 150 GS, Piaggio created its 160 GS in 1962. "Vespa's powerhouse," the 160 GS enlarged both the bore and stroke of the 150 GS engine to 58x60mm, making it capable of 8.2hp at 6500rpm via a Dell'Orto SI 27/23 for a top speed of 65mph. Fuel consumption dropped to 80mpg due to the 160 GS's heavier weight of 232lb.

Although the 160 was a steadier ride than the smaller GS, it didn't conquer the market the way the quicker 150 did. Distinguishing features of the 160 were the added metal trim on the front fender, a mat on the center bridge, a smaller saddle seat with glovebox behind instead of in the left side panel, and a new exhaust system.

Vespa 125 1957-1965 ★★

The classic Vespa 125 was reborn in 1957 with a sleek, new body and entirely enclosed handshifter like its more powerful cousin, the GS. The new 125 featured a revised engine based on the

Piaggio marketed its Vespas with near identical bodywork, which saved on tooling dies for stamping out the pressed-steel monocoques. Different-sized engines were shoehorned into the bodies and marketed to various sectors of the population as a scooter created just for their needs. This was the basic 1959 150 model, ideal for jaunts to the beach. *Classic Scooters Newsletter/Steven Zasueta*

Beautifully plastic poster girl Margaret Lee took her 1963 Vespa Super Sport to the beach. The 10.3hp SS ruled as the top-of-the-line Vespa in the mid-1960s with the major design facelift being the use of an angular-shaped headlamp replacing the rounded lamp that graced the GS and earlier models. This photo from a Vespa pin-up calendar graced scooter shops and the wall of many a male teenager's bedroom—just as Piaggio planned.

150, with a square 54x54mm bore and stroke creating 4.5hp at 5000rpm and pushing the 81kg scooter to 75km/h.

In 1962, the 125 offered a left side panel that hid the spare tire and battery; the side cover could be removed completely instead of the former hinged version with the small glovebox. In 1963, the modernized design with new bodywork smoothed the edges of the old style making the slicker bench seat standard. In 1964, a fourth gear was added.

Vespa 150 1958-1965 ★★

In October 1958, the Vespa 150 sported a new look, following the 125 of the previous year, and an improved engine with 5.5hp at 5000rpm. The square 57x57mm engine wasn't as fast as the GS—it topped out at 51mph—but got better gas mileage and cost considerabley less.

By 1961, the standard Vespa 150 had four speeds and was tuned to 6.9hp at 5000rpm for a 56mph top speed and 100mpg. The no-frills 150 kept to the small, 8in wheels.

In the 1960s, both Piaggio and Innocenti (separately, of course) sponsored international beauty contests on scooters noting that a well-tended putt-putt added much to a tidy image. In Britain, famous movie stars presented the Silver Rose Bowl award to the Miss Vespa Darling. At the English Lambretta National Rally held in Portsmouth, the winner of the Miss Lambretta contest would go on to compete in the prestigious Miss Lambretta International contest.

By this time, Piaggio and Innocenti both financed massive advertising campaigns to promote "scooter culture" in general, and their respective vehicles in particular. The Vespa was advertised as the second conquering of the New World by a Genovese (the first being by Christopher Columbus). Owners magazines funded by the companies were published in a different languages, containing articles on the latest updates, movie stars on scooters, and continental tours. These publications pushed the idea of the sleek, attractive scooter that was fashionable but functional. Fashionable, because no bar between the rider's legs allowed the latest style instead of riding clothes and the covered engine prevented oil spotting clothes. Functional, because a scooter could tour the world but still be parked anywhere.

Piaggio and Innocenti were no longer advertising a product. They were promoting a lifestyle.

Vespa 150 GL 1962-1965 ★★

In 1962, the 150 Gran Lusso was announced with two saddle seats to counter the Lambretta LD 150. The 150 GL had a different engine from the basic 150; it was an oversquare design of

58.5x54mm delivering 6.2hp at 5500rpm for a 53mph top speed via a four-speed gearbox.

Vespa 50, 50 N, 50 S, and 50 L 1962–1966 ★

In 1962, Piaggio launched its entry-level economy scooter, the 50cc Vespa, nicknamed the Vespino, or little Vespa. Piaggio's ads described the 50 in Futurist-like prose as "a brand new Vespa created to allow everyone to enter unhesitat-

In 1965, Piaggio created a hot-rod version of its no-frills 90cc model. The 90 Super Sprint offered power, handling, and speed in a lightweight body packed with a highly tuned engine. The power-to-weight ratio and dummy central gas tank of the 90SS caused scooter racers to protest the model, saying it was a motorcycle in disguise wearing scooter bodywork. They missed the point, racing rules committees allowed the 90SS to start, and it consistently took the checkered flag. Top speed was more than 90km/h or 56mph.

ingly the sphere of motorization." Nevermind the poetic ad language, the 50 became an instant hit and Piaggio's best-selling scooter. By 1993, with a revised 50cc 50S Vintage and 50A with automatic transmission still in production, more than four million 50cc Vespas had been built.

The Vespino was powered by an entirely new motor with rotary port induction requiring a mere 2 percent oil content to the fuel, thus allowing increased performance and power from the elfin engine. The new cylinder was inclined forward at 45 degrees, measuring 38.4x43mm and delivering a faithful 1.5hp. Top speed was 40km/h or 25mph. The three-speed Vespino brought Piaggio's scooters back to Enrico Piaggio's original philosophy of reliable, inexpensive scooters to mobilize every class, every age, everywhere.

The following year two models were offered, the 50 N "for the whole family," and the 50 S "for professional and leisure time," although background checks were not made. The N's three speeds brought it to a top speed of 40 km/h while the 2.5hp S's four speeds made for a top speed of 60 km/h or 37mph. It was a heady speed for the midget 8in wheels.

Vespa 180 Super Sport 1964-1966 ★★★

The engine of the 160 GS was enlarged to make the 181.1cc Super Sport, which replaced the GS as the top-of-the-line Vespa. The 181cc engine was based on 62x60mm, creating 10.3hp at 6250rpm.

The 180 Super Sport obtained a new body-chassis, straying from the classical rounded styling of the GS to the the angular look of the mid-1960s. The crown of the fastest Italian scooter was once again obtained by Piaggio with this scooter zooming at up to 63mph.

A large built-in glove box was added on the passenger-side of the legshield that became the favored spot for mounting a boombox to blast out your own soundtrack as you flashed by the coffeeshops.

Vespa 90 1964–1971 ★

Scooterists often suffered under a subconscious phobia of their Vespa being branded as feminine, especially by the British Rockers. The Vespa 50 and 90, as smaller and easier-to-handle scooter, were often considered sissy models whereas the larger scooters offered the horsepower necessary to console the fragile macho self-image. To assuage this imagined shame, Piaggio developed its Primavera, but a smaller performance scooter was still needed.

Vespa 90 Super Sprint 1965–1971 ★★★★

In the early 1960s, the three-speed Vespa 90 offered manueverability that the larger scooters lacked, but the small scooters didn't have a sport-ing character. In 1965, Piaggio created a Super Sprint, or SS, version of its 90 with a high-performance 90cc engine shoehorned into a lightweight chassis creating a hot power-to-weight ratio.

The body of the 90SS was reworked with a narrower legshield to cut wind resistance, as used on several of Piaggio's racing prototypes in the early 1950s. The spare tire rode between the rider's legs, capped by a dummy gas tank that served as the toolbox. The tank wore Super Sprint badges on both sides.

Although the Vespa 90 Super Sprint had a smaller engine and weighed slightly more than its 125 Primavera counterpart, it boasted a higher maximum speed by 8km/h, topping out at 88km/h or 55mph. The four-speed SS series scooters were designed for competition, often providing better performance than many 200cc competitors.

The 90 provided the added advantage of the engine size falling conveniently short of the new laws in the United States requiring motorcycle licenses for two-wheelers over 100cc. One of Piaggio's original concepts for having the scooter's open area between the legs was for women wearing dresses, but now that the raging style was slacks, this space was unnecessary. Instead, Piaggio gave the scooter a racy motorcycle look while retaining the Vespa design.

Vespa's competition tried to have the SS banned from competition because the area between the rider's legs was closed off with a spare tire and a glovebox that looked like a gas tank. The Federation of British Scooter Clubs ruled in favor of the SS since the dummy gas tank was not structural and allowed the Vespa to keep on conquering its competition.

Vespa 150 Sprint 1965-1969 and 150 Sprint Veloce 1969-1977 ★★

Piaggio replaced its 150 GL with the 150 Sprint riding on 10in wheels and a 150cc (57x57mm) engine that put out 7.1hp at 5000rpm. Four speed was by now standard as well as the bench seat.

In the summer of 1969, the Sprint's engine was modified to produce 7.7hp and 97km/h, the body was updated to be the same as 125 GTR except for the chrome piece on the sidepanels, and they called it the Veloce.

Vespa 125 Super and 150 Super 1965 ★

As the Sprint replaced the GL, the Super replaced the standard 125 and 150 Vespas. The Super was the economical model but still used the sleek design of the faster scooters to make a practical form of transportation. The 125 had a 52.5x57mm engine for 85km/h, and the 150 had the square 57x57mm engine for 90km/h.

Vespa 125 Primavera 1965–1966 and 125 ET3 1967–1977 ★★

In 1965, Piaggio enlarged the 50cc engine to 125cc and retained the 50 chassis to create the 125 *Primavera*, or Spring; Botticelli would have been proud. Piaggio's pride was a hot-rod scooter with a four-speed gearbox capable of hitting a shakey 80km/h or 50mph—a mere 5km/h short of the 150 GL's top speed. An improved gear ratio meant the 125 took only 47.9sec to travel 1km from a dead stop while the 150 managed it in 46.1sec. In the 0-75km/h dash, the smaller Vespa clocked 18.5sec versus 18sec for the 150. In other words, these scooters could beat almost any car off the line for at least the first ten feet.

In 1967, the 121.17cc Primavera became the ET3 packing a potent 5.4hp for an 85km/h or 53mph top speed. The ET3 was so popular, Piaggio revived the model for the 1980s and 1990s as the ET3 Vintage with a 121.16cc engine of 55x51mm now creating 5.6hp via a four-speed gearbox. Wheels were 10in with 3.50x10in tires.

Vespa 125 GT 1966-1969 and 125 GTR 1969-1977 ★★

Piaggio announced yet another version of its 125, the Gran Turismo version with 6.27hp for 88km/h. The GT had essentially the same motor as the 125 Super with higher compression adding to the velocity. Piaggio modified the GT with a round headlamp, more power (7.8hp), more speed (95km/h), a new taillight (borrowed from the 180 Rally), and an R for *rinnovata* (renovated).

Vespa 180 Rally 1968; Rally 200 and Rally 200 Electronic 1972–1977 ★★★

During the late 1960s, interest in scooters waned as higher standards of living in the western world allowed families to buy automobiles. This downward swing hurt Piaggio but doomed Innocenti, which ceased scooter production in 1971. Scooters largely became a thing of the past, remembered as a necessary evil in the tough times following the war. Vespas and Lambrettas were stowed away in the backs of garages and barns throughout the world to make way for the shiny new car; it would be at least another decade before anyone recalled their scootering days with nostalgia.

At the same time, the market for scooters shifted. Vespas became a cult symbol of the growing youth market, winning an image as a mode of transportation primarily for teenagers before they could afford a motorcycle or car. For this growing market, Piaggio created a new speedster, the Rally 200.

The Rally was the hot Vespa of the day. Its brawny engine fathered 12hp at 5700rpm reaching a staggering 101km/h or 63mph (a questionable 1km/h more than the GS, P200E, and the PX200E, according to certain graphs). Piaggio boasted the Rally as the most reliable Vespa thus far, making it perfect for long distance touring.

The Rally 200 was supplanted by the Electronic model, which added electronic ignition to

High pucker factor: a hot-rodded Vespa Primavera in US Air Force thunderbirds colors below the protective gaze of a Thunderbirds' F-16. The Primavera was a powerhouse of a scooter with lots of motor in a small chassis. Stock, it was capable of 52mph; with mod modifications, this primavera blasts off to easily top 65mph. Owner: Steven Zasueta. *Steven Zasueta*

Vjatka: The Soviet Vespa

In the August 1957 issue of Svet Motoru, the Soviet Union announced a new miracle to the comrades: it had created not only a scooter, but a great scooter. Named the Vjatka, to Western eyes it was but a Russian copy of the Vespa.

The Vjatka used a Russian-built Vespa motor of 150cc from 57x58mm bore and stroke giving 5.5hp at 5000rpm with a three-speed gearbox and riding atop 4.00x10in tires. In the 1960s, a 175cc version appeared.

The Vjatka continued in production until the early 1970s when a redesigned version was released. The new Vjatka had a 148cc engine of 57x58mm for 6hp with a three-speed gearbox; although the specifications were the same as the Vespa copy, the new mechanicals were Russian designed.

replace the decrepit mechanical points system. The benefits of the new electronic ignition can hardly be overpraised.

By 1977, six years after Innocenti had given up on the Lambretta, the Piaggio factory at Pontedera produced 613,805 vehicles, ranking fourth in the world behind Honda, Yamaha, and Suzuki, but ahead of Kawasaki. In the same year, Piaggio exported 289,000 Vespas and three-wheeled Apes to 110 countries.

Vespa 50 N, 50 N Special, 50 N Elestart, and 50 Sprinter 1972–1977 ★

These 50cc models updated the 1963 versions with a new look. The Special and the Elestart had squared-off headlamps for that particular 1970s appeal; whereas the 50 N and 50 Sprinter were "obviously classic with timeless elegance," at least according to Piaggio's own view, it was a tough choice. All four of these models came with a bench seat, but lacked much of the power needed to haul two human bodies. The Elestart's battery for an electric start sat on the left side of the scooter, opposite the motor.

Vespa Nuova Linea P125X, P150X, and P200E 1978–1985 ★★★

On April 17, 1978, the Nuova Linea, or New Line, with the Vespa P125X, P150X, and P200E

made its debut in Florence with a grand celebration marking the most major update to the Vespa since the first 98cc model more than thirty years earlier. The P Series was the brainchild of Piaggio's managing director, Ing. Giovanni Squazzini. The P stood for Piaggio, the X for extra qualities, and the E for electronic ignition. The suspension, lighting, and performance were all significantly improved making for a reliable form of transport. The updated electrics produced 12volts with 80watt output from the flywheel magneto and electronic regulator.

The P Series engine featured rotary-valve induction via three piston ports. Riding on two main bearings, compression for each model was 8.0:1 at minimum, offering superior top-end power and smoother delivery throughout the powerband. And now that service stations rarely offered

What the Nuova Linea P Series Vespas lost in traditional styling, they more than made up for in reliability with a modern overhaul of Corradino d'Ascanio's original design to keep it current into the 1990s. The P200 was the top of the line offering rotary-valve induction, electronic ignition, hydraulic shocks, turn signals, and optional turn-key electric start. You could not ask for a better scooter. Owner: Joe Baker.

Other Piaggio Two-, Three-, and Four-Wheelers

Beginning in 1967, Piaggio developed two models of a 49.77cc moped called the Ciao, which was introduced with a one-speed auto clutch or an optional variable-speed automatic clutch. Later descendants of the Ciao were the Bravo, Boxer, and the Sí.

Piaggio also built a line of three-wheelers with the same engine buzz as the Vespa, which were named the Ape, or Bee. These all-purpose vehicles could handle any task with optional equipment including a snowplow, sand dispenser, petroleum fuel tank, fire-fighting tools, and street sweeper with water tank. In some Far Eastern countries, the Ape even challenged the dominance of the rickshaw.

In 1957, Piaggio began production of a line of dwarf Vespa 400 cars with suicide doors, a roll-back convertible top, and two front seats as well as a back bench seat. Powered by an air-cooled two-cylinder two-stroke engine, the car could hit a 56mph top speed (downhill). The 24ci or 393cc engine measured a square 63x63mm; with 6.4:1 compression, power was 20hp at 4600rpm. Gas consumption was 60mpg.

The design featured a rear-mounted engine and rear drive, rack and pinion steering, three-speed gearbox, independent suspension front and rear, drum brakes all around, and a pressed-steel unibody years ahead of other automakers.

The Vespa 400 was exported throughout the world, including to the United States where it was imported by the Boston Vespa Company of Boston, Massachussetts. The car was well received even in the land of land yachts; *Motor Trend* praised it as a "well-engineered miniature." Even with good sales, Piaggio cancelled car production in 1961 and concentrated on its scooters.

miscela, or premixed gas with two-stroke oil, each Vespa had separate reservoirs that automatically mixed the fluids for the engine.

Top of the line was the P200E, based on a 198cc measuring 66.5x57mm with 8.2:1 compression ratio and fed via a Dell'Orto carburetor. Power was up to 12hp at 5700rpm; ignition was completely electronic. Backed by a four-speed gearbox, the P200E could do the American quarter-mile dragstrip dash in 20sec. The 231lb P200E returned 65mpg.

The new body design strayed from the curvaceous lines of the original Vespa to become stunningly modern with angular fenders and sidecover lines. Turn signals were built into the bodywork.

Piaggio took over Moto Gilera in 1979, and reported an annual production of 450,000 scooters in 1980.

Vespa PK50S, PK80S, PX80E, PK125S, PX125E, PX150E, and PX200E 1985–Current ★★

At the 1985 Milan Show, the new Vespa two-stroke direct-injection engine, developed over the previous ten years, was introduced. In that same year, the P Series was updated with two model lines, the K and extra-features X line. The PK125 came with an automatic progressive hydraulic transmission, and a 125 supersports version of the PK was released called the T5.

The PK models all had four-speed automatic transmissions, which caused an uproar in Italy since automatics were considered for people who weren't competent enough to shift. Piaggio knew this might be a problem and offered the PX series as well with a four-speed manual transmission.

In Paris, the reliability of the P Series prompted the founding of Scooter Express, a scooter taxi service that could carry passengers through the crowded streets faster than car cabs and for less money. The scooters were all 1985 white P Series Vespas with a "chrome bar between driver and passenger [to prevent] any possible promiscuity. All drivers are males in their thirties. So far, there are more women clients than men," according to *New York* magazine. The business wasn't all glamor since jealous cabbies assaulted them with tear-gas bombs for taking their business.

The PX200E continued through 1993 with the remainder of the Piaggio Vespa line made up of the 50A automatic, 50 S Vintage, 100 Vintage, 125A automatic, and 125ET3 Vintage.

Cosa 125cc, 150cc, and 200cc 1985–1990; Cosa II LX200 1990–Current ★★★

The Cosa arrived on the scene as the Vespa's replacement in 1985; it brought sighs and tears from throughout the world, and while the Cosa was an excellent scooter, the public outcry prompted Piaggio to reinstate the Vespa in the lineup.

The Cosa revised much of the Vespa's design underneath the skin while retaining its exterior styling lines, although it was now a rolling sculpture in plastic. The stressed-steel unit chassis was retired in favor of a more traditional tube frame covered by unstressed plastic bodywork. Piaggio called this "new technology," and stated that it was based on new advances in the automobile world; it forgot to mention the Lambretta.

The engine was an air-cooled, rotary-disc induction two-stroke in your choice of 125cc for 8.3hp at 6000rpm, 150cc for 9hp at 6000rpm, and 200cc for 11hp at 6000rpm, all backed by a four-speed gearbox. Each model came with an automatic gas and two-stroke oil mixer, denoted as the MA *miscelatore automatico* model; a 125 Cosa was available without MA. Electric start was optional.

Luxury features were plentiful. Turn signals were sculpted into the front legshields and tail and instrumentation went so far as to include a tachometer. And when Italy enacted a helmet law, which immediately cut into scooter sales, the Cosa

Cosa 2 LX200

While many of the newer scooters stray towards the E-Z Boy look, Piaggio continued a forward-leaning racing posture for the rider and retained much of the original classic Vespa design when it launched its Cosa series in 1985. The Cosa, or Thing, was supposed to replace the Vespa but nostalgic tears flowed all over the world and Piaggio brought the Vespa back, even offering a Vintage model in several displacements. This was the Cosa II LX200 of 1993. *Piaggio* offered an underseat hook to hang your helmet from so you wouldn't have to carry it with you while you bought your *cappuccio*.

In 1990, the Cosa line was updated to just one model, the Cosa II LX200. The 197.97cc engine was based on a 66.5x57mm bore and stroke. With 12 volt, 100 watt electrics and riding on 4.00x10in tires, the LX200 could top 110km/h or 68mph.

Sfera 50 and 80; and
Quartx and Zip 1990–Current ★

The Sfera, or Sphere, scooter was introduced in 1990 as the economical entry-level scooter, a modern steel-frame, plastic-bodywork counterpart to the Vespa 50. The engine was a 49cc rotary-disc two-stroke of 40x39.3mm with autmatic gas-oil mix, electronic ignition, automatic gearbox, and electric start. The Sfera was Piaggio's scooter of the future.

The styling was like a spaceship on 2.15x10in wheels with angular, modernistic lines. The seat pivoted forward with a helmet storage area hidden below.

Piaggio continued scooter production into the 1990s with no end in sight and its advanced scoot-

---

Messerschmitt Vespas

Following World War II, the famous aviation firm of Messerschmitt was restricted from building aircraft, so Fritz Fend's design of the Kabinen Roller, or Cabin Scooter, was put into production to keep the firm in business. The Kabinen Roller was a three-wheeled micro car that looked like little more than an overgrown scooter.

When Hoffman Vespa moved onto production of larger vehicles, Piaggio licensed Messer-schmitt to manufacture Vespas beginning in 1955.

The German Vespas differed little from the Italian versions except for the Messerschmitt emblem added under the Vespa logo. Messerschmitt later produced seven different models of Vespas including the Gran Sport. By the mid-1960s, scooter sales were slowing so Piaggio opted to revoke Messerschmitt's dimishing scooter production and export Vespas to Germany from the Pontedera factory in Italy.

KÖNIGIN DER MOTORROLLER

Vespa

AUS DEN HOFFMANN-WERKEN

In an attempt to push their scooters on the German market, Messerschmitt learned from the most effective propaganda machine of all time and used the theme "Deutscheland Überalles" for a scooter ad that read "Überall ist Vespaland." Der Öberfuehrer would have rolled over in his grave.

ers selling as well as ever. It had come a long way since the Donald Duck scooter prototype of 1945.

Piatti UK ★★★

The Piatti was a truly international scooter. Piatti scooters were an attempt by a British manufacturer to break into the Italian-dominated scooter market, and what better way than with an Italian designer? Designed by the London-based Italian engineer Vicenzo Piatti, it was built in Britian by Cyclemaster (Britax), as well as in Belgium by Les Anciens Establishments D'Ieteren.

In spring 1952, after having created the Minimotor for the British Trojan firm, Vicenzo Piatti designed two Piatti scooters: the three-speed 125cc with a top speed between 70 and 78km/h and the two-speed 98cc (built by Vincent, according to certain sources).

The Piatti's saddle could be raised and lowered as on a bicycle, and the nearly vertical front fork was similiar to a child's push scooter. However, the Space Age design gave the impression of a hovercraft, and the wheels almost disappeared under the body as though it was crawling on a cushion of air. The vertical lines of this cigar-shaped scooter did not merely give the impression of breakneck speed, but also facilitated airflow over the engine preventing two-stroke seizure. Elaborate cooling systems were telltale to Italian scooter design and the Piatti with its bridge between the rider's legs and the front and rear grille was no exception.

Pirol Germany ★★

The Dortmund-based Pirol-Fahrzeugfabrik GmbH was originally called Firma Schweppe and came up with one of the great ugly scooters in a rarified strata that can include only the Piatti and a select few others.

The headlamp erupted from the front fender like a pig's snout from a mudpit with the styling carried through to the tail. The rounded front legshield displayed the Pirol logo mounted in the center in the shape of a large crucifix.

Each scooter had a different company's engine, the Pirol 145 of 1949–1951 a 4.5hp Ilo, the Pirol 200 of 1951–1954 had a 6.5hp Küchen, and the Miranda of 1953–1954 had a 9.5hp Sachs. The Pirol 200 was the continuation of the Pirol 145, both with an actual rubber front bumper evoking images of bump 'em cars. The entire rear fender of these scooters hinged up to expose the engine. As Pirol's ads promised, "Der Pirol 200 ist Daher das Fahrzeug für Alle!"

Powell USA

Channing and Hayward Powell built vehicles to the tune of a different plumber. The brothers

The Piatti was quite simply one of the oddest scooters ever built. Its styling bespoke a cigar on wheels with handlebars and a seat perched precariously on top. The Piatti was designed by an Italian for the English market; someone somewhere believed the Italian connection was key to selling a scooter to the Continental-crazed Brits. It was built by the English as well as by Aldimi in Belgium. Owner: Vittorio Tessera.

were based in Los Angeles, the mecca for eccentricity in two-, three-, and four-wheeled vehicles; it was the home of hot rodding and the birthplace of the modern scooter, E. Foster Salsbury's Motor Glide. It was only natural that the brothers would

With extensive paneling on either side of the floorboard, the Pirol looks like it could collapse in the middle if any more weight in the form of a rider was applied. The arcing lines of the rear section separated to fold up, seat and all, for easy access to the engine.

Restored 1939 Powell Streamliner 40 alongside a 1936 Motor Glide and 1939 Crocker. Streamlining has always been a popular term of adulation for anything with curves (or angular) lines, and needless to say, streamlining is an essential feature of a scooter when you hit top speed. Owner: Herb Singe. *Herb Singe*

be inspired to build their own brand of hot-rod motorscooter.

[Much of the information in this chapter comes from the research of Wallace Skyrman, who started the Powell Cycle Registry in 1981.]

Streamliner 40 1939–1940
and 41-J 1941 ★★★★

The first Powell scooter arrived on the scene in the late 1930s and followed the commandments set by the Motor Glide: step-through frame, small wheels, automatic clutch, and a rear-mounted engine. Named the Streamliner Series 40, it used a Lauson 2.3hp four-stroke engine, Tillotson carburetor, and Eismann flywheel magneto ignition. The engine measured 2 1/4x2 1/4in bore and stroke with 6.0:1 compression. Lighting was initially by magneto but altered in 1941 for the 41-J model to a motor-driven generator. Engine cooling was by flywheel fan—"forced blast cooling," according to one brochure.

The Centri-Matic automatic clutch touted in ads was a centrifugal clutch with only one speed; a planetary transmission was optional. Final drive was by chain to the rear wheel, which featured the sprocket built integral with the wheel hub.

The front forks rode on ball bearings in the steering head, a feature that was a long time in coming for most American scooters. The Streamliner also had front and rear suspension before many others. Springing was knee-action on the front forks and on a rear subframe similar to a

swing-arm. Ads also touted its "spring steel frame," probably referring to the natural flex of overextended steel bars.

Options listed in a 1940 flyer included a rear luggage rack, Package Carrier, Tow Back to attach the Streamliner backward to a car's rear bumper, and commercial sidecar. With the 41-J, a tandem seat was offered.

As with the Motor Glide, Powell promoted the ease of scooter operation: one flyer promised that "Everyone who can ride a bicycle can ride a Powell Motor Scooter!" Two foot pedals were all that was needed: one for throttle, the other for the rear wheel's drum brake. Options for the Streamliner included a tandem seat with luggage rack, package carrier, sidecar, and tow hitch for 1941 models.

A-V-8 (Aviate) 1940–1942 ★★★

In 1940, Powell moved to a new factory in Compton, California, and released its new A-V-8 or Aviate scooter, styled as a Harley-Davidson or Indian big twin that had been shrunk in the laundry. This Powell creation would later spark a whole series of such scooters modelled after motorcycles including the Glendale, California, Mustang and Cushman's Eagle line, both of which came postwar.

The A-V-8 was designed for riders who were not afraid to swing their legs over their machine versus the step-through design, which had often been laughed at by true motorcyclists as being effeminate. The A-V-8 featured the motorcycles' rigid hardtail, saddle seat, a separate gas tank, and 4.00x8in tires.

Power was 5hp—a whole lot of horses at the time in a motorscooter—from an odd engine built by Powell from Ford V-8 parts stuffed into Powell's own cast-iron block. As Powell's flyer stated: "Important—pistons, connecting rods, valves, springs, guides, push rods, and fibre timing gears are replacement parts of a popular low-priced automobile." It was difficult to say if that was meant as an enticement or a warning.

Powell's engine measured 3 1/16x2 7/8in bore and stroke for 21ci with 5.0:1 compression. The single-cylinder version of the Ford Flathead was fired by battery ignition—an odditiy for scooters at any time. The engine was turned over by kickstart, although the first push-button electric start for a motorscooter was optional.

The first A-V-8s were built with a variable-speed V-belt drive similar to what Salsbury had developed several years early. The clutch was a three-shoe centrifugal automatic driving a variable-speed transmission via a rubber V-belt, which could be manually shifted into any of four speeds plus a fifth-speed overdrive. Final drive was by roller chain. Yet while Salsbury's variable-drive was a great success, Powell's was not, and most machines found today have been converted to some other type of transmission.

Standard color was harbor green, and a range of options was available: buddy seat, luggage rack, package carrier, windscreen, tow hitch, and delivery and passenger sidecars, the latter with side door.

Powell built the A-V-8 from 1940–1942, during which time a number of other entrepreneurs attempted to make it famous—under their own names. Frank Cooper silk-screened his own decals and sold the A-V-8 as the Cooper Aviate. When the US Army requested bids for a lightweight airborne scooter to drop by parachute behind enemy lines, Cooper took a welding torch, added a maze of reinforcing bars to the Aviate chassis, and offered the military his own Cooper War Combat Motor Scooter. While the Army liked the Cooper better than the Cushman 53, Army inspectors

were unimpressed with the Cooper Motors, Inc.'s "factory," and awarded the bid to Cushman.

When Powell turned its machinery from plowshares (as it were) to swords for World War II rocket and shells production, the Clark Engineering firm bought the remaining stock of 1942 A-V-8s and sold them as its own Victory Clipper scooters. In 1943, the firm of L. Ronney & Sons built A-V-8s as the Ronard Jeepette. And following the war in 1947, Clark was back building A-V-8s as the Clark Cylcone.

Lynx ★★

Following the war, Powell introduced its economy Lynx scooter with a Wisconsin AKN 6hp engine, Wico magneto, and disc-style automatic clutch, riding atop odd-sized 4.00x7in tires.

The Lynx followed the style of the Series 40 but eschewed any bodywork or suspension. The scooter was painted green, the engine gray. As Powell's flyer announced, "Dreams do come true!"

Powell's P-81 was a motorcycle in miniature along the lines of the Mustang and Cushman Eagle. With its 24ci or 392cc engine and 190lb weight, the P-81 had a stump-pulling power-to-weight ratio ideal for dragging big motorcycles out of the mud. As this 1949 *Popular Mechanics* ad stated, the P-81 "Cruises at 45 MPH—with faster pickup than [a] car."

C-47 1947 ★★

The C-47 scooter, built in 1947, returned to a Powell-built powerplant; this design would continue with modifications through 1951 in other Powell models.

Powell's new engine followed true motorcycle lines with a split die-cast aluminum crankcase, a built-up crankshaft, and a cast-iron flathead cylinder. Powell even made its own carburetor and ignition and generator system in an effort to keep costs down. Folklore has it that the piston and some valvetrain parts were again from the Ford V-8, but Powell never made mention of this in its ads. The pistons used were identical to Ford and Mercury pistons except that the Powell's used a flat-top piston whereas the Ford's was domed.

Bodywork now covered the front wheel and ran from the steering head over the rear wheel, but not covering the engine. A saddle seat sat atop the engine trailed by a luggage rack.

P-48 1948 and P-49 1949 ★★

In 1948-1949, Powell produced respectively its P-48 and P-49 scooters with a refined version of the Powell C-47 engine but lacking that scooter's

---

'Danger Rides Two Wheels'

By the mid-1960s, the teenaged set had taken over the scooter market while their elders moved on to four-wheelers. The older generation then looked back at scooters with horror: putt-putts were dangerous.

Earlier in 1957, *Popular Science* reassured tentative buyers that scooters were safe, writing, "Visibility is good; there are no posts to obstruct side vision, and you can see behind simply by turning your head." And even went on to say, "Snow, however, is navigable if you know your stuff."

But just five years later, an *Atlantic Monthly* article disclaimed their safety, writing that, "Scooters are inherently unstable, like spinning tops... On a scooter you lean over, and there you are, upside down in the ditch. You have to influence the scooter around a corner in a series of more or less controlled wobbles." Harsh words like these lead to legislation against scooters in many countries.

Once-mobile teens now had to rest at home with their studies instead of scooting on a Slimline following such outcries as General George C. Stewart of the National Safety Council: "To turn a fourteen year-old child loose on a motor scooter in today's traffic is about as sensible as giving a baby a dynamite cap for a teething ring. I would rather have a fourteen-year-old child of mine turned loose in traffic with a ten ton truck than on a scooter."

---

bodywork. The new 7hp 24ci engine used a cast-iron cylinder barrel with 3 1/6x3 1/4in bore and stroke, a die-cast aluminum crankcase, and a built-up crankshaft. The engine was sparked by a Powell magneto with the kickstart working directly to the camshaft. The Power-Matic automatic clutch transferred power to the rear 4.00x7in wheel via two rayon-cord V-belts.

Powell continued its tradition of eccentric creativity in the dry sump oiling system, which scavenged oil via crankcase pressure from an oil tank mounted to the floorboards. And the lucky rider sat on a seat formed by the aluminum gas tank.

Two models were offered: the Standard with solid front forks, crash bar seat cushion, floor mat, luggage rack, and rear foot rests; and the Deluxe with all of the Standard's features including telescoping front forks, chromed luggage rack mounted on springs so it could double as a buddy seat, headlamp, and taillamp. A side car was also available for either model.

The P-48 and P-49 were odd-looking scooters, an indestructible maze of solid bar stock that made up for its lack of grace by being sturdy—and heavy at more than 200lb for the complete machine. As a P-49 flyer hinted, "It Looks Custom Built," a polite way of saying it was not streamlined, to coin the other buzzword of the era.

P-81 1949–1951 ★★★

In 1949, Powell returned to its miniature motorcycle styling from the A-V-8 in creating its new P-81. This new scooter was half Whizzer, half Indian Chief, arriving on the market at the same time as Cushman's new Eagle. But the Powell offered more power than the Eagle, and rode atop 4.00x12in wheels.

Two P-81 models were offered: the Deluxe and the Special (called the Custom for 1950). The Deluxe engine was based on a 3 1/16x3 1/4in bore and stroke for 24ci, creating 8hp at 3200rpm and a 45mph top speed. Fitted with a larger-bore piston, 10hp at 3400rpm was possible from 26ci. Both models used the automatic clutch but resorted to the tried-and-true chain drive; some last models reverted to the dual V-belt final drive. Continuing its exotic tradition, Powell used the furnace-brazed frame as an oil supply tank to the dry sump system.

For 1949, the P-81 was available in black baked enamel set off by chrome trim with an optional luggage rack. By 1950, you could have a Custom in red, blue, green, or black. As the ads promised, "BIG motorcycle features throughout and at an unbelievably low price!"

During the Korean War, Powell turned away from scooter production and back to war contracts. In 1954, the brothers began building economical pickup trucks and sport wagons designed with hunters and campers in mind. Working with 1940s era Plymouth chassis, they added fiberglass front end, wood bumpers and funky options like a pop-up camper top, fishing pole compartments and more.

From 1967–1972, the final Powell scooter series was built, the 3 1/2hp Model M and 5hp Model L Challengers and 7hp Model J and JL Phantom mini-bikes, using Briggs & Stratton or Tecumseh engines.

It was the end of a long line of fascinating scooters. Like Salsbury, Powell had been innovative. The Powell had an influence on other scooters that went far beyond the small size of the firm and the number of scooters it built. The brothers set the style for miniature motorcycle scooters, offered the first scooter with electric start, and experimented with a broad range of eccentricities. The Powell scooters are rare and collectible today.

Prior UK ★

B. P. Scooters of Wolverhampton offered its Prior Viscount scooter in 1957 based on the German Hercules R200 and built under license. The motor was a 191cc Sachs providing 10.2hp at 5000rpm via a four-speed gearbox.

Ironically, the Hercules had been based on the German TWN Contessa, and when that scooter was imported to the UK, English buyers were confused by the two nearly identical scooters.

Progress Germany ★★

By 1954, Heinkel had already claimed "Tourist" for its scooter, Progress stuck with the *wanderlust* idea and opted for "vagabond," or *strolch*. The most impressive feature of the Strolch 150 and 175 were their headlamps mounted on the front apron but moving separately with the wheel. The Stuttgart company chose 16in wheels for added hill-climbing ability in the mountainous region. The engines were made by Sachs with 6.5hp for the 147cc, 9hp for the 174cc, and 10hp for the 1955 191cc Progress 200. The Strolch roller was also available with a 98cc Fichtel & Sachs engine. The Progress 200 didn't have the pivoting headlamp of the Strolch, and from 1958–1960 all Progress' scooters erased this interesting feature as well.

Progress UK ★★

Carr Bros. Ltd. of Purley in Surrey built German Progress scooters under license beginning in 1956. Three English Progress models were offered, all with Villiers two-stroke power: the 148cc Anglian, 197cc kickstart Briton; and the 197cc electric-start Britannia.

Puch Austria ★★

The grand old Steyr-Daimler-Puch firm of Graz offered its first scooters in 1952, the Puch R and RL. Power was from a 125cc single of 52x57mm delivering 4.5hp at 5100rpm with three speeds and 3.25x12in tires. The R was sparked by flywheel magneto; the RL by battery ignition.

In 1954, Puch sold RL scooters to the Swiss Condor firm as well as working together to develop a three-wheeler with two rear wheels driven by a differential. In 1955, the Puch R disappeared, the RL continued, supplemented by the RLA with electric start.

In 1957, the SR and SRA 150 Alpine line made its debut with a 150cc engine of 6hp at 5500rpm and completely updated bodywork. Again, the SRA added electric start.

In the early 1960s, Puch developed its DS 50 and DS 60 Cheetah scooters; in 1965, it offered its R50 Pony.

Raleigh UK ★★

Raleigh was famous for its bicycles dating back to the high times of Queen Victoria. In 1960, however, the firm decided to risk its reputation by selling a scooter. It contracted with the Italian Bianchi firm to sell its 78cc Orsetto scooter to the English market as the Raleigh Roma—never mind that Bianchi was situated in Milan. The Roma continued through 1964.

Riverside USA ★★

Montgomery Ward came late to the scooter market but it came in style and force. As Sears

Puch's scooter was a marvel of engineering, from the high-quality components down to the hinged rear cover that offered excellent access to the 125cc or 150cc engine—should it ever break down. Owner: Vittorio Tessera.

Rock-Ola offered its stylish line of scooters through *Popular Mechanics* ads, this one appearing in 1938. The scooter followed the tenets set down by Salsbury and competed with the other major Chicago manufacturer, Moto-Scoot. The "revolutionary new 'Floating Ride'" announced in this ad was the dual coil springs on the front forks.

Restored 1938 Rock-Ola scooter with styling betraying the company's roots in jukebox manufacturing. The mesh enclosing the 5/8hp Johnson Iron Horse engine was actually a metal sheet stamped to look like woven wicker—what will they think of next? But the Rock-Ola did have front suspension, via a triangulated forks and spring setup, an early use of such luxury. Owner: Herb Singe. *Herb Singe*

Roebuck named its scooter line the Allstate, Monkey Ward named its the Riverside.

In the late 1950s, Monkey Ward bought Rockford Scooters, which were actually Mitsubishi Silver Pigeons, and were renamed Riverside scooters. Ward sold the scooters mail-order via its nationwide catalog and outlet stores. The scooters were given further model names: the Nassau, Waikiki, and the Miami, which started its life as the C-74 Pigeon.

The identity crisis didn't end with Rockford-Mitsubishi; in the early 1960s, Montgomery Ward sold Lambretta scooters for several years, adding its nameplate to the legshield of the Li Series.

Rockford Scooter Company USA ★★

Beginning in the late 1950s, the Rockford Scooter Company of Rockford, Illinois, was the US importer of Mitsubishi Silver Pigeons, which were relabelled as the Rockford Scooter. Into the 1960s, Rockford imported the Pigeon C-73, C-74, C-76, and C-90 models.

Rockford in turn wholesaled its scooters to Montgomery Ward, where they were sold as Riverside scooters.

Rock-Ola USA ★★★★

Canadian David C. Rockola sparked his Rock-Ola firm in Chicago in the early 1930s building penny scales for the weight conscious. With Prohibition's repeal, Rock-Ola created its first jukebox in 1935 and spun disks on its way to success in the jukebox dance craze of pre-World War II days. Rock-Ola's jukeboxes were attired in brilliant lights, chrome frou frou, and Buck Rogers cool, and when the firm turned to scooters in 1938, it brought along its eye for style.

The Rock-Ola scooter followed the basic tenets of scooter design set down by the Salsbury Motor Glide with its small wheels, step-through design, and rear-mounted engine. Rock-Ola power was a one-cylinder 5.8hp Johnson Iron Horse engine. Clutch action was by tightening a belt.

The Rock-Ola's styling appeared in the engine cover, which was subtly curvaceous with its compound curves—something other makers were wont to invest in. The scooter was set off by two-tone paint, a headlamp, and a taillamp.

All told, the Rock-Ola looked like a roller skate dressed up in a swank metal zoot suit. *Popular Mechanics* ads pictured young girls at speed on the Rock-Ola—showing off both the ease of the scooter's use and more than a fair share of leg as their flouncy dresses were lifted by the breeze of a full 30mph top speed.

Rock-Ola also offered a three-wheel Delivery model based on the scooter rear end but adding a two-wheel front axle and large carrying compartment.

During World War II, Rock-Ola gave up scooter production to punch out ammo boxes and rifle parts for the war effort. Postwar, the firm returned to jukeboxes and forgot about scooters.

Röhr Germany ★

Röhr turned to scooters from farm machinery in 1952, and its Roletta always bore agricultural lines. Equipped with a roaring 197cc Ilo engine, the Roletta had 10hp with a top speed of 90km/h on the 12in wheels and was made until 1957. One of the most distinctive features of the Roletta was the boar's-snout headlamp that looked like an overgrown, lighted zucchini resting on the front fender.

The Roletta was built from 1952–1957 with a 200cc two-cylinder engine creating 10hp.

L. Ronney & Sons USA ★★★

The influential Powell firm created an innovative new scooter in 1940 known as the A-V-8, or Aviate. This scooter was a miniature motorcycle, setting a style that would continue with the Mustang and Cushman Eagle. And since it was such a success, numerous firms either purchased Aviates and sold them as their own or built their own versions under license.

In 1943, the Ronney firm of Los Angeles offered its version of the Powell as the Ronard Jeepette with 4.00x8in tires and a 21ci engine delivering 5hp.

P. P. Roussey France ★★

The frères Pierre and Paul Roussey displayed their elegant scooter in 1952 with long, sleek lines reminiscent of a two-wheeled Citreon. Water cooled the two-stroke motor available in two sizes: 125cc for 5hp or 170cc for 9hp. The design was revamped by les frères with updated models for 1953 and 1955.

Rumi Italy

There's a certain exquisite poetry in moving from manfacturing miniature submarines to building motorscooters. And Moto Rumi's Formichino scooter is perhaps the one motorscooter respected by motorcyclists—probably because it can melt the paint off many 250cc motorcycles of the era with its amazing horizontal two-cylinder two-stroke 125cc engine.

Moto Rumi was gone as quickly as it had arrived. The firm created its first motorcycle in 1949 and left the market by 1962. In those twelve years it built a reputation based on the power of its trademark engine, used across the line in its production motorcycles and scooters. It also created a series of exotic prototype racing machines.

Rumi's motorcycles and scooters were always unique. The engineering was avant garde and innovative; the styling was unlike any other two-wheelers. The features were created by a different mindset—unorthodox frames and forks, handy clocks mounted in gas tanks, odd fittings often individually stamped with Rumi's logo. The Rumi motorscooter was a totally unique creation compared to the Vespa, Iso, or Lambretta of the day.

Officine Fonderie Rumi was created before World War I by Achille Rumi as a specialized foundry based in the center of the city of Bergamo, Italy; after Achille's death, it was headed by his son, Donnino. During World War II, Rumi constructed two-man midget submarines as well as torpedoes for the Italian Navy. For the Italian postwar reconstruction, Rumi turned its engineering skills to the manufacture of motorcycles and scooters. Inspired by the success of Lambretta and Parilla, both located in nearby Milan, it built for

The Scoiattolo was Moto Rumi's first scooter, arriving in 1951 with a unit chassis of stamped steel and Rumi's great horizontal twin 125cc two-stroke engine mounted in the center. The Scoiattolo was offered in Rumi gray or blue. This was a 1953 model, which was available with electric start; in 1954, Rumi unveiled its superior Formichino scooter but surprisingly kept the Scoiattolo in production until 1957. *Gösta Karlsson archives*

the street; envious in rivalry with the four-stroke MV Agustas and Mondials, it built for the race-track.

The Rumi engine was an engineering master-piece, a race-winning two-stroke a decade ahead of the dominant East German MZ and the myriad Japanese designs. It was also a masterpiece of efficiency, weight, and size, as was the Vespa power-plant.

The crankcase was cast in four parts: two central sections that bolted together on the horizontal to hold the gearbox and crankshaft, and two side cases that bolted to the center block on the vertical to hold the clutch and Nassetti flywheel magneto. Separate cylinder barrels and heads bolted to the block, each held in place by four studs.

Bore and stroke of the 125cc was 42x45mm, with the two cylinders timed to fire at 180 degrees. A variety of single or dual carburetors and mufflers or megaphones were available for Standard, Sport, or Competizione models.

This engine premiered in the 1949 Rumi motorcycle, and soon appeared in race tune in the 1951–1954 Competizione Gobbetto, or Hunchback (nicknamed for the mounting of the magneto atop the engine like a humpback), and the long-lived Junior Gentleman production racer. In 1951, Rumi created its first scooter.

Scoiattolo 1951–1957 ★★★

The Scoiattolo, or Squirrel, scooter was introduced at the Milan Fiera Campionaria in 1951, the same year the Lambretta D and fully enclosed LD models bowed. Certainly Rumi was lured to the scooter market by the success of Innocenti and Piaggio, but its Scoiattolo was more of a motorcycle than a scooter, lacking the compactness, efficiency, and simple operation of the Vespa.

Like the Vespa, the chassis and body were a stamped-steel unit without a frame. But the wheels were 14in and gave the Scoiattolo an identity crisis: on one hand, it was an overgrown moped; on the other, a weak-kneed motorcycle.

The engine was Rumi's great 125cc twin with 6.5:1 compression and a single UA 15S Dell'Orto, creating 6hp at 4800rpm. The three-speed foot-change gearbox belied its motorcycle roots; a four-speed was offered from 1953. Top speed was 80km/h.

In 1953, an electric start version was offered with two 6 volt batteries run in parallel and mounted beneath the long saddle seat. In the same year, an aluminum-body sidecar for the Scoiattolo was first offered, running on a 3.25x14in wheel.

The Scoiattolo continued to be offered even after the introduction of the Formichino, which was a vastly superior scooter. Production mercifully ended in 1957.

Formichino Normale and
Formichino Lusso 1954–1960 ★★★★

The Formichino, or Little Ant, was designed by Donnino Rumi and is without doubt a motorscooter masterpiece. Whereas the Vespa was designed for simplicity—of construction, operation, and repair—the Formichino was simply unique.

The chassis and bodywork were of an innovative unit design akin to Corradino d'Ascanio's Vespa. But instead of the stamped steel of the Wasp, the Rumi body was cast from aluminum alloy in three structural sections that were assembled with Phillip's-head studs.

A rear section formed a fender, seat, and engine mount (modified in 1956 into two sections); and two vertically split center section halves held the front of the engine, gas tank, and steering head. Two further, nonstructural cast-aluminum pieces were a headlamp shell and a front fender. The foundry work was done by a Rumi subsidiary, Metalpress, also of Bergamo. The scooter was connected in the center by the engine, taking to an extreme the engineering concept of an engine as a stressed member of a design.

The engine of the first series Formichino breathed through a single Dell'Orto UA 15S carburetor with a split intake manifold. With a compression ratio of 6.5:1, the 125cc created 6.5hp at 6000rpm via its four-speed, foot-change gearbox and a multiple-disk oil-bath clutch. For comparison, the Lambretta LD 125 of 1954 made only 4.8hp, a dramatic difference.

Early Formichinos rode solely on 4.00x8in tires but by 1958, 10in wheels and 3.50x10in tires were optional. Drum brakes of 125mm diameter were fitted front and rear.

The second series Formichino appeared without fanfare in 1956 bearing only subtle modifications. The rear body section was now cast in two pieces with the fender hinged to fold up, easing rear tire changes. A Veglia speedometer unit with odometer was also added.

With the introduction of the Formichino Sport in 1957, the standard model was called the Normale.

In 1958, the Formichino Lusso bowed with luxury accessories but specs similar to the Normale. Accessories included a long, two-person saddle, cast-aluminum passenger footpegs, chrome hubcaps, and assorted chrome trim. A wide range of paint colors was now available: standard Rumi gray, ivory, silver, sky blue, racing blue, gold, yellow, and, of course, *rosso corsa*, or Italian racing red.

Other options were offered through the Little Ant's life, including an extra pillion saddle, full legshields, several types of spare tire racks and luggage racks, as well as an assortment of swank chrome trim pieces, ideal for cruising the *duomo* and essential in the land that made chrome exhaust tips what they are today.

Rumi exported its two-wheelers throughout the world. The US importer was Berti Corporation in New Hyde Park, New York. The Formichino was for sale in the United States as the Little Ant scooter with ads promising a full 65mph.

Also in 1958, Rumi advertised a 150cc Formichino based on a bored 125cc engine, according to Riccardo Crippa's *Rumi: La moto dell'artista*. Bore and stroke was 46x45mm, producing 9hp at 6500rpm. Other sources also claim a 175cc model, but Rumi had a unique way of advertising models that never actually went into production; whether the 150cc or 175cc Formichino went into production or remained a prototype is not known.

Formichino Sport 1957–1960 ★★★★

In 1957, Rumi showed its Formichino Sport at the Fiera Milanese. The Sport featured new cylinder barrels cast in aluminum alloy with steel liners and fed initially by a single 22mm Dell'Orto; later versions came with twin 18mm Dell'Ortos on separate intake manifolds. Power was now up to 8hp at 7200rpm with a compression ratio of 7.0:1 and top speed of 105km/h or 69mph.

While the Normale featured a simple Rumi decal on the side of the headlamp, the Sport had an elaborate insignia with the Rumi emblem of a maritime anchor, reflecting the midget submarine heritage, patriotically backed by the Italian *tricolore*.

Standard tires were 3.50x10in and many race parts were optional by 1959: a range of dual Dell'Ortos and special alloy barrels with chrome bores.

Formichino Economico 1958 ★★★★

In 1958, an odd economy model made its debut, the Formichino ST-EC or Tipo Economico. The chassis reverted to standard steel tubing covered by stamped-steel bodywork in the classic Lambretta style. The E was available solely in British Racing Green with a white flash over the gas tank.

The E used the Normale engine with 6hp at 6000rpm, but top speed was 50mph and gas consumption was 113mpg. According to Crippa, a 175cc ST-EC model was also advertised.

All in all, it was an odd scooter for Rumi, known for its sporting models. In the end, less than 1,000 were believed to have been constructed, all destined for export from Italy, although

Rumi's Formichino was one the greatest scooters ever made. Based on the firm's 125cc horizontal engine and a cast-aluminum chassis, the Little Ant was light, powerful, and quick—top speeds of 65mph were typical. The first series of 1954-1955 had this one-piece rear fender. *Gösta Karlsson archives*

none are believed to have come to the United States.

Formichino Bol d'Or 1959 ★★★★

In 1955, motorscooters first appeared at the premier endurance racing event, the Bol d'Or or Trophy of Gold held at the French Montlhéry circuit. Scooters had been racing all over the continent in backroad duels and small-time road races, but here was international competition and the potential for worldwide glory.

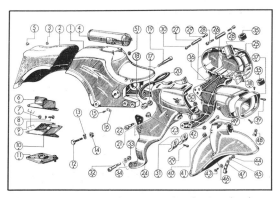

The Formichino chassis was made of cast aluminum sections that were joined in the center by the engine. From 1956–1960, this second series model was available with the separate rear fender that was hinged to swing out of the way for rear wheel changes. Twin carburetors were also available on the second series Formichino. *Gösta Karlsson archives*

Scooter Road Racing:
From the Bol d'Or to NASCAR

Scooterists started racing each other the day two of them met on the road. The first organized races took place in postwar Italy when a scooter offered the ideal entry into road racing on a budget that could not afford the latest MV Agusta motorcycle or even a prewar racer.

In 1950, Innocenti entered a special Lambretta racer in the grueling Milano–Taranto, dash from Milan to Taranto in the bootheel of Italy. Rider Carancini averaged 62.101km/h, bettered in 1951 by Longoni on his Lambretta at 75.948km/h.

The year 1955 saw the birth of true scooter racing with the French twenty-four-hour Bol d'Or, or Trophy of Gold, endurance race was staged at the Montlhéry circuit with scooters competing in classes for standard, sport, and racing models. In that first year, the team of Gerard Daric and M. Brugeilles on a 150cc Lambretta ran in the 175cc motorcycle class finishing 25th overall but first in their class after covering 937 miles at an average speed of 62.87km/h or 39.03mph. In 1956, in spite of legshield-to-legshield competition from Rumis, the Lambretta duo finished 1,948km or 1,210miles at an average speed of 81.18km/h or 50.44mph. Lambrettas, Rumis, and P. P. Roussey scooters consistently ruled the track, and Rumi even named its production racing scooter the Bol d'Or in honor of the race.

In 1952, a special factory Lambretta six-day trial machine, a variation of the 125cc model C, competed in the International Six Day Trial with a large gas tank between the rider's legs instead of the small tank under the seat. In 1961, Lambretta works racer Alan Kimber completed the 1,200 mile ISDT and in the Welsh 3-day Trial was awarded the prestigious scooter award.

Off the English coast, the Isle of Man Scooter Rally attracted hundreds of scooter racers in a competition that mimicked the famous motorcycle Tourist Trophy, or TT, race that circled the island. Innocenti even created its Lambretta TV 200 model to challenge Vespa at the Manx race.

In the United States, NASCAR, the stock-car racing association, sanctioned oval dirt-track scooter racing with the premiere held on July 11, 1959 at the New York City Polo Grounds baseball stadium. Two classes were open to scooters of more or less than 150cc, which could do battle in

WFO at a solid ton on a full-race Lambretta during an American Scooter Racing Association race in the 1990s. Based on your everyday Li 150, this racer sports a bored and ported cyclinder of 190cc, racing clutch, and an expansion chamber like a sousaphone. The frame is handmade from chromemoly tubing topped by an alluminum-alloy gas tank and dressed in full fiberglass fairing and seat section. The stock forks get it into ASRA's Group B Specials, which also approves of the hydraulic disc front brakes. Built by Mick Dailey of GoFast Scooters in Anaheim, California, for Bruce Gajjar; rider and current owner John Quintos of San Francisco was hanging off here. Paul Verlangieri

Classes for standard, sport, and racing scooters were initially set up, and the scooters ran for twenty-four hours with two riders allowed per scooter. At the end, the scooter completing the most laps won, and from 1955 through the last Bol d'Or scooter race in 1960, Rumis ruled. Their finest year was 1958, running against both scooters and motorcycles when the Foidelli/Bois team ran a Rumi Sport 2,095km or 1,302 miles at an average speed of 87.327km/h or 54.258mph to win.

The year 1958 also saw the debut of the ultimate Formichino model, the 125cc Bol d'Or. Based on the Sport, the production racer's engine had a compression ratio of 7.0:1 in alloy barrels with chrome bores pumping out 8.5hp at 7200rpm through two 18mm Dell'Orto carbs; dual 22mm Dell'Ortos were optional. Top speed in production trim was up to a staggering 75mph.

The Bol d'Or ran on 3.5x10in tires, tuned suspension, and was fitted with a long, slim dual seat; a supplementary gas tank was also available, styled like a first series Rumi Junior Gentleman motorcycle. The Bol d'Or was finished in brilliant gold and white and emblazoned with the Rumi Sport decal and *tricolore*.

In tuned competition trim, Sport and Bol d'Or models were typically fitted with short megaphone exhausts, dual 22mm carbs, and polished ports. Top speed was often up to 150km/h or 93.2mph.

V-Twin Prototypes 1960–1962 ★★★★★

In 1960, Rumi announced a motorcycle and scooter line based on a new modular four-stroke engine in three displacements: 98cc (40x39mm for 5.8hp at 7500rpm), 125cc (43x43mm for 6.8hp at 7000rpm), and 175cc (48x48mm for 8.2hp at 6800rpm). The 90 degree V-twin engine featured overhead valves run by pushrods and rocker arms; the V of the engine was mounted in line with the wheels.

The design of the Rumi V-twin scooters mimicked the established look of the Vespa and Lambretta. The body was of stamped steel surrounding a tube frame. Sidecovers were hinged to open laterally. Controls were finally all on the handlebar, with the exception of the foot-operated rear drum brake. Tires were 3.50x10in.

All in all, it looked like the right scooter at the right time. But suddenly Rumi switched gears and quit motor vehicle production. An official account of this change of heart was never made, but Rumi had returned to military contract work, leaving behind the fickle world of motorscooters and abandoning the V-twin scooters to fate in prototype limbo.

At the Köln Motorcycle Show in October 1992, a new Rumi racing motorcycle was shown;

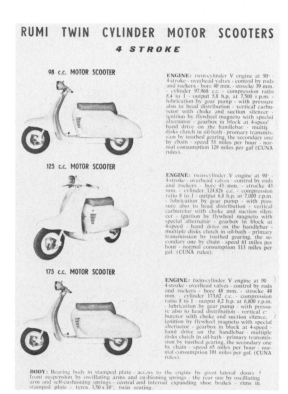

Rumi announced a complete line of four-stroke V-twin scooters in 1960 with a shared chassis for 98, 125, and 175cc versions. The concept was brilliant and the styling was closer to the accepted scooter tradition than Rumi's Formichino, all of which spoke of success. It was not to be; as quickly as it came, Rumi disappeared. The V-twin scooters remained prototypes; only one 125cc survivor is knowntoday. *Gösta Karlsson archives*

is there a possibility of a new Formichino in the future?

Safeticycles, Inc. USA ★★

The Safeticycle Cruiser from La Crosse, Wisconsin, was half scooter, half Ner-A-Car, the odd low-seat American motorcycle of the 1920s. As the firm's debut ad, appearing in the *Saturday Evening Post*, stated, "Nationally Advertised, Nationally Accepted." The first half of the statement was obviously true; the second half was wishful thinking.

The Safticycle was a step-through bicycle riding atop large bicycle wheels; the seat height was below that of the rear wheel. The large wheels and mile-long wheelbase provided "no jumping bumps ...no death grip... no bobble... no bounce," according to a flyer. But not many people took the ad's advice of "Eye it, try it, buy it."

San Cristoforo Italy ★★★

Having a company named for San Cristoforo, the protector of travelers (who was later impeached by the Vatican after having done centuries of good work), must have been good advertising for a scooter.

S. Cristoforo s.r.l. of Milan took over production of Gianca's Nibbio scooter in 1949. The Nibbio had been one of the pioneering Italian scooters alongside the Vespa, and S. Cristoforo kept it in production until 1951.

When the Nibbio first rolled off the new assembly lines it was substantially updated from the Gianca model. The bodywork was all new, as was the 125cc two-stroke engine. With 5hp at 4700rpm and a three-speed gearbox, the Nibbio was now good for 75km/h.

In 1952, S. Cristoforo released its Simonetta 125cc scooter, which was in truth a Nibbio under a new name. The styling was slightly renewed but the motor was retained. The Simonetta was also built in France by Ravat.

Sanko Kogyo Japan ★★

Sanko Kogyo's Jet series of motorscooters was built primarily for the Japanese market in the

Safticycle's Cruiser model was a strange concoction—half bicycle, half scooter. The benefits were obvious (to the copywriter): the large wheels saved the rider from "'death grip' steering" as well as "bobble," the bain of all scooter riders although they didn't know it yet.

1950s. The line bowed in 1953 with the 175cc J5 producing 4.5hp at 4200rpm and riding on 4.00x8in tires. The styling was pure tractor.

By 1954, the Jet J5 had been dressed up with chrome trim, air ducts, and a jet ornament taking off from the front fender. The effect was still the same. In the same year, the Jet J7 was offered to combat the deluxe Rabbit and Pigeon models with an overhead-valve 250cc engine of 70x65mm for 6.7hp at 4500rpm and a top speed of 70km/h.

Salsbury USA

In 1935, the United States was sunk in the midst of the Great Depression with no end in sight. It was the days of *The Grapes of Wrath*, people selling pencils and apples on the streets or willing to work for food; job layoffs were rampant and making ends meet for those with jobs was a tightrope walk.

Onto this stage stepped E. Foster Salsbury with the idea of building a motorscooter to be called the Motor Glide. Salsbury was inspired in 1935 when he saw the great feminist and aviator Amelia Earhart dashing around the Lockheed airport at Burbank, California, on an ancient Motoped, a motorized scooter left over from the 1910s.

Salsbury said in a 1992 interview that at the time he had "No idea what the market for a scooter would be. It was pure invention—very far out for those days." Yet he had an inkling, as he wrote in a corporate newsletter commemorating the scooter's later success: he "conceived the idea that this country needed a good but inexpensive mode of transportation." The Motor Glide was to be economical transportation for those without a car and double as an inexpensive second car for others.

Motor Glide 1935–1936 ★★★★★

Salsbury hired inventor Austin Elmore to construct the first Motor Glide in late 1935 working at Salsbury's brother's heating and plumbing shop in Oakland, according to Salsbury. The scooter used an Evinrude Speedibyke single-cylinder two-cycle engine with a 2x1 5/8in bore and stroke for 5.1ci or 82.5cc. The crankcase was made of aluminum alloy with fuel fed through a single carburetor into a two-port internal rotary intake valve. At a maximum of 3500rpm, the engine created 0.75hp. For simplicity, drive from the Speedibyke engine was via direct roller friction running onto the rear tire.

The Motor Glide used a duplex frame that surrounded the steering head at the front and supported a tube-frame rear section mounting the engine. Pressed-steel floorboards covered the center section.

When the prototype was ready for action, Salsbury packed his wife, daughter, and scooter into his car and drove from Oakland to Palm Springs for a vacation, stopping off at the February 1936 Airplane and Boating Show in Los Angeles' Pan-Pacific Auditorium. Salsbury displayed his scooter to barnstorming aviator Colonel Roscoe Turner who was thrilled by a ride on the Motor Glide; he immediately pronounced the scooter "The greatest woman catcher I have ever seen," Salsbury recalled.

Turner placed the prototype on display at his show booth and it drew instant attention: for child movie star Freddy Bartholomew of *Little Lord Fauntleroy,* it was love at first sight and he ordered one. In fact the scooter was such a success, Salsbury cancelled the family vacation and got to work, contracting a Los Angeles machine shop to begin production.

The Motor Glide Company announced the debut of its scooter in a February 1936 magazine

The Motor Glide was introduced to the world at the February 1936 Airplane and Boating Show in Los Angeles; at the same time, this first ad appeared in magazines showing Col. Roscoe Turner endorsing the first Motor Glide built by Austin Elmore. After riding the Motor Glide for the first time, Turner proclaimed it, "The greatest woman catcher I have ever seen." This early model had direct roller drive onto the rear wheel. The Motor Glide Company was soon to be renamed the Salsbury Corporation. *E. Foster Salsbury archives*

137

Roscoe Turner and the faithful mounted on Motor Glides at the opening of one of the first Salsbury dealers, in San Diego, California, in early 1936. Turner is on his second Motor Glide, one of the New 1937 Model De Luxe High Speed Motor Glides, to quote its full name. Catchy. *E. Foster Salsbury archives*

Salsbury wasted no time in updating the first Motor Glide into the new 1937 Model De Luxe with a semblance of bodywork covering some of the Evinrude motor. The powerplant now had its crankshaft rotation reversed to allow chain drive to the rear wheel. A battery-powered bicycle headlamp had also been added. *E. Foster Salsbury archives*

ad with Turner's hearty endorsement. Turner was an irrepressible and flamboyant aviator who was probably better known as an early master of promotion and showmanship. He did, however, win the 1933 Bendix Trophy and 1934, 1938, and 1939 Thompson Trophy Air Races. He flew accompanied by his parachute-equipped pet lion cub, and was himself nattily attired in gleaming jackboots and a colonel's uniform, which was vaguely legitimized by an honorary commission in a state National Guard. He once crashed his plane in 1936 only to be saved by his huge silver belt buckle, which absorbed the impact, receiving a dent but saving Roscoe's life. Never mind his background, Turner was famous, and his boost for the neophyte Motor Glide must have meant life or death.

Roscoe Turner's new two-wheeled mount weighed 65lb and came "fully equipped" with lights, horn, and collapsible handlebars so it could be stowed in planes, boats, or cars for economical travel. As the ads stated, "Glide along effortlessly mile after mile. Ride it to work; visit friends and interesting places." This was the market sector the company hoped to attract: commercial use, not sport.

But while the rest of the scooter was proving itself, the same could not be said for the roller drive. On the reverse side of a Salsbury archival photo of this first scooter, an unknown hand noted that the drive system "worked fine on dry pavement."

The 1937 Aero Model Motor Glide was introduced in November 1936 by this full-color poster, which also showed off the new Parcel Carrier and Cycletow. With this model, Salsbury truly established itself and a market, inspiring others such as Powell, Moto-Scoot, and Cushman to make their own scooters. *E. Foster Salsbury archives*

Foster Salsbury estimated that only 25-30 of the roller-drive Motor Glides were ever built.

New 1937 Model De Luxe High Speed Motor Glide 1936–1937 ★★★★★

By November 1936, the new 1937 Model De Luxe High Speed Motor Glide was offered in *American Bicyclist and Motorcycle* magazine, available now from the newly formed Salsbury Corporation. The 1937 Model still used the Evinrude motor but with the crankshaft rotation reversed to allow chain drive to the rear wheel.

"Widely acclaimed in the West in 1936—Motor Glide rides forward to national distribution in 1937," according to this first ad. Based from Salsbury's new plant at 1515 East 75th Street in Los Angeles, a production line was now assembling up to six scooters at a time. And Roscoe Turner was back, now astride his 1937 Model.

Salsbury also printed its first full brochure in November 1936 with pictures of Roscoe Turner, the assembly line, and full specifications for the 1937 Model. With the chain drive, the scooter now ran up to 35mph while delivering 125mpg. Beyond the reversed rotation, the engine was the same 0.75hp unit with a flywheel magneto pro-

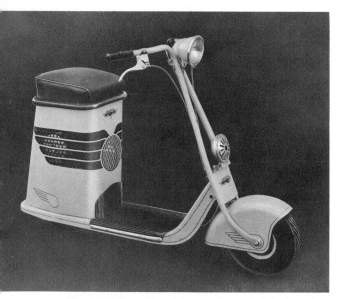

The 1937 Aero Model boasted restyled bodywork to enclose the new Johnson four-stroke engine. It was while shopping for the new powerplant that E. Foster Salsbury contacted Cushman for a bid on its Husky engine; Salsbury declined Cushman's offer, and Cushman decided to enter the scooter market for itself. Oddly enough, Johnson would later merge with Evinrude—Salsbury's first engine-supplier—and buy out Cushman. *E. Foster Salsbury archives*

viding ignition and lighting, a cast-aluminum muffler, and 0.5 gallon gas tank. Tires were General's Jumbo Junior 12x3.50in, and a drum brake was fitted to the rear wheel, operated by a hand lever.

Styling had also developed from the prototype with steel bodywork encasing the motor at the rear; as the brochure stated, it was "Smartly streamlined for style and beauty." Original colors were High Gloss Jade Green or Chinese Red, each finished with "attractive" cream trim and chrome plating; special colors were also available upon request. Accessories included an electric horn, headlight, and taillight.

All of this was aimed at a market looking for an economical vehicle that was easy to use. Ads showing women on the Motor Glide were not just cheesecake, and operating instruction had only two steps: "First—Give the Motor Glide a push and step on. (Automatic compression release makes starting easy.) Second—Give it gas by opening the throttle with your right hand and away you go." The seat was "extremely comfortable," made of coiled springs and "amply padded with felt and hair." The step-through construction was ideal for skirts as there was "nothing to straddle." As Roscoe Turner attested, "Here's the smartest, safest, handiest and most economical motor transportation." What more could you want?

And so many people followed Roscoe Turner's lead. Actress Olivia de Havilland took a Motor Glide for a spin around the Hollywood studio lots. Vacationing Bing Crosby terrorized Honolulu on one. Johnnie "Scat" Davis, heartthrob of "Sweepstakes Winner," went hillclimbing with his. Freddy Bartholomew rode his around Hollywood "like a streak of greased lightning," according to the *Los Angeles Times*. Salsbury capitalized on its location nearby the movie studios in their heydays, terming its scooters "Hollywood's Motor Glides" and stating in ad copy that the scooters were handy everywhere—"and, of course, around movie studios." It was image-building at its best.

Model 1937 Aero Motor Glide 1936–1937 ★★★★★

Nevertheless, Salsbury was not resting on its laurels. By December, after introducing the 1937 Model in November 1936, Salsbury announced a new model, the 1937 Aero Motor Glide with full bodywork enclosing a new Johnson four-stroke engine. This engine had a 2 1/8x1 3/4in bore and stroke for 6.2ci creating 0.75hp at 2400rpm. A flywheel magneto continued to supply spark while no less than four giant 6 volt batteries provided lighting. The Aero glided to a lower 30mph top speed but returned—as proved by an official AMA test—153mpg for your investment of around a nickel per gallon of gas. The Aero was priced at $119.50 while the De Luxe was $155. By early 1937, the original 1937 Model De Luxe was gone as the company concentrated on the Aero.

In the following months, Salsbury also introduced the Parcel Carrier attachment, a large bin that mounted on the rear of the Motor Glide for delivery services. This was followed by three optional Motor Glide models designed for commercial use. The Passenger Side Car Model SC-11 was a bathtub-like sidecar available with a single padded seat and a color scheme matching the scooter. The Express Side Car Model SC-12 followed the SC-11 styling but was merely a commercial carrier bin. Both sidecars rode on the 12in tires of the scooter with "suspension" supplied by the natural flex of the metal frame.

Finally, the Cycletow Model 64 was an ingeniuous set of giant "training wheels" that mounted to the rear end in line with the rear tire; these could be elevated for solo riding or lowered in place for towing of the scooter. Photos showed vacationers trotting along with their Motor Glides in tow and car dealers using them for picking up and delivering new cars. The idea followed Harley–Davidson's 1932 Servi-Car and Indian's Dispatch Tow. The Cycletow became the Model CT-60 for 1938.

With these added accessories, the Motor Glide was finding myriad new customers. A 1937 brochure shows Motor Glides in the faithful service of telegraph riders and messenger deliverers, postal carriers, police patrols, the US Army and Navy, and more. Foster Salsbury estimated that 200–300 1937 Aero Motor Glide units were built and sold in all.

Models 50 and 60 1937–1938★★★

In late 1937, Salsbury introduced on the new 1938 Motor Glide its most revolutionary feature: the Self-Shifting Transmission, as the firm termed its new automatic clutch and transmission torque converters. The primary drive was via a V-shaped rubber belt running between pulleys. The belts shifted between the different-size pulleys for ratios of 14:1 in low to 4:1 in high. The automatic clutch allowed the engine to idle until the throttle was twisted. This automatic transmission technology was startlingly innovative in 1937; the reason it is commonplace today is due to Salsbury's designs, which are still state of the art on industrial engines and vehicles of all sorts, including snowmobiles and the latest generation of Honda four-wheelers.

Two models were offered in 1938, both with the torque converter: the Model 50 with 5/8hp engine and the Model 60 with the 1 to 1 1/2hp engine. And again Colonel Roscoe Turner was at the controls for the new ad campaign, stating that the 1938 Motor Glide "is the last word in personal transportation and far exceeds my fondest expectation for performance."

The bodywork styling for the new 1938 scoots remained similar to the 1937 Aero although the horn was moved atop the steering head and the headlamp ascended to the handlebars. The 1938 models were now finished stock in cream only with green striping; special colors were available at nominal extra cost.

And it all worked. It worked so well in fact that it set the style for all scooters that were to follow, from the Cushman and Vespa onward. Tak-

In late 1937, Salsbury introduced its most revolutionary invention ever: the "Self-Shifting Motor," as the firm termed its new automatic clutch and transmission torque converters on this poster hung in Salsbury dealer showrooms everywhere. This automatic transmission technology was futuristic for 1937. And Roscoe Turner was back, as happy as ever with his new 1938 Model 60 Motor Glide with 1 1/2hp Johnson engine. *E. Foster Salsbury archives*

An original, unrestored late 1938 Model 50 5/8hp lacking its original decals and wing paint motif. The headlamp moved to the handlebars and the horn ascended to the steering head with the 1938 model; late 1938 models had this fatter front fender with the forks projecting through. Owner: Jim Kilau.

ing inspiration from the early American Motoped, English ABC Skootamota, and others, Salsbury and Elmore created a modern scooter that was a success. And all scooters that followed would share at least three of five of the Motor Glide's attributes of a motor placed next to the rear wheel in some form, step-through construction, body-work covering the motor, small wheels, and an automatic transmission/clutch.

One reason for the Motor Glide's influence was that in 1938, Salsbury sent a sales agent to Europe armed with blueprints and photos to discuss licensing production to potential scooter manufacturers. Foster Salsbury said in a 1992 interview that, while he was not on the trip, he believed that Piaggio was among the firms contacted. Piaggio—as well as the others that were approached—declined a Salsbury licensing agreement.

Models 70 and 72 1939–1945 ★★★

For 1939, Salsbury completely revamped the Motor Glide, introducing the Model 70 with Standard Seat and Model 72 with DeLuxe Floating Ride Seat. The engine in both models was a new 2.3–2.7hp Lauson single-cylinder four-stroke measuring a square 2 1/4x2 1/4in for 8.94ci with a compression ratio of 6.0:1. Ignition was by flywheel magneto, lighting by a generator, cooling by air via "forced draft," and oiling by pump. The Self-Shifting Transmission was standard on the Model 72 and optional on the 70. Other develop-

ments included rubber engine mounts and a drive chain automatically oiled by crankcase oil vapor.

The suspension was also updated for unprecedented comfort. "Rubber snubbers" and tension coil springs "effectively cushion road shocks" at the front and rear, promised flyers. And the tires were now 3.50x12in but still with only a rear drum brake.

The most dramatic change was the new "aero-dynamic aircraft designing for style leadership," as Salsbury brochures waxed poetically. These radical styling advances were most pronounced in the new Easy-Lift Streamlined Engine Hood, which truly looked as though it was "styled by the wind" with curves replacing the creases and folds of the older Motor Glides. The sides of the hood were now made of mesh, providing a tantalizing and seductive see-through view of the mechanicals. Motor Glide wing emblems were emblazoned over the fenders and hood mesh sides. The standard color was again Tacoma Cream with green striping and cadmium-plated parts.

The seats distinguished the two models. The Standard Seat of the 70 was a simple pad albeit covered in "durable quasi leather." The Floating Ride Seat of the 72 was actually a thinner pad, covered in Fabricoid, but mounted atop long leaf springs; the leaves doubled as bumpers at the tail. The Tandem Standard Seat was a lengthened version of the single; the Tandem DeLuxe added an extra Fabricoid pad to the leaf springs of the 72.

By 1939, you could order a Model 70 or 72 as fully optioned as your neighbor's Cadillac. The Special Equipment and Approved Accessories list from February 1, 1941, listed the following options: DeLuxe Floating Ride seat (optional for Model 70); Tandem DeLuxe seat; Tandem Standard seat; Tandem seat footrests; Salsbury Self-Shifting Transmission (optional for Model 70); Passenger Side Car; Express Side Car with open top; Express Side Car with hinged cover and latch; Parcel Carrier with hinged cover and latch; hand throttle control with cable; Flex Glass windshield; speedometer; Tow Glide; Vibra Disc horn with button, wiring, bracket, and 6 volt battery; and special paint colors.

The Models 70 and 72 continued their legacy through World War II during which they were built in small numbers. In the war years, as in the Depression years, scooters continued to be pressed into new services with gas rationing making the 100mpg attractive.

To counter Nazi aggressions in Europe, the US Army requested bids for military motorscooters in 1944. Salsbury was one of several makers alongside Cushman who provided scooters; Fos-

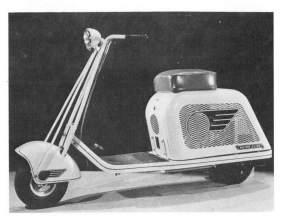

In 1939, Salsbury launched its new line of scooters with a 2.3–2.7hp Lauson single-cylinder four-stroke engine, its own torque converter, and new styling that was far ahead of any other scooter make for its time. This was the Standard Model 70. *E. Foster Salsbury archives*

The new 8.94ci Lauson four-stroke with flywheel magneto and lighting generator as well as reworked Salsbury torque converter. Primary drive was via a V-shaped rubber belt running between pulleys. The belts shifted between the different-size pulleys and the automatic clutch allowed the engine to idle. *E. Foster Salsbury archives*

ter Salsbury estimated that as many as 200 Model 72s were sold to the US Navy for base transportation and communications during the war. For the Red Cross and armed services, Salsbury created a Mono-Ambulance Motor Glide with a covered stretcher on a sidecar chassis.

By 1945, Motor Glide production ended. Salsbury had something new up its sleeve for 1946.

Super-Scooter Model 85 Standard and Deluxe 1946–1949 ★★★★★

It was outrageous. It was radical. It was the motorscooter of the future—and destined to be the most desirable motorscooter of all time.

Its styling was avant garde, years ahead of the Jet Age styling of the 1950s, more akin to a zeppelin on wheels. Yet the wheels were barely visible, hidden beneath flowing, streamlined fender skirts and so, along with the ease of the Self-Shifting Transmission, you felt as though you were not so much gliding—you were flying.

Salsbury spent the war years producing a small number of civilian scooters but had concentrated on materiel for the war effort. The firm also designed the Turret Truck, a motorized forklift with a revolving front end; it was licensed to Hyster Company in 1949.

Among its other work, Salsbury also developed an experimental wind tunnel for the aviation industry, which was used in early aerodynamic studies for fighters and bombers. Lessons learned in the new field of aviation aerodynamics would set the stage for the design of the new Salsbury scooter.

In 1944-1945, Salsbury sold his scooter business to the Los Angeles defense-contracting firm

AVION, Inc., which in turn changed its name to Salsbury Motors, Inc., in 1946 and became a subsidiary of Northrop Aircraft Corporation.

Based from a new plant in Pomona, the new Model 85 scooter was introduced at a press preview in late 1946 on Fargo Street, the "steepest

The DeLuxe Model 72 differed from the Model 70 in its "Floating Ride" seat that perched the cushion atop dual leaf springs for Gold Wing-like comfort circa 1939. *E. Foster Salsbury archives*

To announce its revolutionary new Model 85 super-scooter in 1946, Salsbury photographed it in front of Los Angeles' Pan-Pacific Auditorium where it had first shown its scooter to the world in 1936. This was a DeLuxe model with full front fender and windshield, chassis number 504. *E. Foster Salsbury archives*

improved hill" in Los Angeles, according to Steve Hannagn Associates, Salsbury's new PR firm thanks to Northrop, which promoted the event. The 85 climbed the 32 degree slope with ease "although the grade is enough to stall many automobiles." The show was meant to impress the press with Salsbury's idea of a motorscooter "as a second car for moderate-income families."

Northrop called its new Model 85 Super-Scooter the Salsbury scooter; not the Motor Glide by Salsbury. Obviously, Northrop believed Salsbury was an established name—and it didn't want further confusion with Cushman's Auto Glide.

The Model 85 had been designed by engineer Lewis Thostenson during the end of World War II. Thostenson had been one of Salsbury's original engineers and continued on at Northrop; Foster Salsbury headed the scooter sales team for Northrop.

The Model 85 was available in Standard and DeLuxe versions, both using the same mechanicals but the latter with a plexiglass windshield and fully developed front cockpit. The engine was a Salsbury-built 6hp four-stroke single-cylinder set at an angle toward the rear of the scooter. It featured the exclusive Straight-Shot carburetion

system, a short, but admittedly angled intake manifold. Nevertheless, the 1946 brochure promised the power "will take you up steep hills at car speed."

The torque converter was standard on both models, and for further ease of operation, the 1946 brochure didn't even use the words throttle or brake when describing the two control pedals: they were simply the Stop and Go pedals. The 85 DeLuxe, however, could be ordered with an auxiliary hand throttle.

Perhaps the most interesting feature of the new 85 was the front and rear forks, which were one-sided with stub axles inspired by airplane strut design. But the suspension was provided by two, different-rate coil springs housed *within* an elongated steering head. At the rear, a single coil spring did the damping. The 85 had come a long way from the Motor Glide.

It was the bodywork of the 85 that caught your attention first and foremost. Both versions were bejewelled with a chrome bumper and a similar rear-end design. Within the tail bodywork was a spare tire and luggage compartment "ample for most shopping trips"; on top was a padded, leather-covered seat.

The Standard featured a large fender that enveloped the front wheel and lead up over the steering head in one smooth, bodacious expanse. The DeLuxe added a large cowling over the front fender surmounted by a plexiglass windshield. Where the headlamp on the Standard was free standing, the DeLuxe headlamp was recessed into the cowling.

The design was pure Buck Rogers: at a time when Northrop was experimenting with its advanced XF-89 Scorpion jet fighter, the Salsbury scooter shared the Jet Age styling. And it was large. The size was unprecedented among scooters; it was certainly big enough to be a second car!

Northrop produced the Model 85 for two years during which time Foster Salsbury estimated 700–1,000 units were built and sold, including units exported to Germany. But as Salsbury recalled the Model 85's demise, "Demand fell off when cars started becoming available again and Northrop halted production." It was a sad finale for a great scooter.

Salsbury's influence on all other scooters that followed cannot be overestimated. Austin Elmore and Foster Salsbury dictated the design of the modern motorscooter with their 1936 Motor Glide.

Saroléa Belgium ★★★★

Saroléa was one of the grand old motorcycle manufacturers that failed to find a market postwar. In 1956, Saroléa showed its Djinn scooter at the Salon de Bruxelles. Named for a desert spirit, the Djinn was a Rumi Formichino disguised by the Belgian maker's decal on the aluminum-alloy bodywork and Belgian Englebert whitewall tires. Saroléa built the Djinn in cooperation with Rumi in the late 1950s for the Belgian market.

Scootavia France ★★

M. A. Morin's heavy-looking scooter had the unusual advantage of principal parts made of magnesium and molded alpax. The engine originated as a 125cc Ydral, but from 1952 to 1954 (the last year of production), changed to a four-speed 175cc AMC engine. The lines of the rear of the scooter bore a strong resemblance to the DKW Hobby. The overgrown front fender, later copied by Peugeot, looked like a Parisian police hat with a bladelike visor where a bumper would usually lie. Although probably not sharpened, it would be exceptionally dangerous cruising down the Champs Elysées if an unaware tourist thought that stoplights were heeded in Paris.

A Salsbury–Harley-Davidson dealership with a Model 85 DeLuxe on the Art Deco show stand and a Standard on the floor. Note the display engine on the stand as well as the Salsbury posters in the showroom. *E. Foster Salsbury archives*

In 1946, Salsbury was acquired by Northrup but the Model 85 had been designed by Salsbury engineer Lewis Thostenson during the end of World War II. Here at an outing along the California coast with a Model 85 DeLuxe, left, and Standard; note that only the DeLuxe has the added seat for the pillion riders. Also note that this wholesome group of scooterists was driving and drinking—drinking milk, that is. This was the audience Northrup and new sales chief, E. Foster Salsbury, saw as their scooter's audience. *E. Foster Salsbury archives*

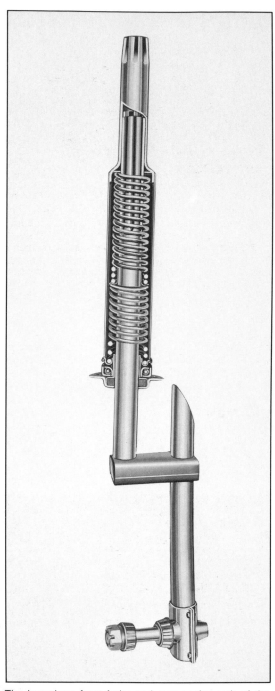

The ingenious front forks and suspension unit of the Model 85 was years ahead of the McPherson strut that would become standard on most automobiles in the 1980s. The two, different-rate coil springs were mounted inside the steering head. The stub axle held the front wheel, which ran on two Timkin roller-bearing races. *E. Foster Salsbury archives*

Servos Germany ★

Servos' lightweight scooter was called a "Volksmotorroller" in ads, the two-wheeled contender to the Volkswagen.

Built from 1953–1954, it was powered by a miniscule 36cc Victoria engine mounted atop the front fender and driving the front wheel via a chain.

Showa Japan ★★

The Showa Marine scooter was launched in the late 1950s with a scooter chassis and body riding atop large, 14in semi-disk wheels. Power came from a 125cc two-stroke.

SIM Italy ★★★

The Societa Italiana Motorscooters of Reggio Emilia introduced its first scooter in 1951 as a venture planned to mimic the sales success of Piaggio and Innocenti. The SIM Gran Lusso scooter was a joint venture with Giovanni Moretti, a small-scale producer of motorcycles and later, cars; engines came from the Austrian Puch firm.

The design followed the classic scooter tenets: a tube frame covered by steel bodywork, although on the Gran Lusso, the complete tail section hinged forward for engine access. The styling lacked any pretensions of elegance, going instead for practicality.

An artist's conception of a sidecar for the Model 85 DeLuxe, according to an archivist's notation on the backside of the photo. It is not believed that the sidecar unit was ever actually built as demand for the Model 85 tapered off quickly after only two years' production when new cars became available again post-World War II. Production of the Model 85 ended in 1949 and neither Northrup nor Salsbury ever ventured back into the scooter market. *E. Foster Salsbury archives*

The Puch engine was a split-single design of 125cc with two bores of 38mm and a single stroke of 55mm and fed through a sole carburetor, providing 5.5hp at 4500rpm. The gearbox had three speeds with a left-foot selector pedal. The Gran Lusso was also built in France under license by Guiller.

In 1952, SIM added to its line with the Ariete, or Ram, scooter. Like the Lambrettas of the time, the Ariete lacked bodywork and had shaft drive via single-sided rear wheel support of light alloy. The engine was a two-stroke by SIM of 150cc from 57x58mm delivering 7.5hp at 5200rpm.

In 1953, an Ariete Sport version appeared with full bodywork inspired by the homely Gran Lusso styling.

SIM-Moretti flyers announced that its scooter was "The most elegant! The most perfect!" While that may be debatable, the SIM scooters never sold in the numbers projected and production was halted in the mid-1950s.

Simplex USA ★★★

The Simplex Automatic scooter was a big scooter with an automatic transmission—items that the Simplex Manufacturing Corporation of New Orleans belived would help its scooter infiltrate the American motorcyclist's mindset when it was first offered in the late 1950s. As a 1957 ad stated, it was "a motorcycle man's motorscooter." Problem was, a motorcycle man wanted a motorcycle. The Simplex remained an anomaly from both markets: it was too large for putt-puttniks and too small for the Hells Angels.

Based on large, 4.00x20in wheels and a mile-long 48in wheelbase, the Simplex was a scooter with an identity crisis. The chassis was step-through and the 150cc engine was well hidden from prying hands beneath a simple fold of sheet-metal. The automatic transmission carried power to the rear wheel via a rubber V-belt.

The first Simplex motorscooter of 1957 carried its gas tank atop the rear fender behind the seat and was steered by low-profile handlebars. By 1960, the scooter had been refined with the gas tank hidden from view and protective legshields added. For the motorcycle man, Harley-Davidson-style high bars were added, topped by an optional windscreen for high-speed use.

Simplex also offered its Servicycle motorbike alongside the scooter based on the same engine but with styling that was half Whizzer, half Indian Chief, and sold only half of its builder's dreams.

By 1962, Simplex was offering its Sportsman T63 scooter mini-bike.

Success or failure, the Simplex motorscooter was a fascinating machine. And because it was

SIM colloborated with automaker Giovanni Moretti and Austrian engine builder Puch to create its Gran Lusso scooter in 1951. The Puch engine was a split-single of 125cc with two bores of 38mm and a single stroke of 55mm and fed through a sole carburetor, providing 5.5hp. But SIM had two problems: Piaggio and Innocenti, who ruled the Italian scooter market by the start of the 1950s. Despite a promising scooter, the SIM-Moretti never traveled far. *Vittorio Tessera archives*

never a marketing hit, there were not many of them built, so today they are quite rare and highly prized. All made more so by their eccentricity and obscurity.

Simson East Germany ★

Under the brand of AWO, Simson presented in 1955 the Punktchen with a 49.5cc engine made by in Magdebourg at the Karl Marx factory.

The Simplex Automatic scooter was an oddity from a company that specialized in oddities. The 150cc engine nestled below the seat on the crude tube frame, which held the large 20in wheels at both ends. Owner: Jim Kilau.

The KR50 (Klein Roller or little scooter) of 1959 used 16in wheels as opposed to its predecessor's tiny wheel diameter. The 46.7cc engine gave 2.1hp at 5500rpm with a right kick start. Simson didn't have to worry about being late in the scooter market since it appeared that the other East Bloc makers often worked together with their state-owned business.

In 1973, Simson returned to the scooter fold with its Schwalbe KR51-1, KR51-1S, and KR51-1K models. Although in typical scooter style, the Simson's design was just a mishmash of lines and easily forgettable.

Speedway USA ★★

Speedway Motor Corporation of Kansas City, introduced its scooter and miniature motorcycle following World War II to compete with Cushman. By 1946, the firm had built some 300 scooters with production planned at forty-five scooters a day for 1947.

Both the Speedway scooter and motorcycle used the same one-cylinder air-cooled engine, which pumped out 6hp for a 60mph top speed.

Sportcycle USA ★

The midget Sportcycle was available in the late 1930s through *Popular Mechanics* ads for a mere $39.

Sterling France ★

Sterling's Sterva took after the Moto Rumi Scoiattolo scooter, saddle bags and all. The Ydral engine was offered either as a 125cc on the Sterling JV125 model or as a 175cc on the Sterling JV175, the larger with a 6 volt battery. If the rider bored of the Ydral, Stervas also came with a 125cc SAAB engine (made by Etablissements René Briban), a 125cc Nervor and a 175cc Sachs. The Belgian company Van Hauwaert also made Stervas under license with a Minerva label on the scoot.

Sun UK ★

Sun Cycle and Fittings Co. Ltd of Birmingham traced its lineage back to bicycle production at the turn of the century. In 1957, Sun entered the scooter fold with its Geni based on a 99cc Villiers 6F two-stroke engine delivering 2.8hp at 4000rpm with a two-speed gearbox shifted by foot lever and 15in wire-spoked wheels.

In 1959, the Geni was joined by the Sunwasp scooter, obviously trading on the Vespa's renown. The Sunwasp was a svelte scooter dressed by bodywork shared with Dayton and Panther's Princess. Mounted in the tube frame was a Villiers 173cc 2L two-stroke providing 7hp at 5000rpm with a three-speed gearbox and Siba electric leg.

Leading-link forks suspended the front 10in wheel and a swing-arm was at the rear. Drum 6in brakes were used at both ends.

The Geni and Sunwasp lasted into 1960, longer than Sun's motorcycle line. But the firm was soon sold to Raleigh and retired from business.

Suzuki Japan ★

Suzuki eschewed scooters in its early years but offered its 50cc Address model in Japan and Europe in the 1990s.

Swallow Japan ★★

Swallow's Pop scooter first appeared on the Japanese market in 1955 with the 165cc 30C T-165, a long name for a little scooter. The Pop rode on 3.50x10in tires and created 6.15hp at 4400rpm. Its styling was sleek and bejewelled by chrome trim with turn signals mounted on the legshield and tail.

In 1956, Pop was back with two new models: the unclothed 80cc CP and the full-bodywork 125cc CM, both riding atop 2.50x18in tires. While the CM followed typical Japanese scooter styling, the CP was a radically ugly hybrid of scooter and motorcycle styling, which set a design point for the future Pops with abstract swallow-shaped air ducts on the sides. The most interesting feature of the Pops was the swing-arm rear end with dual shocks mounted underneath the seat in the style of the Vincent Rapide.

The 125cc Pop was restyled for 1957 with two-tone paint and 3.50x10in tires. By 1958, the Pop 125cc was up to 5.8hp at 5000rpm from its 52x58mm 125cc engine.

A 175cc Pop appeared in 1958 as well with styling identical to the 125cc. Riding on 3.50x10in tires, the 175cc of 62x58mm created 8.82hp at 5600rpm.

By the early 1960s, Swallow was gone, never having been able to build its nest in the Japanese market controlled by the large scooter makers Fuji and Mitsubishi.

Swallow UK ★★★

Swallow was a famous sidecar builder that ventured into the scooter market with its Gadabout appearing in late 1946 at the same time as the Vespa made its debut in Italy, and the Corgi was first promised for the UK market.

The Gadabout was a basic bare-bones scooter blending the front-end styling of a Lambretta Model A with the rear end of a Cushman 30 Series. A rigid duplex frame held unsprung front forks and a square cushion above the engine, which was covered by a folded sheet of steel that served as the tail section. Tires were 4.00x8in with 5in brakes at both ends.

The engine was a two-stroke 122cc Villiers 9D of prewar design backed by a three-speed gearbox. Weighing in on the heavy end, the scooter moved at a snail's pace compared with the Vespa of the time. A commercial sidecar was optional.

In 1950, the Mk II was offered with a Villiers 10D engine. Leading-link forks with bonded rubber suspension gave a better ride. In 1951, the 197cc Major joined the line with a 6E Villiers designed as a workhorse to pull the sidecar.

But by the end of 1951, the style, speed, and reliability of the Italian scooters had left the Gadabout and Major in the dust, and so Swallow returned to sidecar building, offering a small passenger sidecar for the Italian scooters.

Terrot France ★★★

M. Samuel Renaud presented the first Terrot scooter, the VMS, at the Salon de Paris in October 1951, a rounded pontoon-shaped scooter in the style of 1950s American cars. The two-speed 98cc engine produced 2.6hp with the right foot control being first gear and the left for second.

Terrot's VMS2 of 1953 had seats for two with an enlarged motor of 125cc for 3.5hp; the VMS3 of 1954 had the same engine with left side kick and three-speeds. The Scooterrot of 1955–1957 was marketed in Britain by P & M Panther with its elaborate system of gear selection as an added luxury.

Magnat-debon, a subsidiary of Terrot, produced the Terrot as well with the S1 of 1952 as the 98cc VMS, the S2 and S25 as the 98 and 125cc VMS2, and the S3 in two versions as the 125cc VMS3 classic and the VMS3 "présélective," aka the Scooterrot.

Tote Gote USA ★

In all of the hallowed motorscooter hall of fame, the Tote Gote was the sole scooter conceived as a motorized packhorse with travois to haul dead deer out of woods after a hunting expedition.

Thirty-year-old Ralph Bonham of Provo, Utah, built Tote Gotes in the early 1960s, which sold to hunters like himself who were almost cured of hunting by having to drag 200lb deer carcasses out of the mountains. The muscular Tote Gote could yank a 400lb load up a 45 degree slope, perhaps in anticipation of Bonham's dreams to bag an elk.

Triumph TEC UK

Triumph was one of the most prolific and beloved motorcycles in the world. Its great vertical Speed Twin engine was designed by Edward Turner and remained in production for some four decades. And then Triumph created a scooter.

Tigress TW2 and TW2s 1959–1965 and TS1 1960–1965 ★★

In 1957, Triumph, then owned by BSA, announced a prototype scooter, also designed by Turner. By October 1958, near-identical Triumph Tigress and BSA Sunbeams models were offered, each in two versions, a 175cc two-stroke single and a 250cc four-stroke twin.

The TW2 250cc shared engine parts with the 175cc from the clutch back, but the block and heads were cast in aluminum and were special to the four-stroke twin. The TW2s added electric start.

Performance of the overhead-valve vertical twin 250cc engine was all the Meridan factory could have wished for. In fact, the 250cc prototype was so fast it had to be detuned for production.

The frame of both models was a basic tube affair with an odd bolt-on headstock. The suspen-

The Terrot scooter looked like a primped French poodle on wheels. Dressed in its bulbous body and painted in funky red and white two-tone, the Terrot turned many a head when it putt-putted down the Champs d'Elysee. Even the forks front and rear were enclosed and painted to continue the motif. Owner: Vittorio Tessera

sion was hydraulic front and rear. And the body-work made it the "Sleekest smoothest scooter *ever*," according to Triumph at least.

The Tigress TS1 did not reach the public until 1960. Its 175cc engine was a creative amalgamation, a toolroom special based on the BSA Bantam with the Triumph Cub gearbox. A four-speed gearbox drove the rear wheel via an enclosed duplex chain, much like the Lambretta Li. Top speed was 55mph.

But the Tigress was not a success, arriving in the market with too much too late. The scooter boom had been in the early 1950s; by the 1960s, commuters were riding motorcycles or cars and scooters were forgotten by most.

Everyone within Triumph seemed to understand this except the top management. Don J. Brown, sales manager for the US West Coast importer, Johnson Motors, wrote a confidential three-page letter in 1958 prophesizing the scooter's failure. Brown stated that "My own view has been from the beginning that we are facing a 'market drift' from what... this country needs in the way of scooters.... " In fact it was a market drift from what any country needed.

But the Tigress did find one ready market: circuses loved the scooter. The heavy-duty body and hydraulic suspension made the Tigress ideal for trained bears to circumnavigate the circus ring to the crowd's never-ending awe.

Triumph Tina 1962–1965 ★

Triumph released its Tina as an automatic 100cc scooter for first-time riders.The V-belt transmission drove the rear hub with automatic ratio changes; the only controls were throttle and brakes. Another boon to Learners was the start/drive control that wouldn't allow the scooter to move unless it was in the "on" position.

The Tina's engine was a two-stroke single with the horizontal cylinder directly in front of the 8in rear wheel.

Triumph T10 1965–1970 ★

The T10 was a slightly redesigned Tina with the safety start/drive switch moved under the seat so the scooter would only go when the driver was seated. Other cosmetic changes were made as well, such as the front brake control moved to the left handlebar.

The T10 stayed on for five years but was never a success next to the ever-improving Italian designs.

Triumph TWN Germany

Triumph was founded by two Germans, Siegfried Bettman and Maurice Schultz in Coventry, England, in 1897. When Triumph started mak-

Out for a Sunday ride on a Triumph Tigress TW2. The concept behind BSA's Sunbeam and Triumph's Tigress was the engine: four-stroke, two-cylinder, and 250cc. These scooters were designed to offer a luxury scooter with motorcycle power. The idea was sound, the timing was not. Innocenti and Piaggio had sparked the scooter market in the late 1940s; by the time BSA-Triumph entered the fray they had missed the boat by more than ten years. *Mick Walker archives*

After the failure of its Tigress, Triumph tried to keep at least some grasp on the scooter market, offering its T10 in 1965. Yet while the firm had mistimed its Tigress by more than ten years, its timing sure didn't get any better five years later. The T10 was viewed more as cheap form of transportation rather than flaunting the prestige of the earlier scooters. Owner: Vittorio Tessera

ing motorcycles in 1903, they opened a factory in Nürnberg, both making Triumph motorcycles. In 1929, the British half split with the German company taking the name of TEC Triumph (Triumph Engineering Co. Ltd. or simply TEC in Germany), and the German side was named TWN Triumph (Triumph Werke Nürnberg or simply TWN to the British).

Tessy Standard, Luxus, and Super (Superlative) 1956–1957 ★★★

The Tessy had a "floorboard tunnel" or bridge between the rider's legs to facilitate airflow and two luggage carriers, one mounted on the stationary front fender. The Super was the luxury model with a 6 volt battery and electric starter instead of the Luxus' magneto. The Super also was more powerful with 8.5hp reaching 80km/h as opposed to Luxus' 7hp and the Standard's 6hp.

The Triumph factory in Nürnberg offered the Tessy in two color schemes, two-tone in beige and brown or light and dark blue, both with only the teardrop side panel in the darker color.

Contessa 1955–1957 ★★★

The Contessa's engine was based on the TWN Cornet—"the whispering motorcycle," according to TWN publicity. At the 38th Brussels Salon, the 200cc Contessa debuted in January 1955 with four speeds and a special selector that allowed the rider to get to neutral from any position. The Contessa was the true deluxe model with twin pistons moving in unison making for 9.5hp for 95km/h, 10in tires instead of the Tessy's 8in, a long, 52in wheelbase, and a 12 volt electric starter.

In 1957, when TWN had seriously over-produced the number of two-wheelers that the market could bear, it concentrated on typewriters and office equipment, perhaps envisioning the impending Information Age. Gründig took control of TWN in 1958, however the Contessa design was acquired by its rival Hercules who renamed it the Viscount and replaced the engine with a 200cc Sachs.

Trobike UK ★

The Trojan firm of Croydon was an English Lambretta importer that decided to build its own scooter in 1960. The Trobike was the result, based on an open duplex frame with a 94cc Clinton two-stroke and 5in tires. Predating the mini-bike craze of the mid-1960s, the Trobike lasted only a few years on the market.

Troll East Germany ★

The boxy Troll 60E, 100E, 120E, and 120D scooters were "the ideal vehicle for women," as well as for, "country doctors, country vicars, mid-

An assortment of 1955 TWNs shows an eager cyclist trying to hear the putt-putt of the whispering Contessa motorroller. The bulging legshield unsuccessfully hides the spare tire but adds yet another bulbous curve to the 200cc German Triumph powerhouse. *Roland Slabon archives*

The Soviet-made Tula Tourist was propelled forward and upward by a 11hp 200cc Tula engine with Tula electric start and a Tula gearbox, as Tula's flyers were proud to point out. All parts were made in the Soviet Union but the Tourist did travel about, being exported to select European countries, such as the Benelux group, as shown in this flyer. *Vittorio Tessera archives*

wives, nurses, merchants, shoppers and messengers." In other words, the East German government thought these unimaginative scooters were

the cure-all for just about anybody's transportation problem.

The small 60E used an engine from the VMO factory near Lamspringe, others all used Ilo engines, so had considerably more power. The Troll 100E produced 3.6hp for a top speed of 60km/h for the cardboard box-styled scooter. The 120D and 120E had 4hp for a top speed of 65km/h and 70km/h and still had the design of a World War I combat vehicle, less cannon.

The Troll was kept alive into the 1990s by IFA, the "Nationally Owned Motor Vehicle Industry of the German Democratic Republic." IFA also produced the infamous two-stroke Trabant automobile, a true spiritual sibling of the motorscooter.

Trotwood USA ★★

The Trotwood was an anomaly even in the world of scooter oddities. Built by Trotwood Trailers Inc. of Trotwood, Ohio, in the late 1930s, early 1940s, it was a "brand new design," according to ads, which was an understatement that would follow the scooter out of production.

The engine rode on the front forks and drove the front wheel; the whole front end was covered in a curved sheetmetal "trunk"—the catchword of the era for this kind of weird design was "streamlined."

From there things got even stranger. The driver sat atop a rear package compartment with feet in a step-in bathtub-like affair. Two rear wheels followed the front end around, both with drum brakes.

As the ads assured the dubious, the Trotwood was "Needed by merchants everywhere."

Tula Russia ★★★

The year 1957 must have been the date when Soviet planners decided that motorscooters were the vehicles to transport the comrades. In the USSR, both the Tula and Vjatka made their debuts; in Poland and Romania, scooters were also introduced. Perhaps *perestroika* will someday bring the secret planning papers to light.

The Tula 200 scooter was annouced in the August 1957 issue of the Russian motoring magazine *Svet Motoru* but what was not announced was that the scooter was a copy, replica, or rip-off—call it what you will—of the Goggo-Isaria scooter.

The T200 was powered by a Goggo-derived 197cc air-cooled two-stroke of 61x66mm, which was equipped with an electric starter, and rode atop 4.00x10in tires. With 8hp, it could hit 86km/h.

The T200 had a long career—or sentence, depending on your point of view. Introduced in 1957, it continued in production through the 1960s and was relieved in 1973 by the Tula Tourist.

The Tourist ran on the same mechanicals with the electric starter but updated the styling to 1959 with a look more than vaguely similar to the Lambretta TV 175 Series II. The Tula Tourist even went capitalist, being exported to various European countries in the 1970s.

URMW Romania ★★

The Romanian URMW 150 scooter was introduced in 1957 with an engine based on the Polish Osa scooter. The 150cc engine featured a horizontal single cylinder and three-speed gearbox mounted in front of the rear wheel. Top speed was 80km/h.

Paul Vallée France

Paul Vallée productions distributed and marketed by SICRAF (Société Industrielle de Construction et de Recherches Automobiles de France), made scooters that were essentially borrowed Lambretta designs but under no contract with the Italian company for extra profits.

S.149 1949 ★★

The first model, the S.149, was essentially a 125cc Lambretta A or B with a darker paint job. Apparently Innocenti didn't mind, possibly thinking that imitation is the truest form of flattery, that is as long as Paul Vallée didn't try to sell them in Italy. In 1952, Paul Vallée's second scooter was nearly identical, chrome trim and all, to the dressed Lambretta LC except for the mechanics with a 125cc Ydral engine.

BO.54L and BO.54 GT 1953 ★★

Possibly while designing his three-wheeled car, quaintly named the Singing Cleric, he got away from the Italian influenced design and came up with the decidedly French BO.54. Appearing at the Salon de Paris in 1953, the BO.54 had sleek lines with a front fender like a retriever's nose, and was available in a tasteful two-tone (the BO.54L). An Ydral 125cc or 175cc powered the BO on its 8in wheels. Just when M. Paul Vallée had an originally design, he ceased coming up with any further scooter ideas.

Varel Germany ★

The Small Varel factory in Oldenburg bowed in 1951 featuring a 43cc engine pumping out an impressive 0.8–1hp on their FF scooter. The engine sat atop the front wheel in the style of the great French Velosolex moped, making it one of the few front-drive motorscooters.

Velocette UK ★★★

Veloce Ltd. of Birmingham built the Velocette, a long line of well-engineered motorcyles famous for their powerful single-cylinder engines and black and gold livery. In the late 1950s, Veloce developed its LE and Vogue models for the utility market. In 1961, the firm created a motorcycle that was later covered in bodywork, becoming the Viceroy scooter.

The Viceroy's engine was an interesting two-stroke flat twin of 248cc based on a square 54x54mm bore and stroke. Reed valves fed the oil-fuel mix into the crankcase and an electric starter turned it over. The Viceroy engine was also used in a version of the DMW Deemster scooter.

The engine was mounted in the Viceroy just behind the front wheel for optimum balance and coupled with the flat twin engine design, which produced little vibration, the Viceory was a smooth-running scooter.

A four-speed gearbox was driven by a duplex chain, feeding power through a clutch via a shaft

The whitewalled tires added to the clean image of the Victoria Peggy scooter, which was aimed at the female market. Moto Parilla's Levriere scooter influenced the large 200cc engine and body of the Peggy.

drive to bevel gears at the rear wheel. The gearbox also doubled as a rear suspension pivot arm. The wheels were 12in diameter with 6in brakes on both ends.

The frame was a hefty tube affair, belying its motorcycle heritage. With the flowing bodywork in place, the Viceory was a massive—and heavy—scooter.

But the scooter arrived on the scene too late. Veloce made the same wrong decision that Triumph-BSA-Sunbeam made in developing a scooter. The Viceroy last until 1964, and Velocette last only another seven years.

Venus West Germany ★★

The Venus factory in Donauwörth focused solely on scooters during its three-year existence with three models having the same simple but attractive design. Venus offered three models: the Venus MS 150 and MS 175 of 1953–1955; and Venus DS 100 of 1954–1955.

Each model used Sachs engines, the larger MSs with two seats for passengers and an optional electric start (called the MSA model). A notable design feature on the MS model was the "second fender" that extended the line on the side of the floorboard up to the front wheel's moving fender. The DS 100 with 97cc engine pumped out 2.7hp for a maximum speed of 55km/h; the MS 150 had a 147cc 6.5hp engine; and the MS 175 had a 174cc

Yamaha's long-lived Riva line featured lightweight and easy-to-operate scooters, making it ideal for the youth market Yamaha targeted for its scooter sales. This 1993 Riva Razz SH50E-B boasted a reed-valve 50cc engine with electric start, automatic Autolube fuel-oil mixer, automatic transmission, turn signals, and a "clean" two-stroke engine. The scooter had come a long way. *Yamaha*

engine with 9.5hp. Both MSs boasted a top speed of 90km/h.

Victoria Germany ★★

First introduced at the Frankfurt International Motorcycle show, the Peggy of 1955-1957 was a hit with its powerful 198cc horizontal engine. The design was similar to the Zündapp Bella, which in turn was based on the Parilla scooter. Perhaps Victoria borrowed the Parilla design directly considering that in 1956, Victoria had an agreement to use Parilla engines in some Victoria-Parilla motorcycles displayed at the Frankfurt Show.

The 10hp Peggy's push-button gear change allowed it to reach a top speed of 95 km/h. Due to financial problems, Victoria decided to keep producing the Peggy scooter in 1956, after discontinuing it for a few months.

Volugrafo Italy ★★★★

Società Volugrafo of Turin built the Aermoto, a lightweight military parachute scooter with dual front and rear wheels and a low-set frame similar in style to the Welbike. The engine was a single-port 125cc two-stroke with a two-speed gearbox.

Wabo The Netherlands ★

The Dutch Wabo scooter was powered by a choice of British Villiers two-stroke engines: the 99cc 4F with two-speed gearbox or the 147cc 30C with three speeds.

Walba Germany ★★

The 2.8hp Walba 100 of 1949-1950 hardly had an impressive style, but as one of the first scooters produced in Germany, it offered an important mode of tranport for the *volks*. In spite of its heavy 63kg weight for its small size, the 98cc Ilo engine pushed it to a fast top speed of 75km/h on its 8in wheels.

From 1950-1952, Walba offered its Kurier, Tourist, de Luxe, and Commodore models. Although the engines weren't updated much more than enlargements from the Walba 100, the design of the body was much improved.

With a fake turbine engine and martian-like front section, the Walba turned into a futuristic design that was right out of Fritz Lang's *Metropolis*. The phony turbine air intake makes the scooter into a small personal transport unit. Remember, this was the same era as when citizens believed they would soon be able to wear jet packs on their back to fly anywhere.

The Walba was armed with Ilo motors: the Kurier with a 118cc for 4hp and 75km/h, the Tourist and the de Luxe with a 122cc for 4.5hp and 70km/h, and the Commodore with a 173cc for 7.65hp and 85km/h. In 1952, the Walba was redesigned but kept its decorative turbine under the wing of Faka.

WFM Poland ★★★

The Warszawska Fabryk Motocycli built the Osa M50 scooter at its Warsaw factory beginning in 1957. The engine was a 149cc two-stroke giving 6.5hp at 5000rpm via a three-speed gearbox. Tires were 3.25x14in, although they were all but hidden beneath the bulbous front fender and rear bodywork.

Yamaha Japan ★

Perhaps the oddest expansion sideline was Yamaha's foray into the world of motorcycles and scooters. Torakusu Yamaha founded the Nippon Gakki firm in 1955 to produce musical instruments. With an education in clock making and a fascination with motorcycles, Yamaha's original plans had gone the way of all good intentions by 1960 and while musical instrument building continued, Yamaha created its first cycle and its SC-1 motorscooter.

The SC-1 was powered by a 175cc of 62x58mm bore and stroke producing 10.3hp at 5500rpm and riding atop 3.50x10in tires. The front forks were an odd triangulated, one-sided affair both front and rear. A speedometer, choke knob, and ignition key fit in the dashboard on the inside of the legshield with the headlamp mounted on the apron.

The styling of the SC-1 was designed as only the Japanese know how to do, mixing modern and old elements into a rolling sculpture of chrome and sheetmetal.

The SC-1's companion was the moped-scooter MF-1, which also arrived in 1960 with a 50cc two-stroke engine and 2.25x25in tires.

In the 1980s, Yamaha created a wide-ranging series of modern small-displacement scooters designed largely for the youth market worldwide. Models in 50, 80, and 125cc included the Razz, Riva, and in Europe the Beluga. At the 1992 Bologna show, Yamaha displayed its Fly One *scooterone*—a larger scooter—with a 150cc four-stroke engine.

In 1993, Yamaha showed its Frog scooter with retro chic styling. Powered by a 250cc four-stroke engine, its was dressed in snappy two-tone with dual headlamp-like frog eyes.

Zanella Argentina ★

The *fratelli* Zanella were born in Belluno, Italy, moving to Argentina in 1948 to start metallurgy company, Zanella HNOS y CIA. In 1957, they built their first motorcycles, with most of the parts imported from Italy. By the late 1950s, Zanella was producing its own scooters, which were also exported to neighboring South American countries.

Zündapp Germany

"Der Roller für den Motorradfahrer," the scooter for the motorcyclist claim usually failed for most scooter manufacturers, but Zündapp was the exception.

In 1951, Zündapp wanted to jump on the scooter bandwagon and developed a scooter prototype which was never to be developed. Instead, they looked to the reigning champion, Italy, for their first scooter design, building 150cc and 200cc versions instead of the original less than 125cc prototype. Seeing that Vespa and Lambretta were already being sufficiently copied, they turned instead to Moto Parilla scooters and brainstormed ideas from its attractive design. The first Bella is almost indistinguishable from the 1952 125cc Parilla scooter.

Bella R150 1953–1955, R150 Suburbanette 1953, and R200 1954–1955 ★★★

The Bella was a hit when it first came out and was supposedly the most talked about scooter at the international Frankfurt show of 1953. The 147cc model with Bing carburetor had 7.3hp at 4700rpm for a maximum speed of 50mph. The frame of the Bella was a large diameter tube arching over the rear engine and had pressed steel body work attached to it as well as a 8.5 liter gas tank. The 12in wheels, the foot shifter for the four gears and partial "bridge" between the rider's legs give the Bella a near motorcycle image.

When Zündapp began production of the 200cc Bella, they increased the flywheel generater

As the single most popular Zündapp two-wheeler ever produced, this ad shows off all the medals won by the 200cc Bella in 1953. Zündapp was tooting its own horn saying Zündapp is "überall."

from 60watts to 90watts and the battery from 7amp to an 8amp battery for more reliable current to the ignition and the lights. The headlamp was moved higher up on the front apron with the horn below it. The R200 was offered with a delivery van trailer or as the "Bella de luxe" model with a Steib LS-200 sidecar. Zündapp produced more than 18,000 R150s, almost 27,000 of the R200, and only 370 Suburbanettes.

Zündapp designed the Suburbanette for the American suburbs and sold them only in the United States. Its main difference was that it had higher handlebars, a dual seat, a front mudguard (to show off the telescopic forks), but did not have the all the paneling that the other Bellas had.

Bella R151 and R201 1955–1956 ★★★

Following the huge success of the first line of Bellas, Zündapp attempted to expand its line of

The 1953 Zündapp Bella 198 was the ride of many a cool couple in the 1950s. The Bella design showed the sleek lines of Zündapp's glorification of the Parilla Levriere scooter, upon which it was largely based. *Mick Walker archives*

scooters by producing a 125cc scooter which never hit the production line. Instead, the Bella was just updated with some considerable changes since it was the scooter "you are proud to be seen on" according to Zündapp's publicity. Electric start from 12 volt electrics were added along with restyled bodywork and dual seats as well as an improved air duct system to keep the two-stroke engine cool. The front leg shield design was smoothed out as well as the metal reinforced. A new Bing carb was added resembling more an automobile's system than the previous motorcycle style set up. Another new feature included two attachment points for a Steib sidecar with an interchangeable wheel with the Bella that could be added after buying the scooter.

Zündapp produced only 2,500 of the 150cc model, realizing that the market demanded power so they manufactured 27,000 of the 200cc R201, the most of any of model Bella.

Bella R153 and R203 1956 ★★

After seeing the success of Harley-Davidsons and Indians in the American market, Zündapp made a special version of this model sold only in the United States with a kickstart and huge chopper handlebars. Exclaiming in an ad in *Motorcyclist* that "the World's outstanding motorscooters [were made] for shopping, work, school, fishing (will fit your boat) [sic]."

Although swing forks had been available on the domestic German models, these improved forks weren't available abroad until 1956 when Zündapp updated from the telefork which was to remain the standard for future Bellas. "Horsepower is up on some other German scooters, such as the Bella (10.7hp)." (*Popular Science*, July 1957, p.71) The 8hp Bella 150 came with a 6 volt battery and generator as opposed to the 10hp Bella 200 with 12 volt battery and electric starter which cost a quarter more than the 150. The German models had smaller handlebars and standard electric start. By now Zündapp realized the market for scooters was becoming saturated with other makes, so they made only 24,900 of the third series and produced fewer and fewer Bellas every year.

Bella R154 1956–1958 and R204 1957–1959 ★★

This 198cc Bella's cylinder inclined at 30 degrees like the Zündapp S Series motorcycles giving it 12.4hp at 5400rpm for a maximum speed of 65mph. In 1958, the more powerful R204 was considered "amongst the best scooters on the market" (*Motor Cycling*, Jan. 1, 1959).

Bella R175S 1961–1964 ★★★

Only 2,000 of this model were produced with the 174cc, 60x62mm bore and stroke, producing 11hp at 5400rpm

In 1956, the Zündapp Bella was available in both 175cc and 200cc versions. The sophisticated power and quality engineering of the Zündapp set it heads above most competitors. This 200 Bella is mit seitenwagen, which was optional. *Mick Walker archives*

200 551-026 and 560-025 1959–1962 ★★★

The fastest Bella that existed with 13.4hp, unfortunately, sales had plummeted and only about 2,000 of each of these models were made.

Roller 50 and RS50 1964–1984 ★

These two scooters took the place of the Bella, but could not replace it as the best-selling machine for Zündapp during the 50s. These two new scooters were based on the Lambretta Slimline with the easily removable side panels, headlamp on the handlebars, 10in wheels (from the safer 12in wheels of the Bella) and handlebar gear change. One of the only differences from the Lambretta, besides the much smaller engine, was the fancy two-tone seat on some of these Zündapps. The two scooters had a 49cc engine based on the Zündapp Falconette moped with the smaller three-speed Roller 50 at 2.9hp at 4900rpm, and the four-speed RS50 Super at 4.6hp at 7000rpm. The RS50 was later updated slightly and renamed the RS50 Super Sport.

Unfortunately, the company fell on hard economic times in 1985 after producing 130,680 scooters and the entire Zündapp stock and machinery were sold to China. Approximately 1,500 Chinese went overland to Munich by train to pack up all the equipment to ship to the People's Republic. During the two weeks of loading, the Chinese workers slept in the packing crates to save money.

Sources/Suppliers

American
Vintage Motor Bike Club
Joyce Lee, Secretary-Treasurer
537 West Huntington
Montpelier, IN 47359 USA
 US club for "out-of-production" motorbikes and scooters, from Cushman to Whizzer, Simplex to Salsbury

Classic Scooters of America
Steven Zasueta & Edwin Moore, Editors
PO Box 152366
San Diego, CA 92195 USA

American Scooter Road Racing
 Association
6244 University Avenue
San Diego, CA 92115 USA

Cushman
Cushman Club of America
Tom O'Hara, secretary
PO Box 661
Union Springs, AL 36089 USA

Ray Gabbard
Route 6, Box 95
Portland, IN 47371 USA
 Cushman information and parts

Cushman Reproductions
Dennis Carpenter
PO Box 26398
Charlotte, NC 28221 USA
 Cushman parts, accessories, tires, manuals and more

Roger McLaren
193 3rd Sytreet
Excelsior, MN 55331 USA
 Cushman restorations and parts

Rich Suski
7061 County Road 108
Town Creek, AL 35672 USA
 Cushman parts, accessories, tires, manuals and more, as well as parts for other vintage American motorbikes and scooters

Doodle Bug
Jim's Scooter Parts
Jim Kilau
593 North Snelling Avenue
St. Paul, MN 55104 USA
 Doodle Bug parts and manuals, as well as Cushman parts and manuals

Fuji
Erik's Scooter Service
3235 Byron Street
San Diego, CA 92106 USA
 Rabbit parts and service

Heinkel
Deutsches Motorräd Register
W. Conway Link
8663 Grover Place
Shreveport, LA 71115 USA
 The vintage German motorcycle owner's association with excellent quarterly newsletter full of history and classified ads

Innocenti
West Coast Lambretta Works
Vince Moss
6244 University Avenue
San Diego, CA 92115 USA
 Performance accessories, racing and some restoration parts for Lambrettas

Vittorio Tessera
Via Marconi, 8
20090 Rodano (MI) Italy
 Premiere source for information on vintage Lambrettas and Vespas, as well as most other types of European scooters. Also operates a Lambretta museum and runs the Italian Lambretta Club and Registro Storico

Stefano Panciroli
Via Casali, 8
42100 Reggio Emilia, Italy
 Probably the world's best source of vintage decals for scooters and motorcycles of all makes, although specializing in European manufacturers

Marco della Torre
Via Mare Adriatico, 15 (S. Teresa)
65010 Spoltore (PE) Italy
085/20.92.76
 Lambretta collector and parts specialist

Lambretta Preservation Society
M. Howard Karslake
"Kesterfield", Northlew
Nr. Okehampton
Devon EX20 3PN England
 Registry, technical information, and Lambretta museum

Scooter Lambretta Club de France
Annie et Michel Rigaud
F-10320 St. Jean de Bonneval, France

Lambretta Club Nederland
Moeraskreek 11
3206 GE Spijkeniesse, The Netherlands

Mustang
Mustang Motorcycle Club of America
Alan Wenzel, Vice President
530 South Industrial Boulevard
Dallas, TX 75207 USA

Mustang Motorcycle Registry
Steve Counter
3720 Flood Street
Simi, CA 93063 USA

Piaggio
Vespa Supershop Inc
2525 University Avenue
San Diego, CA 92104 USA
 Vespa parts as well as Malossi carburetors and other high-performance equipment

First Kick Scooters
1318 4th Street
Berkeley, CA 94710 USA
 Specializes in vintage and modern Vespas with mail-order parts service

Vespa Motorsport
3450 Adams Avenue